Qur'an and Bible
Side by Side

A non-partial anthology

Compiled and introduced by

Marlies ter Borg

with an introduction by Andrew Rippin

and reflections by Khaled Abou el Fadl

Qur'an and Bible Side by Side
A non-partial anthology

marliesterborg@gmail.com
Printed in the United States of America
by CreateSpace, Charleston, December, 2011

This book is a non-illustrated version of
Sharing Mary, Bible and Qur'an Side by Side
CreateSpace, Charleston July, 2010

This is a peer reviewed book see p.350

ISBN-10: 1466459816

ISBN-13: 978-1466459816

The Library of Congress Catalogue
LCCN: 2011961995

Bisac code REL041000
Religion / Islam / Koran & Sacred Writings

1.Bible and Quran 2. Islam 3. Koran stories

This anthology is available online at
www.bibleandkoran.net
www.koranandbible.net
IKON
Radio Netherlands Worldwide

Qur'an and Bible Side by Side

A non-partial anthology

compiled and introduced by

Marlies ter Borg

with an introduction by Andrew Rippin

and reflections by Khaled Abou El Fadl

with contributions by:

Barbara Stowasser
Mehmet Pacaci
Awraham Soetendorp
Herman Beck
Moch Nur Ichwan
Martha Frederiks
Karin Bisschop

"This anthology is an invaluable resource in underscoring that despite differences and at times conflicts, the Bible and the Quran reveal a Judeo-Christian-Islamic tradition whose shared beliefs and values form the basis for greater mutual understanding and respect."

John L. Esposito, Georgetown University
The Prince Alwaleed Center for Muslim-Christian Understanding

"Written, not in a polemic spirit of proving one religion to be superior to another, but in the spirit of reconciliation... this book is highly recommended for anyone interested in interfaith dialogue."

Simon Ross Valentine, Church Times, UK

"...the compiler of this book was motivated...to clear existing misconceptions and promote understanding and cooperation between two of the world's most widely followed religions...she deserves much credit for her invaluable contribution to inter-religious study and dialogue especially that between Islam and Christianity."

Muhammad Khan, Muslim News, UK

"An important anthology of Biblical and Quranic texts, supported by carefully formulated comments by competent Islamic and Christian academics.Thus the stories are shown,in their subtle differences, to possess a spiritual commonality.

Revd. Dr Reinhardt Kiste, Dialog der Religionen, Intereligios,

"Ter Borg, neither a theologian nor involved in any community of believers, approaches her subject with great intellectual curiosity and a strong sense for the expressive eloquence of the holy texts.."

Elma Kronemeijer, Nieuwe Moskee, Netherlands

This book "must be praised for its novel approach...(it) brings home ...an idea stressed by recent scholarship... that the Qur'an is in constant conversation with the Biblical tradition. The work succeeds in awakening curiosity and will surely prove a useful resource for interfaith education."

Diego A Sarrio, Washington, Islam and Christian-Muslim Relations

“Part of God’s charge and test to human beings is that they would know how to disagree and debate (*adab al-ikhtilaf*) without falling into strife and animosity (*fitna*).”

Khaled Abou El Fadl, *The Search for Beauty in Islam* [xvii]

Qur’an and Bible Side by Side

This anthology is a non-illustrated version of

Sharing Mary, Bible and Qur’an Side by Side

It was prepared with special respect to those Muslims, Christians and Jews, who may not or cannot relate to figurative images (of persons and especially prophets) in their religious experience. Here again they share common roots, to be found in the Hebrew Bible.

“You shall not make for yourself... any likeness of anything that is in heaven above, or that is in the earth beneath, or that is in the water under the earth;” Exodus 20:4-5

I refer those who welcome figurative art in the religious sphere to: *Sharing Mary,* which has many black and white illustrations from Jewish, Christian and Muslim sources; and to a book of full color illustrations titled *“Bible figures in Islamic art,”* forthcoming in 2012.

From the Reviews

The contributors accept as a given the impossibility of...objectivity. They are convinced, however, that a modicum of fairness is possible. Based on the texts cited in this collection, the Qur'an clearly comes across as less dogmatic than is generally presumed, especially in the West. Indeed, ter Borg is of the persuasion that the Qur'an is more sensitive to women's issues and generally less violent than is usually thought.

Suitable for both public and academic libraries. Recommended for lower-level undergraduates through graduate student and general readers.

Professor emeritus, M. Swartz, Boston University
Choice, Current Reviews for Academic Libraries, April 2011

Together with the appealing irenic approach of the whole work, these texts make the book into a successful contribution, whose practical usefulness must not be underestimated, also for non-native English speakers.

Professor Alexander Toepel, university of Tübingen, Germany in CIBEDO-Beiträge" Nr. 1/ 2011Christlich-Islamiticshe Begegnungs- und Dokumentationsstelle der Deutschen Bischofskonferenze

... graceful assessment of the great sources on which Muslims and Christians find daily inspiration. (This book) indicates that believers share values such as peace and forgiveness. In this time of political turmoil and violence,...an excellent call for an inter-religious encounter.

Dr. Gurkan Celik, director of the Dialogue Academy, Netherlands

This long awaited and timely book with scholarly reflections from inclusive Muslim and Christian theologians is a groundbreaking resource for all who would grow in understanding of their Islamic neighbours... an informed, brilliantly researched work, revealing a most resonant interpenetration of scriptural traditions and shared sacred stories.

Brother Bart Seaton SSF, Anglican Society of St. Francis, Australia

Ter Borg strives for impartiality, placing the Bible and Qur'an stories side by side on an equal footing...in a time in which such a neutral perspective is urgently needed. Ter Borg approached experts in the field... for brief reflections on separate themes. This has led to highly readable interludes with a recognizable personal touch.

Rev. dr A. van der Hoek, Netherlands

Contents

Part one: Introduction - Bible and Qur'an in Dialogue

Alpha: The Beginning

Part two: Stories in the Hebrew Bible and the Qur'an

Part One

Introduction

Bible and Qur'an in Dialogue

"Part of God's charge and test to human beings is that they would know how to disagree and debate (*adab al-ikhtilaf*) without falling into strife and animosity (*fitna*)."

Khaled Abou El Fadl, *The Search for Beauty in Islam* [xvii]

This Conference was founded on the beauty of the Book, and our Civilization was the civilization of books. Our way to God is guided by the Book, and we found our worth only in books. Our God manifested through the Book, and our identity was defined by books. So how can we become the corrupters of the Book and the betrayers of books?

Khaled Abou El Fadl, *The Search for Beauty in Islam* [p.193]

From Creation to the Last Day

The story behind the stories

Browsing through this anthology might make the reader wonder whether these stories are simply a string of beads, following one another in a more or less chronological order, or something more. Indeed there is a sense to the sequel, a storyline, which is presented in a nutshell here, to be refined and elaborated on later in this book.
The common storyline begins even before creation, when God was above the waters. In both books the universe is created in six days or divine periods. On the seventh day an interesting difference occur. In intermezzo ii. Herman Beck gives us a humorous anecdote from his experience as a Christian teaching in Indonesia, on the need of God to have a rest. Another difference concerns the creation of woman. Barbara Stowasser shows in iii. how the Biblical story of woman created from the male rib influenced the Islamic interpretation of the Qur'an.

The main difference between the Qur'an and the Christian Bible however starts where Adam and his wife Eve do wrong. In both books they disobey God's command not to go near that one tree. In the Christian version, as explained by Paul, mankind falls into sin, only to be saved by Jesus Christ, Son of God and as such Himself divine. In the Qur'an version Adam and his wife repent and God forgives them, giving them another chance to live a righteous life on earth, thereby earning and regaining the garden of Eden. It is this different ending of the story of Paradise Lost that explains the different status given to the son of Mary. In the New Testament he is born the Son of God. who dies on the cross and is resurrected to save us from our sins.

1. A Bridge of Stories – Marlies ter Borg

You have before you a unique anthology of stories told in both the Bible and the Qur'an. It starts obviously with creation, which in both books took six Days or divine periods. It continues to describe the creation of man and woman, who in both books dwell in the Garden of Eden, until they are forced to leave paradise through a fault of their own. It figures the sons of Adam, Cain and Abel, and the first murder. Then the great flood is described which destroyed human and animal life on earth, except for those who had boarded the ark of Noah. In both books Abraham nearly sacrifices his son, and Lot confronts the lusty masses of Sodom. Joseph is left by his jealous brothers, sold as a slave to Egypt, there to rise to power. Both books relate his near seduction. Moses is put to water by his anxious mother in both books, later to save his people from Egyptian oppression. David fights Goliath in both books, becomes King and is a gifted psalmist. His extremely capable son Solomon receives the queen of Sheba in both books. Job suffers and is healed and even Jonah gets swallowed by a big fish in both Bible and Qur'an.
The parallels continue in the New Testament. Zacharias receives heavenly news about the miraculous birth of his son John as Mary does about Jesus. Both are well-loved and respected in both Christianity and Islam. Jesus lives a life of peace and healing, supported by his disciples in Bible and Qur'an. In both books God lifts him up to heaven, there to act as witness or judge on Judgment Day. Both books show how the inevitable reckoning of the individual's life and deeds follows upon the Day of destruction, when earth and sky make way for heaven. Those on the left descend into hell in both books, and those on the right are lifted into paradise.
Thus this anthology follows the well known stories from let us say, the first Day to the Last; from the Creation of the Universe to its destruction', followed by the final Judgment. All these well known stories are told 'in their own words. Quotes have been taken from Qur'an and Bible and arranged to show the very similar storyline developing on both sides,

According to the Qur'an Jesus or 'Isa is emphatically not the son of God because God the Creator, unlike humankind, or any other creature, neither begets nor is begotten. Indeed. 'Isa is a great prophet, born of the virgin Mary. The Quranic Jesus received a Holy book as did Moses and Muhammad. He is also called the Christ, the anointed one in the Qur'an. But there Jesus does not die on the cross. 'Isa is lifted up to Heaven as he is in the Bible. Neither he nor Muhammad or any other human being is, or indeed needs to be the Savior. In the Qur'an it is up to individual men and women to show remorse and to regain paradise by deserving it, as Adam and his wife did before them.

Such are the diverging storylines behind the stories, similar in so many respects, different in a few. These are the two necklaces Islam en Christendom have created from the gorgeous beads offered them. Most of stories in this book stem from the Tenach, renamed as the Old Testament or Hebrew Bible. Thus it is very fitting that Awraham Soetendorp throws his light on the Hebrew prophets (vii.) and the figure of Jesus, (xi) . Apart from the gentle suggestions done by a handful of experts, from Academic, Jewish Christian and Muslim background, in the intermezzo's , this is as much guidance as the reader will find in this book. There is a wealth of commentaries available elsewhere. Here only the stories themselves are offered, so many gems from which to pick and choose. It is for the reader, plodding steadily from beginning to end, from Alpha to Omega, or browsing through the chapters at will, to compile a personal necklace from the gems Bible and Qur'an have on offer.

which the reader can follow from one chapter to another. The quotes are arranged here in a novel way: systematically side by side. The Bible quotes being the oldest are placed reverently on the left. The more recent Qur'an quotes are placed on the right. Sometimes the stories are not entirely parallel. Thus the Quranic story of fratricide refers to the sixth commandment which, in the Hebrew Bible, is linked to the story of Moses. Such digressions are recognizable by the different shade. The same method of selection and arrangement is used to deal with three legal issues that have been at the center of recent controversy: the position of women, penal law and international law, especially regarding war.

Law is often prohibitive. It tells us what not to do. A special chapter is reserved for a more positive approach to human behavior: common values and virtues, formulated in both books to encourage motivating men and women to 'do their best'.

The first and last chapter, aptly named Alpha and Omega, deal with common attributes ascribed to God in both Bible and Qur'an. They act as it were as the starting and ending point of a rainbow, a divine arch reaching over the stories and issues in which humankind is the central focus. The attributes of God are described 'the Author's own words'. For I am not the author of this anthology, simply its compiler.

For the reader's convenience, this compilation has been structured so that each chapter can be read separately. The parallel structure and subtitles make it possible to follow the similarities and differences closely, step by step. The stories are kept brief; some elaborations and most repetitions that occur in the Qur'an and the Bible are omitted, to increase readability. Careful mention of sources makes it easy for the reader to go back to the textual context of both books.

Each chapter is introduced by a short preview, explaining what the reader can expect. The characters are introduced. Similarities and differences in the storyline are briefly mentioned. These introductions are as short and objective as possible. I make no attempt at interpretation. Neither are the stories placed in the context of other relevant texts such as from the Talmud, Church Fathers or the Hadith. This important interpretative

activity is left to the reader. No judgment is made, on the assumption that the readers can and will make their own judgment, in a variety of ways. That a variety of interpretations of the texts are possible and indeed often enlightening is shown by the guest introductions and intermezzos. In chapter 2. Nur Moch Ichwan from Indonesia elaborates on the concept of tolerance, which lies at the root of this book, as it lies, in his view, at the root of Islam. In chapter 3. I specify the methods and limits of this book, as any author should in an academic publication. In chapter 4. Andrew Rippin discusses the academic and historic context of this 'side by side', which although novel in its own way, is nevertheless embedded in the past. Whilst stressing the limits and value of the approach he ends with an invitation to hear the musicality of both texts in their individuality.
Interfaith dialogue is very much a personal matter. It is a dialogue between humans, each with their own background. This is why I have asked a handful of experts from a variety of backgrounds to write a short piece on a specific theme, appearing in one or more specific chapters. These experts are not only academics, but have concrete practical experience in the dialogue between Academics, Christians and Muslims. They were asked to give us an anecdote from their experience, showing how reading texts from the 'other' faith entails a typically human, emotional response. Thus in ii. Herman Beck, a Dutch Islam expert and practicing Christian, tells us how his Indonesian students reacted to reading the creation story from Genesis. In iii. Barbara Stowasser explains how surprised her students' surprise at the egalitarian character of the Qur'anic story of Adam and his wife. In iv. Khaled Abou el Fadl expresses the longing for brotherhood, as a counterpoint to the story of fratricide. In vi. Awraham Soetendorp comments on the common theme of killing or saving one individual. In vii. he discusses the concept of 'prophet', ending with Miriam, the sister of Moses and Aaron, as a fitting comment on the title of the book, and transition to the New Testament.
In viii. I grant myself room to show how sharing the stories about Mary produces a surprising new image of the mother of Jesus as a highly educated woman. In intermezzo viii. Soetendorp explains what Jesus can

mean to a Jew. Mehmet Pacaci, takes on the difficult subject of Judgment Day in x. And in xi. he relates how a shadow fell over his audience of Christian Methodists when he dealt with the concept of hell. As a backdrop to the legal chapter on women, Martha Frederiks, a Christian expert from Holland with a missionary background, expresses in xiii. her surprise at finding stories about inspiring women in the Qur'an. Khaled Abou el Fadl closes the row with reflections on attributes of God, found in both Qur'an and Bible. Andrew Rippin's students ask "Who is speaking?"
Thus a small sample is given of ways in which stories can inspire and surprise readers as they did experts in the field working in an interfaith setting. This is of course no more than a sprinkling, a small posy of daisies in a field full of flowers. The target was not completeness but freshness. It must be refreshing, even to those with knowledge of Islam, Judaism or Christianity, to read the stories as they appear side by side. Too often we come to texts with minds formed by interpretations into which we are ready to bend any and every quote we encounter. In this anthology the reader is asked to postpone judgment, to take a fresh look at stories which have over the centuries provided new inspiration time and again. Apart from their religious meaning, the texts assembled in this anthology are part of world literature which, ancient as they may be, deserve a fresh look.

In spite of my objective of being objective, I must confess to an underlying subjective stance which has governed not only the selection, but the very idea of producing this anthology. My aim has been reconciliation through mutual understanding. It is the same drive that inspired the quotes from Obama and El Fadl which introduced this book. That there are and have been tensions between the faiths, from whose books I have plucked the quotes, is no news. In this anthology I chose to highlight similarities, whilst respecting differences. I approached these, not on a high level of abstraction -which is the prerogative of theology,- nor on the concrete level on which the media like to focus, -but on something in between, accessible to all human readers. I have focused on the tales which unravel around well loved characters whom the faiths share. I feel and hope that these charming and dramatic stories, common to both Bible and Qur'an, -

but presented here in a novel way, i.e. brotherly and sisterly side by side, - will act as so many bridges, ready for anyone willing to cross.

i. Sharing Stories - Intermezzo by Karin Bisschop

From the start our work together was an example of how people with different religious views and backgrounds can come together and produce something valuable and informative without giving up their own convictions. We have different religious views, but Marlies and I never saw that as an obstacle but rather as an incentive to stay alert and check the background information and sources we worked with. We didn't have to win each other over; we respected each other as friends and coworkers and gave each other a look into our lives. We crossed bridges together but we didn't burn them behind us. The bridges are there for everybody to cross, they are neither wobbly nor unsafe. And it's not a one-way-road!

The first chapter we worked on was the story of Mary/Miryam and Jesus/Isa. Marlies send it to my website www.moslima.nl by email on December 17th 2005, with a request to publish it. This was our first contact. After this first story Marlies would send me a new chapter weekly. I would read through the Qur'an verses, give her new verses to work with and suggest other angles. Slowly the columns grew longer and the chapters laced up to beautiful strings of pearls made of verses.

Every story was special and all were dear to us, but some chapters where more laborious than others, like the one about the prophet Lut/Lot, which can hardly do without interpretation, but which has been interpreted in many ways. We had to keep our introduction objective but in the same time we couldn't ignore the implications of the verses.

Other chapters gave us only joy, such as the one about paradise, which can also open up for those of other faiths as long as they believe in One God. I remember discussing whether it might snow in paradise, and imagining together how beautiful that would be.

2. Tolerance and Pro-existence

understanding each other's language

Moch Nur Ichwan

"Is Father Hermen already a muslim?" The question came from Rev. Djaka Soetapa. Father Hermenegildo de Almeida looked dazed. Wasn't he a Catholic, a priest in East Timor? Yes, he had enrolled as a student at the State Islamic University of Yogyakarta, in which non-Muslims are allowed to enrol. He was following my course on Contemporary Religious Movements. But that was only to broaden his knowledge, in the context of an MA in religious studies. He had no intention of converting to Islam. And now this Reverend Djaka Soetapa, honorary lecturer at the same university, was calling him a muslim! To make matters worse, Rev. Djaka added: "I have been a muslim for a long time." Father Hermen laughed politely, but he stood perplexed.

I, on the other hand, knew exactly what he meant. He was referring to the subtle distinction made by the progressive Muslim intellectual Nurcholish Madjid between islam and Islam; between muslim and Muslim. He used the capital letter for the organised religion initiated by Muhammad. The small letter he reserved for what is much more important: submission to the Good, to God. He understands

"*Inna 'd-dīna 'indallāhi l-Islām*" [3 Al-'Imran, 19]

as

*"The Religion before God is **islam**, (submission to His Will)"*

This verse does not refer to organized religion but to a far more fundamental submission to the Divine. Indeed this and the next verse argue that the People of the Book, that is Jews and Christians, can be muslims in principle, though they might stray from God in practice.

"And say to the people of the Book and those who are unlearned: "Do you submit yourselves?" If they do, they are in right guidance..." 3 Al-'Imran, 20

According to Nurcholish every religion which teaches submission to God is islam. Everyone who submits to the Divine, to the Truth, to the Good, is a muslim. On the other hand, if a Muslim, that is someone who confesses Islamic faith but in practice sins against humankind and against God - a Muslim who for instance kills innocent people - is not a real muslim (with a little *m*).

When this Indonesian intellectual presented his ideas in the 1980s, he was criticised by many Muslim activists. They accused Nurcholish of being secular and having gone astray. However many Muslims supported his interpretation. A number of non-Muslims, spokesmen of other faiths said that if this was the concept of islam, they were "muslims" as well.

Rev. Djaka was among them.

Most non-Muslims are astonished and perhaps even irritated by the Qur'anic statement that Abraham was a 'muslim'. The relevant verse reads:

"Abraham was not a Jew nor yet a Christian; but he was true in Faith (hanif), and bowed his will to God's (which is islam), and he was not of the idolaters."

3 Al-'Imran, 67

Revealed in Medina, the verse implies, first of all, that there was a *hanif* or religious movement in Mecca and Medina, which adhered to Abrahamic monotheism; and, secondly, that there was a debate between Jews and Christians in Medina, in which each party claimed for itself the most intimate relationship with Abraham.

"You People of the Book! why do you dispute about Abraham, when the Law and the Gospel were not revealed till after him?" 3 The Heifer, 65

The Qur'an argues that it was impossible to claim that Abraham was a Jew. Or, as Karen Armstrong[1] puts it:

"Living before the Torah and the Gospel, Abraham was neither a Jew nor a Christian but represented a simpler faith that reflected the unity of God."

However, as a matter of fact, Abraham initiated some of the major parts of the Jewish religion. Yet, the children of Israel (Jacob) had to wait for Moses to receive God's law (Thora). Of course Abraham couldn't be Christian in the literal sense, for he lived centuries before Jesus Christ was born, although Christians might call themselves 'sons of Abraham in faith.' In the same way one could hold that the term Muslim is irrelevant for anyone who lived before Muhammad received the Qur'an.
But the Qur'an claims that both Abraham and indeed Jesus and his disciples were muslim in the inclusive sense explained above.
Muhammad's religion presented in the Qur'an as similar with, and indeed a continuation of Abraham's religion. Muhammad explicitly builds on prophets living either before Abraham, such as Adam and after him, such as Moses and Jesus. All of them were characterized by their submission to God.
Written with a small *i*, islam is a *perennial religion* flowing from Adam to Muhammad, and far beyond, however its particular expressions might be called. In this sense all the messengers and prophets of God whom we meet in the Qur'an, are muslims, chosen bearers of messages of 'islam'. So in this anthology we meet Abraham and his son Ishmael who pray:

"Our Lord! make of us muslims, bowing to Your (Will), and of our progeny a People muslim, bowing to Your (Will);" 2 The Heifer,128

In the Qur'an we meet Jesus surrounded by his disciples.

---

[1] Karen Armstrong, "Foreword: Abraham: Meeting Guests, Meeting God," in Joan Chittister, Saadi Shakur Chishti, Arthur Waskow, *The Tent of Abraham: Stories of Hope and Peace for Jews, Christians, and Muslims*, Boston: Beacon Press, 2006, xi.

"Said the Disciples: "We are God's helpers: We believe in God, and you bear witness that we are muslims (obedient to God ed.)." 3 Al-'Imran, 52

But is this inclusive approach developed in the Qur'an valid only for the three monotheistic faiths, the so-called Abrahamic religions? Does the generous approach hold only for Jews and Christians, for the People of the Book? What about other religions?
It is interesting that the Qur'an says:

"For We have assuredly sent amongst every People (umma) a Messenger (with the Command), 'Serve God, (the Divine, ed.) and eschew Evil'." 16 The Bee, 36

This does not necessarily mean that in every *umma* there is only one messenger (the term used is messenger [*rasul*], and not prophet [*nabi*]). It could be two, such as Moses and Aaron, who in the Qur'an were messengers both for Israel and Egypt[2]. It means that the number of God's messengers is at least as many as the peoples or *umma* existing in the world. That means there are *umma* which have more than one messenger. The Qur'an says that it mentions only a few of messengers God sent to humankind; many messengers are not mentioned.

"We did aforetime send Messengers before thee: of them there are some whose story We have related to you, and some whose story We have not related to you." 40 The Believer, 78
The Qur'an even explicitly mentions both Semitic-Abrahamic messengers and 'untold messengers'.

"We have sent thee inspiration, as we sent it to Noah and the Messengers after him: We sent it to Abraham, Ishmael, Isaac, Jacob and the Tribes, to Jesus, Job, Jonah, Aaron, and Solomon, and to David We gave the Psalms. Of some Messengers We have already told thee the story; of others we have not - *and to Moses Allah spoke direct."* 4 The Women, 163-164

[2] (19 Mary, 51-53; 23 The Believers, 45; 26 The Poets,13; 28 The Narrations, 34), or more (36 Ya Sin, 13-14).

This implies that they are included in the same overall religion of 'islam', (written for our purposes with a small i).

Seen from the perspective of human history, there were many "*umma*" outside the Arabian Peninsula. Of course God knew about them, He is All knowing. From archaeological artefacts, we know that there were *umma* who lived in Africa, Latin America, the Malay-Indonesian Archipelago, China, Europe, and so on. If God has sent a messenger to every *umma*, those *umma* had and have their own messengers. All those messengers taught their people to follow the path of truth and righteousness, to submit to the Divine. So, in the inclusive sense, all those religions can be considered as islam, and their followers can be muslims in the sense that Abraham and the disciples of Jesus were.

However, one may ask, why are the norms and devotional ways of various religions and peoples so different? To this question, the Qur'an has a clear response: pluriformity is willed by God.

"To each among you have we prescribed a Law (shir'a) and an Open Way (minhāj)." 5 The Table Spread, 48.

What further differentiates those *umma* are their religious rites; (*mansak;* pl: *manāsik*).

"To every people We appointed rites, that they might celebrate the name of God...But your God is One God: submit then your wills to Him (in islam)."
22 The Pilgrimage, 34

Such difference of *mansak* is not to be disputed or discarded, 22 The Pilgrimage 67 since it is willed by God. For every umma there is a messenger who teaches particular norms (*shir'a*), methods (*minhāj*), and rites (*mansak*), but all have the same basic value, i.e. submission to the Divine. Many religious adherents get trapped in the rigidity and imagined superiority of their particular norms, methods, and religious rites. They forget the basis of every religion, that is submission to the Divine; islam. In this context it is relevant that humankind is in essence a "single people" (*umma wahida*).

"Mankind was one single nation, and God sent Messengers with glad tidings and warnings..." 2 The Heifer, 213
If He wanted to, God could easily forge the different nations into a single people, with a single set of rites and laws, all following the same Messenger. But He chooses to do otherwise. God sanctions diversity and calls upon men and women to strive for the virtues in different ways[3].

"If God had so willed, He would have made you a single people, but (His plan is) to test you in what He has given you: so strive as in a race in all virtues. The goal of you all is to God; it is He that will show you the truth of the matters in which you dispute." 5 The Table Spread, 48

It is not up to human beings to decide what is right in morals and religious matters. Only God can know the Truth about the differences disputed by and among religious communities.
The appreciation of variation does not imply that anything goes. It is of even greater importance to find common terms or *kalima sawā'*. 3 Al-'Imran, 64
It is the unity and similarity (formulated in Islam as the submissiveness to God), that should be emphasized, and not differences in norms, methods, and rites. For whatever our differences, we will all return to the One. Underneath the variety in norms and rites lies one basic human and divine value: Righteousness.

"O mankind, We made you into nations and tribes, that you may know each other (not that may despise each other). Verily the most honoured of you in the sight of God is (he or she who is, ed.) the most righteous of you." 49 The Inner Apartments, 13

This emphasis on tolerance of religious diversity does not mean that a follower of Muhammad should be skeptical of his or her faith or abandon the particular norms and rites belonging to it. On the contrary, Muslims should develop a strong faith in their own religion and spiritually submit their life to God as long as it lasts. Yet, the deeper his or her belief is, the

---

[3]See also 10 Jonah, 19; Hud 11:118; 16 The Bee 93; 21 The Prophets, 92; 23 The Believers, 52; 42 Consultation, 8; 43 The Gold Adornments, 33.

more tolerant a Muslims or Muslima will be towards other religions. For by submitting to God they submit their claim to Truth to God. By understanding islam with a small letter as a universal subjection to the Divine, he or she discovers it in other religions and recognizes real muslims amongst their adherents.
Such inclusive understanding is in line with the general cosmological teaching of the Qur'an which stipulates that all creatures—not only human—on earth and in heavens submit themselves to God, willingly or unwillingly.

"...all creatures in the heavens and on earth have, willingly or unwillingly, bowed to His Will (accepted ***i****slam)..."* 3 Al-'Imran, 83

Submission to God is the very essence of the "Religion of God" for the whole universe. For natural creatures, including the natural dimension of humans, this submission is reflected in their compliance to natural law, which is also God's law. Thus the sun rises and sets and humans are born and die. But for humans, as rational and moral creatures, the willingness is essential. They possess freedom of choice, and therefore carry the responsibility for their own deeds. Unlike natural creatures, humans have reason by which they are able to differentiate between good and bad, right and wrong. Within this context, therefore, the concept of "no compulsion in religion" is very essential. For humans, choosing freely to submit to God's law is what matters.
A comparable approach is also to be found on the Christian side. Here the relevant term is 'anonymous christian' (written here with a small c in analogy to muslim) introduced by Karl Rahner. He states that people outside Christianity have the possibility of receiving God's salvation through Christ, although they are not baptized, (have no 'Christian' name), and even if they reject Christianity.

"Anonymous Christianity means that a person lives in the grace of God and attains salvation outside of explicitly constituted Christianity — Let us say, a Buddhist monk — who, because he follows his conscience, attains

salvation and lives in the grace of God; of him I must say that he is an anonymous Christian;"

In Rahner's view a Christian simply can't believe even for a moment

"that the overwhelming mass of his brothers not only those before the appearance of Christ right back to the most distance past (whose horizons are constantly extended by paleontology) but also those of the present and of the future before us, are ***unquestionably and in principle excluded*** *from the fulfillment of their lives and condemned to eternal meaninglessness? He must reject any suggestion, and his faith is itself in agreement with his doing so. For the scriptures tell him expressly that* ***God wants everyone to be saved."***

Here Rahner refers to saint Paul:

"God...will have all men to be saved, and to come into the knowledge of the truth." 1 Timothy 2:4

Influenced by Rahner's concept of 'anonymous christianity', the Second Vatican Council (1962-1965), affirmed the possibility of salvation outside the Church. In essence, 'anonymous christian' refers to the same as the word 'muslim'; to a man or woman who chooses to let him- or herself be led by Divine inspiration and natural law to strive for Peace (Salaam). Many will appreciate that the inclusive stance implied by these honorary titles is not something negative if based on true understanding and sincerity; that is, if it is free from political manipulation, a sense of superiority and a drive for dominance. These are titles which are earned by those who practice an inclusive approach.

Of course, a Christian might resent being called a 'muslim' as a Muslim might resent being called an 'anonymous christian'. However why should we not try to communicate peacefully and constructively using our different inclusive 'religious language games'? Such inclusive terms as 'muslim', 'anonymous christian' or indeed other similar expressions from other religions form an important element in developing a tolerant understanding of other religions, as a condition for co-existence and even pro-existence; the notion that the others' difference is a value rather than a fault. The first step is the refusal to force others into conversion with the use of positive and negative sanctions; physical force, financial pressure or the offering of advantages in the welfare and educational field. This kind of conversion has been practiced throughout history by Muslims and Christians alike. It is emphatically rejected in the Qur'an.

"Let there be no compulsion in religion." [2 The Heifer, 256]

Is there a common complimentary name which could be used by the Children of Abraham without psychological barrier? It is interesting that both the Qur'an and the Bible share a similar term for Abraham, that is, "the friend of God" (*khalīlu 'Llāh*).

*"Who can be better in religion than one who submits his whole self to God, does good, and follows the way of Abraham the true in faith? **For God did take Abraham for a friend.**"* [4 The Women, 125]

Quite similarly, the Bible reads:

*Abraham believed God, and it was accounted to him for righteousness. And he was called **the friend of God**.* [James 2:24]

In other places, the Bible says: "Your friend Abraham." [2 Chronicles, 20: 7] and "my friend Abraham" [Isaiah. 41:8] The mention of Abraham in the Qur'an is related to the dialogue between the Abrahamic religions, implying that Abraham is their "common father". This also means that the "common term" between these religions should use shared "Abrahamic language" and "examples". Therefore it is important for these religions to learn about their father Abraham. The Qur'an mentions three major characteristics of Abraham: submitting his whole self to God, doing good, and having true faith. In the context of Abraham, true faith here refers to monotheistic faith. Because of these attributes Abraham is regarded by God as "the

friend of God". And whoever possesses these three attributes has 'quality' in religiosity.
In the Bible, Abraham is said to have two characteristics: believing (faith) in God and righteousness. Despite "submitting the whole self to God" (islam) is not mentioned explicitly, it is actually implied in both believing in God and righteousness. Believing in God requires submission to Him. The Qur'an has made it explicit according to its *weltanschauung*.
In Jewish, Christian and Islamic scriptures and traditions the title "friend of God" is given only to Abraham, and not to other Messengers. Because Abraham is the father of the adherents of these religions, it is logical that the latter could be called "children of the friend of God". Despite this, it might be proposed that the title "friend of God" could be used also as compliment for all Children of Abraham: Jews, Christians and Muslims. The difference is that Abraham's title was given by God, and that this compliment is now used by children of Abraham for each other.
The Qur'an verse forbidding compulsion in religion implies that coercion in religious affairs is neither effective nor morally right, nor indeed acceptable in the eyes of God. That insight lies at the center of peaceful co-existence. Pro-existence goes an important step further. It opens up the mind and indeed the soul to the fascinating differences between the rites and norms of different faiths, and to their underlying similarities. Especially when performed in dialogue, as happens in this book, this search can be exhilarating and enriching. Let me end with a quote from that great peace-loving man, Mahatma Gandhi:

"To be a good Hindu also meant that I would be a good Christian. There was no need for me to join your creed to be a believer in the beauty of the teachings of Jesus or try to follow His example," [4]

Let this be an inspiration for Muslims and Christians to share Abraham, Jesus, Muhammad and their teachings, as aspects of their common heritage.

---

[4] Millie Graham Polak, *Gandhi, The Man,* 1931, G. Allen & Unwin

3. Qur'an and Bible Side by Side

method and limitations

Marlies ter Borg

Surprising though it may seem, a side-by-side anthology of Bible and Qur'an quotes was not available in the English language until it appeared the Dutch site www.bibleandkoran.net in December 2007. I was very pleased to be able to cooperate with the Dutch Ecumenical Broadcasting Company IKON who, together with Radio Netherlands Worldwide, was putting the complete Bible and the complete Qur'an on an equal basis on the same website for the first time in history. In fact they performed this feat not only in Dutch, but also in English and in Arabic, with of course the complete Qur'an its native language. This feat was preceded by one and a half millennium of enmity.

Against this historical background the side-by side published in 1889 by a German professor of Evangelical Theology, Johann-Dietrich Thyen [1989] was a breakthrough. Unfortunately it was never translated into English, or edited in a way to make it accessible for lay persons. Neither was it developed in a dialogue with Muslims. It was the work óf Christian expert fór Christian experts and showed, apart from an admirable honesty and diligence, a slight bias. For example Thyen give the chapter on John/Yahya the Biblical title of '*Johannes der Täufer,*' (John the Baptist); but there is no such thing as baptism in the Qur'an, for there is no original sin which has to be washed away. The *'Sündenfall'* a title Thyen gives to the story of Paradise Lost takes place only in the Christian Bible. The Jewish and the Muslim interpretation of the story lack the concept of original sin.

The Intellectual Crusade against the Qur'an

Over the centuries the enmity between Christians and Muslims has acted as a barrier to a non partial side by side anthology. As explained in the next chapter, Muslims revere the Law and the Gospel as authentic messages of God to Moses and Jesus, tragically lost to mankind. However the áctual Bible is criticized as God's word tampered with, making the Qur'an the only authentic message of God. For centuries the Christian attitude to the Qur'an was likewise negative. The first Latin translation, by Robertus Ketensis commissioned by Peter the Venerable of Cluny, appeared in 1143 after the first Crusade, as sentiment moved towards the second. This translation, *'Lex Mahumet pseudoprophete'* tended to exaggerate even harmless texts to give them a nasty sting, preferring improbable, unpleasant meanings over likely and decent ones. It served as a refutation of Islam, and as a source of knowledge for missionaries. It inspired Dante to place Muhammad in deep hell, with his entrails hanging out, punished as sower of discord. Inferno XXVIII, 19-42, 1308-1321 A second Latin translation was issued in 1698 by Ludovico Marracci, a confessor to Pope Innocent XI, with an introductory essay titled 'Refutation of the Qur'an'. This version chose the most negative translations to the to give a very dark picture of the Qur'an. Marraci's self-stated goal was to discredit Islam. His translation was the source of most later European translations

In 1499 in Granada some 5000 Arabic manuscripts including the Qur'an were publicly burned at the orders of Ximénez de Cisneros, Archbishop of Toledo. The German poet Heinrich Heine referred to this incident in the famous lines *"Where books are burnt one ends up burning people."* These words, often taken as a prophesy of the Nazi regime, were spoken by Hassan, servant of Al Mansor the ruler of Cordoba. Heinrich Heine, '*Almansor. Eine Tragödie*,' 1821 Such public book burnings did not occur often, but the Qur'an was placed on the catholic index. When it was abolished in 1966, reading the Qur'an by Catholics was still simply 'not done'.

Accessible

Whilst giving all due honor to Thyen, this anthology pretends to go a step further, a few steps in fact. In the first place, it is not just for experts but explicitly, and perhaps even first and foremost, for lay persons. Indeed it gives the lay reader a relatively easy way of catching up on knowledge withheld for centuries of blackening and prohibition. If Bible and Qur'an are to be considered as part of World Literature, it is about time that they be made easily accessible for every willing reader. Easily means more than making Bible and Qur'an available in the lay person's language. It implies more than putting them on internet so that search programs can be applied. Even simultaneous search of both books made possible by IKON on www.bibleandkoran.net can be no more than an instrument, often leading to surprises but as often simply proving what the reader already suspected. When IKON looked for a way of lowering the threshold even further, they stumbled upon our stories. So they decided to publish this anthology together with the complete Bible and the complete Qur'an on internet. Thanks to Radio Netherlands Worldwide it was simultaneously published in English and Arabic. It is this same desire to help lower thresholds for a sensible discussion on Bible and Qur'an which lies at the root of the anthology lying before you. *Qur'an and Bible Side by Side* is an improved and extended English version of the Dutch book; it is available online.

Non partial

Secondly, this anthology strives for impartiality, placing Bible and Qur'an stories side by side on an equal basis. I try to refrain as much as is humanly possible from interpretation or evaluation. This attempt must be understood in the light of the historical experience of deliberate misinterpretation described above.

Given my position of religious and institutional neutrality it might well be easier for me than it was for Thyen, a Protestant academic working, however critically, in the tradition of Luther. In other words, I have the fortune (and misfortune) of having no constituency, whose members might scold me, raise eyebrows or even remove finances.

The relationship of the Protestant movement to the Qur'an was hardly more favorable. Although he opposed a crusade against the Islam as a religion, Martin Luther did feel the need to fight Islam on the spiritual level. However, instead of banning the Qur'an, he wanted to make it available for scrutiny. Thus at his instigation, Ketensis' translation was republished in 1543 in Basel. Luther wrote a preface. For him Muhammad was Gog, (with the Pope c-starring as Magog), the satanic enemy sent by God as a punishment. In the Bible Gog is destroyed and finally buried in Israel, in a graveyard *"so large that it will block the way of anyone who tries to walk through the valley which will then be known as 'the valley of Gog's Army'."* Ezekiel 39:11 Incidentally Gog also appears as Yajuja in the Qur'an as a destructive force let loose just before the Last Day. 21, The Prophets, 96-97 Luther could not help noticing similarities between Qur'an and Bible, but this only strengthened him in his opinion that Islam "had been patched together out of the faith of Jews, Christians, and the heathen." He compared Islam with the small horn of the fourth Beast.

"This horn had the eyes of a human and a mouth that spoke with great arrogance." Daniel 7:7

The particular arrogance of Muhammad was, according to Luther, his refusal to accept Jesus as divine, and to offer salvation on a rational basis of good deeds, rather than grace. Thus the difference in the stories mentioned annex to chapter 1 became the basis for hatred and fear.

Many later European translations of the Qur'an merely translated Ketenensis' Latin version into their own language, as opposed to translating the Qur'an directly from Arabic. As a result early European translations of the Qur'an were erroneous and distorted.

To end this rather gruesome tale of centuries of hatred it is worth returning to Heine, to his introductory poem to the same play Almansor:

"Christians and Muslims fought against each other, North against South. Love came at last and bought Peace."

Dialogue

A third step forward was that this book was developed with and is directed to Muslims as well as Christians and Jews. A maximum of impartiality was achieved by an ongoing dialogue. Thus for the original anthology printed in Dutch in 2007 and put online on www.bibleandkoran.net a Dutch converted Muslima, Karin Bisschop, acted as sparring partner. We discussed every chapter, mutually catching each other out on any signs of partiality. We corrected each other whenever one of us was secretly slipping away from the principle that we were dealing only with the Qur'an and Bible, rather than with the Talmud, Hadith, Church Fathers, or what we had, in some way or other, understood to be the right interpretation of certain passages.

This method reached its climax when we agreed that there is no literal command in the Qur'an to wear headgear (head scarf, or hijab), and that the religious duty to do so needs some further interpretation. For the Qur'an only tells women (and men) to behave and dress chastely. Thus women are required to cover their breasts. They may not display their beauty, except to a small circle of intimae. [24 The Light, 31] But whether this implies covering head and hair is not decided in the Qur'an. Muslimas give a variety of interpretations of this passage. Karin herself sees herself, on the basis of an additional Hadith, obliged to wear a headscarf out of doors. In the course of our cooperation our 'non-interpretation' of this passage hit the headlines. Karin, who runs a website for Dutch Muslimas called www.moslima.nl, was sharply criticized by some of its visitors. However Karin held fast to our position, integrity above loyalty to her own constituency. For the task we had set ourselves focused on the Qur'an and Bible and did not include the Hadith or indeed any form of interpretation. We explicitly left the interpretation of the selected quotes from the Holy Books to the reader, and to whatever expert authorities he or she was willing to acknowledge.

After the anthology was put online in Dutch, English and Arabic, I received a host of comments from all sides and a variety of countries. Any sensible and constructive suggestion was seriously considered. Verses were added at the request of readers, but no verses were scrapped. Leaving accusations aside from Christian fundamentalists that we were putting the word of God next to the work of Satan, we took advantage of all sensible criticisms to lift the anthology on a higher intellectual level.

During the second phase of the project, the preparation of an English publication in print, several comments were received from experts in the field, who were ready to contribute some thoughts to this book. Andrew Rippin represents academic Islam expertise in his introduction on the academic and historic context of this side-by-side. The readiness of Khaled Abou El Fadl to scrutinize my legal chapters, giving me very relevant advice, meant a great deal to me. He gave me permission to quote from *The Search for Beauty in Islam*, from which several mystical reflections have found their way into this anthology.

Moch Nur Ichwan elaborates on how the term 'muslim' with a small letter m was given as a compliment by one Indonesian Christian to another. Tafsir expert Mehmet Pacaci writes about the Last Day, mentioning his experience in lecturing to American Methodists on 'Hell'. Martha Frederiks wrote on her fascination with women in the Qur'an. Herman Beck gives us a charming anecdote on lecturing to Muslim students in Indonesia on the creation story. Barbara Stowasser ends her revealing essay on Eve with her students' reaction to the story. Finally Awraham Soetendorp writes from a Jewish perspective on the prophets, on Miriam, sister of Moses and name sake of Mary and on Jesus. These 'guest authors' were asked to write, not in a polemic, academic but in a friendly way, from their own personal experience. They were invited to elaborate on a theme of their choosing from a side-by-side chapter, using their expertise, but in a personal way.

For interpretation is, in this age of individualism, ultimately a question for the individual believer. Of course religious authority and religious inspiration play an important role, but even they are ultimately of the individual's own choosing. Internet makes accessible interpretations which differ from those in one's direct surroundings. The multi-cultural reality of today, interfaith dialogue and even confrontation force us to open up to ideas we did not grow up with. There are choices to be made on many issues. Indeed we reap today the fruits of a religious individualism which finds its roots in Bible and Qur'an. The individual authors who are willing to share their thoughts with the reader of this book are especially interestin, not only on account of their expertise and research, but because they have lived and worked in a Christian-Muslim setting. Thus the anthology was tested and corrected during the process of its production in order to make it as correct and impartial as possible. To quote an anonymous peer reviewer:

"One should appreciate a balanced and unbiased language and content of introductions for each topic. The passages from either of the Holy Scriptures are selected carefully both to provide a proper content of them and to preserve neutrality over them."

A beginning, not an end

For many readers this book is an introduction. Hopefully they will be inspired or provoked to further reading, thinking and debate. In no way is this anthology final or comprehensive. I did not set out to be in any way all-embracing or to produce something definite. An anthology, by definition a selection, is simply a bouquet of handpicked flowers, arranged in a certain way. Thanks to the careful mention of sources, checked again and again by a variety of persons, the reader can go back to the Biblical or Qur'anic context from which the quotes were taken. He or she can trace the elements of the bouquet to the infinitely fuller flower gardens from which they were picked. This anthology is obviously not complete, nor is it the only possible anthology. Other authors might make other selections and arrangements. Why not? Pretending that this anthology presents some kind of ultimate or perfect truth would be a sign of pride. No text written or compiled by humans, - let alone an anthology of verses selected from Bible and Qur'an - can pretend to contain infinite truth and divine wisdom. Even God needs more than one book to express his wisdom, as is beautifully expressed in the Qur'an:

"...if the ocean were ink (wherewith to write out) the words of my Lord, sooner would the ocean be exhausted than would the words of my Lord, even if we added another ocean like it, for its aid." 18 The Cave,109

A book about religious texts - not a religious book

This book is not about religion. Judaism, Christianity, or Islam is simply not its subject. Many other books cover the varieties these religions have shown over the ages in a way far better than the present author could ever do. This book is not about people and their beliefs and belief systems. Only incidentally are religious practices mentioned, for instance in introducing those stories which are linked to religious feasts. This book is no more that an anthology of texts that play a great role in three religions. It is not about religion as such. The relations of Jews, Christians and Muslims are highly complex. They have been studied extensively from a variety of angles. Each of these world religions consists of a pluriformity of movements and schools, authorities and dissidents, and builds upon a vast literature of interpretation. This anthology goes back to what, in the midst of these sectarian and academic debates, is sometimes snowed under: the actual texts of Bible and Qur´an.

Although it draws on religious books, it is itself not a religious book, in the sense that I am trying to promote my own religious convictions. Of course, as a European, I could hardly escape from the influence of the dominant religion of my the time. I was brought up in England with a mild form of Christianity,- Methodist, Congregational and Anglican, - all in a peaceful mix. During my teens in Holland I lost my faith, although I never regarded it as inimical. As a philosopher I again started reading the Bible, together with the Qur'an, experiencing them as fascinating and mutually enriching literature of the highest level. Whatever one believes, one can hardly escape from the fact that the intriguing and touching stories of Bible and Qur'an deserve the name of Literature with a capital L. They have, even in their mutual enmity, played a tremendous role in European culture, and can still inspire by their dramatic stories and wise sayings.

Most contributors to this book do depart from a clear religious conviction. Their goal however is not to convert but to communicate. This holds for

Christian contributors such as Martha Frederiks and Herman Beck, as well as for their Muslim counterparts, Karin Bisschop, Mehmet Pacaci and Moch Nur Ichwan, and of course Rabbi Awraham Soetendorp. Of course, Abou El Fadl is a Muslim, but his reflections reach out to humanity as such.
Whoever is looking for proof that his or her own convictions, his or her Holy Book or religion is superior to that of another will be disappointed. So will they who seek to discredit religion as such. For this book does not seek to prove anything of the sort. In fact it does not set out to prove anything. Conclusions are conspicuously and emphatically lacking. Neither does it try to compare books which are so different in terms of history or structure or in terms of the status accorded to them by the respective believers. Qur'an and Bible Side by Side is simply an anthology. It is not relevant for my compilation of the quotes, that Muslims see the Qur'an as the Word of God, whereas most Christians today see the Bible as a divinely inspired but human product.. In this anthology no evaluations either of equivalence or superiority are given. Although I might, as indeed any reader might, prefer the development of one story over and above another, as the editor I withhold judgment. Anyway, my opinion would be too trifling and minutely personal to have any relevance. If asked what I think or believe, I must conclude with the philosophers stance; I know that I do not know.

Exegesis, Tafsir - figurative, historical and contextual interpretation
This book has been compiled with utmost care, in the philosopher's tradition of respecting texts. It does not focus on interpretation, exegesis or tafsir, nor on the historical context of Bible and Qur'an. This is not to underestimate the importance of such approaches. For instance, the figurative or metaphorical interpretation of texts has a rich history in Jewish, Christian and Islamic tradition. Verses from the books themselves make clear that they entail figurative or symbolic language.

"I will open my mouth in a parable." Psalm 78:2

"These things I (Jesus ed.) have spoken to you in figurative language;" John 16:25

"He it is Who has sent down to you the Book: in it are verses basic or fundamental (of established meaning): others are allegorical." 3 Al-'Imram, 7

According to Mehmet Pacaci such quotes refer to the expression of the transcendent and unseen world in human language. Qur'an interpretation (Tafsir) distinguishes between muhkamat *ayat,* or literal verses and verses which are *'mutashabbihat',* indicating a profound symbolism. It is this symbolic language that humans must use when discussing what no living man has seen: God, the Last Day, Hell and Paradise. For instance

'a Parable of the Garden which the righteous are promised.' 47 Muhammad, the Prophet 15

This symbolic or figurative approach to interpretation follows from the idea God transcends all that is visible or thinkable by man.

"And there is none like unto Him." 112, Purity of Faith,4

Ibn Rushd, that great Muslim philosopher persecuted by his own people, argued eloquently for a figurative understanding of Qur'an texts. This approach figurative was developed to great heights by the Sufis. They understand verses calling for slaying Pagans (9:5) to mean fighting against evil forces in one's own soul. In Christian tradition figurative interpretation of the Bible dates from the 3rd century, from Origen, and was developed by Ambrose and Augustine.

The Jewish philosopher Moses ben Maimon or Maimonides, (1138–1204) a contemporary of the Muslim Ibn Rushd 1126-1198), living in Islamic Cordoba introduced an historical analysis of the Bible, showing that some images of God had a certain utility or relevance in certain periods, which they lost in later, higher stages of development. Thus an angry, jealous God can be understood as relevant when the people of Israel were still combating their

polytheistic tendencies. As Jews settled into monotheism a more loving God came to the fore.
Historical analysis is also common in Tafsir, where detailed research is done as to the specific circumstances of Muhammad at the time of certain revelations. Thus verses on slaying Pagans are to be understood in the context of the conflict between Muhammad and the polytheists of Mecca. Their meaning is not to be transferred to a 21st century setting. The Qur'an itself contains the notion of the historical development of revealed truth, and the idea that verses can be substituted by later verses.

"None of Our revelations do We abrogate or cause to be forgotten, but We substitute something better or similar:" 2 The Heifer, 107

Historical analysis also flourishes on the Christian side, and is well developed by secular analysts. Biblical and Qur'anic images are explained in terms of the social, cultural, political or economic context in which they were written.
Another form of interpretation is con- or intertextual, whereby verses are placed into perspective by linking them to other verses. It was Spinoza, the former Jew living in Holland, who excelled in this type of what is now called hermeneutical analysis,. He explained verses in the New Testament by reference to similar verses in the Hebrew Bible. All I can add to contextual analysis in this book is to suggest that it be extended to include similar verses from Bible and Qur'an. This could lead to valuable insights.
Having underlined the importance of figurative, contextual and historical interpretation, I must stress that the interpretation of texts given in this book is minimal. I leave Exegesis and Tafsir are to those who are better equipped than I am to deal with them. Perhaps this new combination of Bible and Qur'an texts - side by side - will raise new questions to work on.
This book, with its relatively modest objectives, can be fruitfully used together with these various approaches practiced by other experts, for the very reason that it leaves interpretation and contextual and historical analysis to the reader. Its usefulness might be more extensive because of what is left unsaid. It simply offers - to a large variety of readers - a

refreshing look at Bible and Qur'an texts, by presenting them in a novel way: together. It is this new way relating of Bible and Qur'an texts that might inspire new research in the field of interpretation.

The only thing I add is to each chapter of parallel quotes on a story or issue is a short introduction, describing the plot and mentioning the differences in the way it sometimes unravels. Similarities and differences are touched upon as objectively as possible. Only those references to translation issues, to exegesis, tafsir and tradition, deemed absolutely indispensable to understanding the texts are included. If, as in the legal chapters, more is added, a variety of interpretations is offered, so that the reader can make his or her own choice.

Balanced selection

The selection of texts has been a quest for balance. As far as is possible, given the difference in structure and history, Bible and Qur'an are equally represented, in terms of both quantity and quality. Although the Bible obviously has many more words than the Qur'an, an attempt has been made to make the columns on the left and right of more or less equal length. Care has been taken to ensure that under the heading 'Bible' in the left column, the Hebrew Bible or Tenach and the New Testament are all adequately represented. As explained above, every effort has been made to avoid bias in the selection of quotes.

Above all, I would like to emphatically counter the assertion that I have the desire –as do some others writing on this subject - to prove the superiority of the Bible over the Qur'an, or vice versa. As I was compiling this anthology, it soon became clear that the idea of a 'contest' between the Qur'an and the Bible was absurd. Indeed, the texts I selected from these books turned out to be so complementary that their combination resulted in enrichment. Often, reading the left column clarifies the one on the right, and vice versa.

There appears to be a sharing of values on several levels: first, in the loving respect shown to the same characters, from Adam to Jesus or 'Isa; second, in the expression of nearly identical story lines; and finally, in the ideas wrapped up in the stories, which are explicitly elaborated in the chapters on values and attributes of God. Indeed the chapters Alpha and Omega describing characteristics attributed to God were a significant result of ongoing dialogue, the idea being suggested by Mehmet Pacaci and seconded by Khaled Abou el Fadl. It is inspired by the idea of the 99 names of God and the 13 attributes in the Jewish Yigdal Hymn.

What's in a name?

That Allah and God are the same or even similar is not for me to say. Perhaps not even a thoughtful believer can venture such a statement. For what, in the final analysis, can we human beings know about the divine? But we can talk about the names we give to God.

God or Allah?

On 14th August 2007 the Dutch Bishop Muskens proposed calling God Allah. "God doesn't care what we call him. He is above that kind of thing. People have invented different names in order to quarrel with each other." He called into memory that 'Allah' simply means 'The God'. He didn't imagine the name 'Allah' would be accepted by the Catholic Church immediately, but in a hundred years or so things could be quite different. NRC Handelsblad 19 August 2007

A description of different names or characteristics attributed to God/Allah can be found in the last chapter of this anthology, Omega. Here I simply wish to point out that the names *Allah* and *God* are used by both religious groups as the situation demands. Thus on the Arabic version of the Dutch site www.Qur'anandbible.net Allah is used all round, simply because it is used in the Arabic translation of the Bible. In Indonesia Christians use the term 'Allah' to communicate with their Muslim counterparts. In America Muslims use the word God. In this anthology I use the name *God* for the Jewish, the Christian and the Muslim deity in my introductions. In the

quotes I follow the translators, who use the word God and Allah respectively.
What holds for the name of God also holds for the names of the various characters that people this anthology. For brevity's sake I often use their English names. The Arabic names appear often in the quotes from the Qur'an. In the table of contents English and Arabic names stand brotherly and sisterly side by side.

The Sources

The texts compiled in this book are very diverse in their origins. The Bible stories contain texts from the Hebrew Bible, or the Tenach, which includes the Torah, or Law. These go back, at least in part, to the Israel of 1000 years before Christ. It is said that they cannot be fully understood without the Midrasj and Talmud, the record of rabbinic discussions about Jewish Law and ethics, which unfortunately falls outside the limits of this anthology, as do writings of the Church fathers, modern theology, and the vast volumes of Qur'an interpretation or Tafsir. In all these cases the reader is warned not to jump to conclusions! Genesis, on which I draw extensively, may be the first book of the Bible, but is probably not the oldest. It was reportedly written down during the Babylonian exile, about 500 years before Christ.
Many quotes are taken from the New Testament, recorded between 50 and 130 A.D., which contains the four Gospels, letters from the apostle Paul, and the Revelation of John. The great variety of documents written around these books, such as the Gospel according to Thomas, I leave aside. I do once cite from Mishnah Sanhedrin, a legal Jewish text from the end of the 2nd century A.D. For newcomers, the *LORD* in the Bible refers to *God* or *Y(a)hw(e)h (I am).* In the introductions, I use the term '*God'*.
The Qur'an dates back to the seventh century A.D. and was, according to Islamic tradition, revealed to Muhammad by the Archangel Gabriel over a period of 23 years, starting in 610 A.D. The Islamic era begins with Muhammad's emigration to Medina in 622 A.D which is counted as 0 A.H. The first revelation occurred while Muhammad was still living in

Mecca, during the month of Ramadan, which is commemorated each year through fasting and reflection. For newcomers:
I, We, He - refers to 'The One God' or Allah. Allah is the one speaking in the Qur'an, revealing his message to Muhammad via the angel (messenger) Gabriel.
Of course, given the time difference, the Qur'an could not have been mentioned in the Bible. On the other hand the Bible is mentioned in the Qur'an, and Jews and Christians are called the People of the Book. The book resulting from the revelations to Muhammad supposedly contains an affirmation of the best from the Torah and the Gospel, and the Psalms of David. The significance of these earlier books is underlined in the following:

"If you were in doubt as to what We have revealed to you, then ask those who have been reading the Book from before you..." [10 Yunus, 94]

However this veneration does not refer to the Bible as we know it, which according to Muslim tradition, has been tampered with by human beings with human motives. Nevertheless, to understand stories written in 'shorthand' in the Qur'an, and issues only touched upon or even less than that, Muslims sometimes fall back upon the more elaborate Biblical texts on the subject in question. Indeed, Biblical notions have found their way into the Hadith or sayings of Muhammad, and are used both in the interpretation or Tafsir of the Qur'an and in the development of Islamic Law.
The Bible was created over many centuries and displays a wide variety in structure and style. In comparison, the Qur'an is a marvel of simplicity, created in one and the same breath, as it were. Intended for recitation by the faithful, it includes many repetitions and quick changes of subject. Its mercurial character makes it very difficult for outsiders, and perhaps even for insiders, to follow the storyline or the logic of arguments. Here Sharing Mary anthology can offer support.
The differences in structure and history between the two books make it difficult to spot similarities at first glance. It was only by 'cutting and

pasting' that I discovered the clear and very similar lines of the stories and arguments. There are a surprisingly large number of parallel stories in the Qur'an and the Bible. All of them are represented in this compilation, although some of the longer ones have been abbreviated. Experts or believers might miss beautiful elaborations etched into their brains. They can easily go back to find them in the Bible and Qur'an.
The Qur'an then is the youngest book. Meanwhile Jewish and Christian thought had been developing, with ideas and story elements not found in the Bible finding their way into the Midrasj or rabinnic Tenach interpretation; or in the various apocryphal gospels elaborating or varying on the officially accepted ones. Surprisingly these non-official elements sometimes turn up in Qur'an texts. Although a thorough investigation of these connections falls outside the scope of this anthology, I couldn't resist mentioning them incidentally.

Translations

Many excellent Bible and Qur'an translations have been published. After due consideration, I selected Abdullah Yusuf Ali's widely respected rendering of the Holy Qur'an. Thanks are due to Tharike Tarsile Qur'an Inc. (New York, USA) for their wholehearted permission to use the updated version of 2008. Words added by the translator to provide clarification are in brackets. Additions made by me to facilitate the reader's understanding of the storyline are marked as follows: (ed.)
As for the Bible, there are many excellent translations into English. However many are carefully guarded by copyright rules. Thus I was forced to use three different translations for the left column. The overall result was, however, very fortunate. Thus the New King James Version, (NKJV) published by Thomas Nelson, Inc. in 1982, is used for the stories, thus remaining within the 1000 verses allowed without explicit permission. For 'modern' controversial issues I used the Contemporary English Version, (CEV), thus staying within their 500 verse limit for use without explicit permission. For the chapter on *Common values and virtues* and for the chapters on God; *Alpha and Omega,* the ancient King James version is

used. I thank The Britsh Crown and Cambrigde University for the cordial permission- strictly speaking unnecessary for publication outside the UK- to use that beautiful age old Biblical language from 1611 for the chapters which do indeed taste of eternity.
My ultimate reason for choosing this combination of three Bible translations is the combined beauty of the language. If Khaled El Fadl searches for beauty in Islam, I still search for it in the Bible, the Holy Book of my childhood. Thus whereas the CEV is clearer for the contemporary legal chapters, for me, the baby Jesus was never "d*ressed in baby clothes and lying on a bed of hay*" [Luke 2: 4-12] as the CEV would have us believe. He was most definitely "*wrapped in swaddling clothes, lying in a manger.*" as the NJKV clearly states. That beauty can coincide with practicality is shown by the fact that swaddling clothes are back in fashion, proven by medical experts as a remedy against unrest of the infant generally and cot death in particular. Perhaps our forefathers were wiser than we were taught to believe.
I have taken the liberty with both books to cut and paste for the reader's benefit. Three dots indicate an incomplete sentence. Often complete sentences have been removed, to sustain the tension and keep the focus on the storyline. The extensive use of omissions is not due to lack of respect. On the contrary, they keep the storyline clear and exciting, without burdening the reader with irrelevancies. He or she can easily go back to the source from which the quotes were plucked. They have been noted with care.
All translations have their limitations. In a sense, they can be no more than a rendering of the original text, written in Hebrew and Aramaic (Hebrew Bible), Greek (New Testament) or Arabic (Qur'an). Translation issues have been spelled out by the experts. It is only incidentally that I refer to various translation options, as the subject demands.

Reconciliation while respecting differences

However much one tries, an anthology can never be completely objective. Subjective preferences and one's own social context play a role. I have chosen to bring the Bible and Qur'an texts as closely together as possible,

and to underline the conciliatory tendency so clearly present in both books. This is not to wash away differences; on the contrary such a practice is degrading for the believers. My intentions in the cultural and political context of today are perhaps To bridge misunderstandings, to seek common ground, and to be respectful about differences.
The beautiful texts collected in this anthology will strike a chord with many readers from a variety of backgrounds. They will hopefully contribute to inter-faith and inter-cultural and academic dialogue, which is intensifying in many places all over the world. A constructive dialogue does not unfold as a matter of course. It needs effort, and more especially openness, kindness and patience, as El Fadl notes in a comment on this Qur'an verse:

*"O mankind! We…made you into nations and tribes (*li ta'arafu) *that you may know each other (not that you may despise each other).* 49 The Inner Appartments,13

'Li ta'arafu' means to get to know one another. But the word *'arafa'* (to know) is quite profound. It connotes kindness, goodness, tolerance, and patience…To know is to learn and teach – learn about others and teach about ourselves. To learn and teach, that is *'ta'aruf'*. And neither learning nor teaching can be accomplished without kindness, tolerance, and patience. Khaled Abou el Fadl.p.19

The selection of quotes from Bible and Qur'an presented in this anthology is not a definite statement, not an end, but, hopefully a beginning. This anthology evolved over more than half a decade into what lies before you now. The quotes I have collected flow together into a beautiful image of what many believe to be the work of the Divine, which others simply recognize as great literature. Hopefully this anthology will inspire religious and secular readers alike.

4. The historic and academic context

Andrew Rippin

A long history of comparing the Bible with the Qur'an precedes the "side-by-side" presentation that is the feature of this book. The process may even be said to start with the New Testament's citations of the Hebrew Bible and the Qur'an's views of both of its predecessors. The Gospel writers looked to the biblical record of the past for scriptural predictions that were fulfilled in the coming of Jesus. Muslim scripture suggests that possession of revealed books is a criterion of true religion; it thus recognizes the Jewish Torah and Psalms and the Christian Gospels as defining characteristics of the earlier faith communities and as a basis for the construction of a new one. While acknowledging the inherent value of these scriptures, accusations are made in the Qur'an of Jewish and Christian "tampering" with the text of scripture, thus arguing for the validity and truthfulness of the Qur'an as the only valid inheritor of the status of being God's word. The basis on which this argument was made required the scriptures to be brought together and compared as to their contents. This basically polemical approach towards the comparison of scripture continued in medieval times, and became a stock part of both Christian and Muslim attitudes towards each other's texts. For example, a defense of Christianity written in Arabic by a certain al-Kindi in the 9th century brings forth explicit comparisons between the Bible and the Qur'an when making arguments that not a single truth can be found in the Qur'an that is not already known elsewhere. Likewise on the Muslim side, writers such as Ibn Hazm (died 1064) critiqued the biblical text for its wrongful portrayal of the prophets of the past, seizing on biblical suggestions that Abraham told lies and Lot and David were immoral, for example. This kind of assessment has been explored fully by Hava Lazarus-Yafeh in her book *Intertwined Worlds: Medieval Islam and Bible Criticism* Princeton University Press, 1992 in which she argues for a significant role for Muslim thinkers in the development of biblical criticism in Europe (in people such as Spinoza) precisely because they were examining the Bible in comparison to the Qur'an.

Not all medieval thinkers took a negative view, however. Walid Saleh has examined the work of the Egyptian intellectual, al-Biqa'i, who died in 1480. This analysis "A Fifteenth-Century Muslim Hebraist: Al-Biqa'i and His Defense of Using the Bible to Interpret the Qur'an," *Speculum* 83[2008], 629-54 shows that a Muslim reading of the Bible could take a positive approach, although a controversial one, given the reaction of some of al-Biqa'i's compatriots at the time. While al-Biqa'i certainly understood the Qur'an to be the ultimate judge of truth, he also recognized that the Bible can help explain much of the Qur'anic text by filling in details that are not explicit, especially in the stories of the prophets.

A Muslim thinker such as al-Biqa'i might be seen as a precursor of 19th century European developments in the study of the Qur'an. Such studies are usually said to have commenced with Abraham Geiger, a rabbi and the founder of the German Jewish Reform movement. In 1832, Geiger published an award-winning work with the title "What did Muhammad take from Judaism?" published in English translation under the title *Judaism and Islam* in 1898

This book traces the sources of the Qur'an within Judaism, and to a lesser extent, Christianity, and, in doing so, attempts to demonstrate that religion developed in accord with human social concerns and conditions; and thus from the perspective of an emerging Reform Judaism, should continue to do so. All the stories of the prophets and the ethical impulses of the Bible and the Qur'an could be traced back to ancient mythological structures of which those texts were stages in a long historical evolution.

Geiger's work was the beginning of an extensive series of academic works tracing the "sources" of the Qur'an in the Bible and the later biblical tradition (in its full sectarian diversity). Such studies now tend to be viewed as reductive in approach in that they allow no scope for the creative spirit of an individual prophet and they convey a strong sense of illegitimacy of any independent existence of a subsequent tradition because of its "derivative" nature. The main emphasis in historical scholarship today is to move away from a comparison of the text of the Bible to that of the Qur'an and recognize that the Qur'an stands at a particular historical moment within a long tradition of biblical interpretation. The Qur'an is viewed as emerging within the context of near eastern late antiquity, capturing a much broader scope of human mythological activity as its background than a simple comparison to the Bible might suggest.

This 'side-by-side' anthology of the Qur'an and the Bible, then, must be understood as a venture of a different sort than that found in medieval polemic, 19th century reductiveness, or 21st century multi-cultural contextuality. The first thing to remark is the key difference between it and other contemporary scholarly endeavors: that it focuses solely on the text of scripture. Such an approach has certainly been subject to criticism because it suggests a particular orientation to religion that is characteristic of the modern world (and especially Protestant Christianity) which tends to equate religion with its scripture. In reality, religions in their institutional forms are so much more than that, for they also involve the many varied expressions that the human communities derive from their texts. The focus on scripture also tends to suggest that members of religions are somehow bound to their texts in ways that limit their actions in the world such that they cannot act in other ways. To be a "true" Muslim, or Christian, or Jew, one must not be seen to be contradicting the scripture, it seems to suggest. For example, if the Qur'an says that owning slaves is fine, then to be a true Muslim one must accept that and preferably even own one! If God condemns homosexuality in the Bible then that is a guidance that must be followed! However, historically, the religious communities did not see themselves in this manner when it came to scripture and nor do all religious people take that view today; they all construct traditions and sources of authority to supplement and even correct scripture. Certainly this has changed for some believers in the modern world. Some contemporary Jews, Christians and Muslims see their religion as a personal, internal attitude that is stimulated, fostered and maintained through a relationship to their scripture only. So while the attitude towards scripture that sees it as foundational to life in the manner of a political constitution has impacted religion, it is important to remember that this does not capture the full sense of being Jewish, Christian or Muslim in the modern world as all believers understand it.

A "side-by-side" text of the type presented here has particular merits as well as a significant heritage. One model for it may be seen in the way Christian scholars have developed such an approach when dealing with to the three (or four) "synoptic" gospels. In that context, the format can be revealing for historical purposes. In the case of presenting Bible and the Qur'an together, however, the time frame that separates the two of them means that caution is needed. Juxtaposing the texts in this manner and attempting to draw any sort of historical conclusions can lead to some serious misinterpretations of the data. Of course, we may well assume that at least some Jews and Christians at the time of the emergence of the Qur'an were quite familiar with their canonical biblical texts and thus the textually based comparison as suggested by a "side-by-side" approach is not wholly anachronistic. However, the reader must guard against the misleading implications of a reductive approach in drawing any conclusions from the "side-by-side" comparisons that suggest either direct borrowings or apparent misunderstandings. History tends to make things far more complicated than that type of comparison implies. The reader needs to be cautious, and recognize that these religious traditions are alive and have strong traditions of interpretation and adaptation that can move the ideas and traditions of those living communities a significant distance from the apparent sense of the scripture. The end result of this process of interpretation will sometimes exaggerate the differences between the two texts but, on other occasions, will bring them closer together.

There is probably no better example of this than the story of Jesus and his crucifixion. The account itself is a major point of contestation between Christianity and Islam, given that Christian theology has tended to depend on the historical reality of Jesus' death on the cross for its theology of sacrifice and redemption. The oft-cited denial of Jesus' crucifixion in the Qur'an, then, has made this a point for some aggressive debate between polemicists. However, the history of the way these verses have been interpreted in Islam, as has been explored in Todd Lawson's *The Crucifixion and the Qur'an: A Study in the History of Muslim Thought*,[Oneworld 2009] makes it clear that such a stark understanding and portrayal of the differences between the two religions on this point simply does not do justice to the full dimensions of the Muslim side of the debate. And surely it is important to remember that many Christians, too, can affirm their strong belief in the significance of Jesus while at the same time not embracing a notion of redemptive death on the cross. This emphasizes the point made here previously that the reader must guard against the inclination to think that believers are somehow tied to an interpretation of, or an attitude towards, scripture that emerges out of an apparent sense of the text just because the 'side-by-side' view suggests similarities or differences.

Ultimately, a 'side-by-side' text such as this serves to further certain common religious goals. It draws attention to the commonalities of traditions and the richness of mutually supporting scriptures within the near eastern religious milieu. Of course, there are differences, too, and those become apparent within this approach as it draws attention to the uniqueness of the each text when it deals with the same traditional material. So, what then should a 'side-by-side' text such as this do for the reader? What is its purpose? Put simply, it should awaken curiosity. Rather than rushing to judgment over right and wrong, the reader must be encouraged to ask 'Why?'; 'What does this mean?', 'Of what significance is this?' If we are to speak of religious traditions being mutually enriching because of their differences and similarities, those characteristics cannot be simply left on the level of saying, 'that's interesting.' The reflective process has to go further.

One of the challenges of structuring a 'side-by-side' text such as this is the level of repetition within the Bible and the Qur'an themselves. The instances in the Bible are well known, as evidenced in the case of the book of Chronicles and the four Gospels, and even explicit on occasion, given the name of the Book of Deuteronomy, or 'second law'. The Qur'an's use of parallel passages has been remarked upon in scholarship but never fully resolved as to what it means historically. Do the stories originate in different folk-tale traditions? Do they reflect different audiences during Muhammad's lifetime? Are they intended to illustrate different theological points? The full sense of such duplication cannot be accommodated in this type of 'side-by-side' analysis and yet, within both scriptures, repetition is a central rhetorical feature and is an integral part of the way in which the overall message is conveyed. In a detailed scholarly analysis of the matter, John Wansbroug[h] argued for a strong sense of literary formulaic structuring, likely reflective of an oral compositional environment for the Qur'an. *Qur'anic Studies: Sources and Methods Scriptural Interpretation*, Oxford University Press, 1977; reprint Prometheus Press, 2004 This, he suggested, is displayed by the parallelisms displayed especially in the prophetic stories. In his analysis of the stories of the Arabian prophet Shu'ayb (Moses' Midian the father-in-law equivalent to the Biblical Jethro) as found in the Qur'an, 7:85-93, 11:84-95, 26:176-90, 29:36-7 Wansbrough saw a standard scheme found in prophetic literature in general. Such passages start with a commission of the prophet and a formula of legitimating, followed by a diatribe or accusation and a threat or prediction of destruction. Dialogue ensues with an altercation, a counter-argument and a final expression of resignation. The conclusion provides a rejection and fulfillment of the threat, and an epilogue and final assessment. The complexities of the text of the Qur'an and the Bible provide challenges to the reader on many levels in coming to a full appreciation of the literary depths upon which these texts draw. Certainly one of the merits of the 'side-by-side' presentation is to display some of this in a revealing manner, while not attempting or even pretending that this unlocks all the secrets.

Nor can a 'side-by-side' version of scripture convey all of the contents of either the Bible or the Qur'an. It is necessarily a selection. Such a selection must to be done, as it is here, with a great deal of care so as to reflect, as much as is possible, no sense of an agenda that serves the purposes of one faith community over another; nor indeed a secular attitude of ridicule towards both. The chapters of this anthology show the deep commonalities in the stories of the past shared by the religious traditions; and the fundamental motifs of monotheism contained in descriptions of creation and the judgment day under the guidance of the one God. Again, we should not pretend that this is all that these books are about. Such arrogance is entirely misplaced. Rather, the 'side-by-side' presentation must be viewed as an invitation to read more, to see the stories in their overall context, and to hear (as far as translations allow) the rhymes, rhythms and verbal musicality of both texts to their fullest and in their individuality.

Alpha: the Beginning

נִבְרָא אֲשֶׁר דָּבָר לְכָל קַדְמוֹן
לְרֵאשִׁיתוֹ רֵאשִׁית יןוְאֵ: רִאשׁוֹן

"He preceded every being that was created."
Jewish Yigdal Hymn

"I am Alpha…the beginning…the first"
Bible, Revelation 22:13

"He is the First…"
Qur'an 57 Iron, 3

In the beginning, there was only God, but the promise was there. The ultimate goal was given. God was also the Last, even when He was only the First. Both books relate how even before the universe had been created, God's spirit was moving over or enthroned above the waters.

Bible	God/Allah	Qur'an
"I am Alpha and Omega, the beginning and the ending," saith the Lord, "which is, and which was and which is to come..." Revelation 1:8		He is the First and the Last, the Evident and the Hidden. 57 Iron, 3
And the Spirit of God moved upon the face of the waters. Genesis 1:2		...and His Throne was over the waters. 11 Hud, 7

Part Two

Stories in the Hebrew Bible and the Qur'an

5. Creation

Heaven and earth and everything in between were created, out of the void by a Divine Word.

First, God created light. Then, He created the Sun and the Moon and in so doing He created day and night. God created time. Then, heaven, earth and the seas were separated. The earth was covered with plants. He made sky, water and the earth teem with birds, fish and land animals. That is the story of the creation in both books. The Qur'an adds that everything was created from water, and that heaven unfolded into seven heavens.
In the Bible, men and women were created in God's image. The Qur'an emphatically rejects this resemblance between God and humankind.
The book of Genesis tells us that God affirmed what He had created. *"He saw... that it was good."* [Genesis 1:9] The Qur'an emphasizes the care and generosity of the Creator. The wonders of creation are "signs for people who believe" that they can trust God's mercy.[16 The Bee, 79] The wonders of the creation should encourage people to excel. Its purpose is

"that He may try you, which of you is best in conduct." [11 Hud, 7]

In both books, the creation took place in six days (periods) of Divine time. These were no ordinary days, for day and night, indeed time, were created during the process of creation itself.
What happened after these six miraculous Days? The Bible mentions a seventh Day: the Sabbath, a day of rest for God and for human beings. In the Qur'an, God did not rest, for he knows no fatigue. After six Days of creation, He settled himself on his throne. The notion that God is never weary is also expressed in Isaiah.
The book of Genesis emphasizes that after six Days the Creation is

complete, perfect. The Qur'an holds that after these six miraculous Days, God continued to create, again and again. A second creation take
s place with each new spring, each new birth. Finally, on the Last Day, He raises humankind from death in a third creation.

In the Bible, the Creation comes at the beginning, in the book of Genesis. The Qur'an contains repeated references to the creation in several different surahs.

Both books give humans a special responsibility to care for everything that God created. In the Bible, humankind may rule over the Creation on behalf of God in the way God would, for he was shaped in His image. The Qur'an speaks of humankind as vice-regent. He does not own the earth, to do with as he pleases, but must care for the Creation in God's name.

God created heavens and earth
In the beginning God created the heavens and the earth.
The earth was without form, and void; and darkness was on the face of the deep. Genesis 1:1-2
Then God said, Let there be…: and there was... Genesis 1:3
For He spoke and it was done; Psalm 33:9

Day and Night
Then God said, "Let there be light"; and there was light. And God saw the light, that it was good; and God divided the light from the darkness. God called the light Day, and the darkness He called Night. So the evening and the morning were the first day. Genesis 1:3-5

God made the sky
Then God said, "Let there be a firmament in the midst of the waters, and let it divide the waters from the waters."
Thus God made the firmament, and divided the waters which were under the firmament from the waters which were above the firmament; and it was so.

Creation a sign
And among His signs is the creation of the heavens and the earth… 42 Consultation, 29

He it is Who created the heavens and the earth in six Days. 11 Hud, 7

…glory be to Him…when He decrees a matter, He says to it: "Be," and it is. 2 The Heifer,116-117

Light and Dark
Praise be Allah, Who created the heavens and the earth, and made the Darkness and the Light… 6 The Cattle,1
He created the heavens and the earth in true (proportions):
He makes the Night overlap the Day, and the Day overlap the Night… 39 The Crowds, 5

Heaven and earth
…He comprehended in His design the sky, and it had been (as) smoke:
He said to it and to the earth: "You come together, willingly or unwillingly."
They said: "We do come (together), in willing obedience."

And God called the firmament Heaven.
So the evening and the morning were the second day. Genesis 1:6-8

Land and ocean

Then God said, "Let the waters under the heavens be gathered together into one place, and let the dry land appear"; and it was so.
And God called the dry land Earth, and the gathering together of the waters He called Seas. And God saw that it was good. Genesis 1:9-10
This is the history of the heavens and the earth when they were created...before any plant of the field was in the earth and before any herb of the field had grown. For the Lord God had not caused it to rain upon the earth...but a mist went up from the earth and watered the whole face of the ground. Genesis 2:4-6

Trees and grain

Then God said, "Let the earth bring forth grass, the herb that yields seed, and the fruit tree that yields fruit according to its kind, whose seed is in itself, on the earth:" and it was so.
And the earth brought forth grass, the herb that yields seed after his kind, and the tree that yields fruit,

So He completed them as seven firmaments... and He assigned to each heaven its duty and command. 41 Fussilat,11-12

Water and earth

It is He Who has let free the two bodies of flowing water: One palatable and sweet and the other salt and bitter. 25 The Criterion, 53
And it is He Who spread out the earth, and set thereon mountains standing firm and (flowing) rivers. 13 The Thunder, 3

And We send down water from the sky according to (due) measure, and We cause it to soak in the soil...
And We send the fecundating winds -then cause the rain to descend from the sky, therewith providing you with water...though you are not the guardians of its stores.
3 The Believers,18; 15 The Rocky Tract :22

Abundant fruits

...and fruit of every kind He made in pairs, two and two... 13 The Thunder, 3

With it We grow for you gardens of date-palms and vines: in them have abundant fruits: and of them you eat (and have enjoyment).
Also a tree springing out of Mount Sinai, which produces oil, and relish

whose seed is in itself, according to its kind.
And God saw that it was good.
So the evening and the morning were the third day. Genesis 1:11-13

for those who use it for food.
23 The Believers, 19-20

It is Allah Who causes the seed-grain and the date-stone to split and sprout. He causes the living to issue from the dead... 6 The Cattle 95

Lights in the sky

Then God said, "Let there be lights in the firmament of the heavens to divide the day from the night; and let them be for signs, and for seasons, and for days, and years; and let them be for lights in the firmament of the heavens to give light on the earth"; and it was so. Then God made two great lights: the greater light to rule the day, and the lesser light to rule the night. He made the stars also. God set them in the firmament of the heavens to give light on the earth, and to rule over the day and over the night, and to divide the light from the darkness. And God saw that it was good. So the evening and the morning were the fourth day. Genesis 1:14-19

Sun, moon and stars

Don't you see how Allah has created the seven heavens one above another, and made the moon a light in their midst, and made the sun as a (Glorious) Lamp?
71 Noah, 15-16

He has subjected the sun and the moon (to His law): Each one follows a course for a time appointed.
39 The Crowds, 5

And We adorned the lower heaven with lights... 41 Fussilat, 12
It is We Who have set out the Zodiacal Signs in the heavens, and made them fair-seeming to (all) beholders. 15 The Rocky Tract, 16
It is He Who makes the stars as beacons for you, that you may guide yourselves, with their help, through the dark spaces of land and sea:
6, The Cattle 97

Animals, wild and tame

Then God said, "Let the waters abound with an abundance of living

Fish, birds and cattle

And Allah has created every animal from water: of them there are some

creatures, and let birds fly above the earth across the face of the firmament of the heavens."
So God created great sea creatures, and every living thing that moves, with which the waters abounded according to their kind, and every winged bird according to its kind. And God saw that it was good. And God blessed them, saying,
"Be fruitful, and multiply, and fill the waters in the seas, and let birds multiply on the earth."
So the evening and the morning were the fifth day.
Then God said, "Let the earth bring forth the living creature according to its kind: cattle and creeping thing, and beast of the earth, each according to its kind"; and it was so. And God saw that it was good.
Genesis 1:20-25

God created man in His image
Then God said, "Let Us make man in Our image, according to Our likeness";
So God created man in His own image; in the image of God He created him; male and female He created them.
Then God blessed them, and God said unto them, "Be fruitful, and multiply; fill (replenish KJV) the

that creep on their bellies; some that walk on two legs; and some that walk on four. 24 Light, 45

Do they not look at the birds, held poised in the midst of…the sky? Nothing holds them up but (the power of) Allah. 16 The Bee, 79
And He has created cattle for you: from them you derive warmth, and numerous benefits, and of their (meat) you eat.
And you have a sense of pride and beauty in them as you drive them home in the evening, and as you lead them forth to pasture in the morning.
And they carry your heavy loads to lands that you could not (otherwise) reach except with souls distressed.
16 The Bee, 5-7

Nothing like unto Him
(Allah) Most Gracious! He has created man. 55 Most Gracious, 1, 3
He is Allah, the One and Only;
And there is none like unto Him.
112 Purity (of Faith),1, 4

(He is) the Creator of the heavens and the earth: He has made for you pairs from among yourselves, and pairs among cattle: by this means does He multiply you: there is

earth, and subdue it; Then God saw everything that He had made, and indeed it was very good. So the evening and the morning were the sixth day. [Genesis 1:26-28, 31]

nothing whatever like unto Him... [42 Consultation,11]

Seventh day: Rest

And on the seventh day God ended His work which He had done, and He rested on the seventh day from all His work which He had done. Then God blessed the seventh day and sanctified it... [Genesis 2:2-3]

Remember the Sabbath day, to keep it holy. Six days you shall labor and do all your work, but the seventh day...you shall do no work. For the LORD...rested the seventh day. [Exodus 20:8-10]

The everlasting God, the LORD, the Creator of the ends of the earth, neither faints nor is weary. [Isaiah 40:28]

Allah not weary

Your Guardian-Lord is Allah, Who created the heavens and the earth in six Days,

And is firmly established on the Throne (of authority). [7 The Heights, 54]

We created the heavens and the earth and all between them in Six Days,

nor did any sense of weariness touch Us. [50 Qaf, 38]

Perfect creation

Thus the heavens and the earth, and all the host of them, were finished. [Genesis 2:1]

Then God saw everything that He had made, and indeed it was very good. [Genesis 1:31]

Continuous creation

Don't they see show Allah originates creation, then repeats it... [29 The Spider,19]

...even as We produced the first Creation, so shall We produce a new one. It is He who begins the process of creation, and repeats it... [21 The Prophets, 104; 10 Yunus, 4]

ii. Reading the Creation Story together

Intermezzo by Herman Beck

It's always a great pleasure to work in a context of religious diversity. Reading each other's relevant texts together with believers from another tradition is an enriching experience. Their refreshing perspective and different historical experience force you to look at your own familiar texts in a new way. As a protestant Christian I had the privilege of teaching as a visiting professor at the IAN Sunan Kalijaga, an Islamic State University in Yogyakarta in Indonesia. It was my task to introduce PhD students to the Western approaches in religious studies; in particular historical critical analysis and the method of literary-critical method of studying religious documents. In this approach holy books are studied as are other literary texts. Questions are asked about the historical context in which they were written, so as to promote their understanding.

In our group we decided that the reading of the first two chapters of Genesis would offer a good exercise to get to know these Western approaches and show the problems that might arise.

I was expecting that my students would be a little uncomfortable at this approach, for they believe that the Qur'an is the word of God whereas I like many Christians believe that the Bible was written by different people in a variety of historical settings, although God's truth might shine through these human words in one way or another.

That there are two different creation stories in the Bible was no problem for my Muslim students. In the Qur'an the creation story also appears in different verses, without a perfect consistency between them.

They were also familiar with the problem that, whilst on the one hand, God created the Universe from nothing, (*creatio ex nihilo*), there was on the other and already something there: the waters (chapter alpha). That was familiar to them for in the Qur'an God's throne was over the waters before creation started. Even the six days of creation they did not take literally, for day in this context was a divine unit of time, rather than a week day as we know them. Our day and night appeared only in the course of creation, when God created sun and moon. So reading the creation story Genesis 1 presented no problems to my Muslim students. On the contrary they liked the Genesis version, which, compared to the scattered verses in the Qur'an, was more complete and beautiful. However we got into trouble when we came to Genesis 2:2, which reads:

"And on the seventh day God ended His work which He had done, and He rested on the seventh day from all His work which He had done."

When they read that, my students simply burst out laughing! That made me a bit unsure of myself. I had after all only been in Indonesia for a short while, only three months in fact, and I couldn't figure out what they were laughing about.

"Did I say something silly?" I asked.

"No No, it isn't you we are laughing about; it's the absurd idea that God Almighty, the Creator of heaven and earth, should need a rest. How on earth could God be tired?"

In the Qur'an it is quite different. God is almighty, unlike humans. There is nothing like unto him. So God cannot be tired like a human being. Humans have needs, God is self sufficient. Saying that God needed a rest is giving him human needs. That is absurd.

This made me realize that due to my own education and socialization, I took things for granted, which on second thoughts might need rethinking.

Thank goodness, after searching the Bible, Marlies and I finally found, for this anthology, tucked away in the book Isaiah, a quote about God never tiring,.

"Hast thou not heard that...
the Creator of the ends of the earth, fainteth neither is weary". Isaiah 40:28

No I hadn't - until I came to Indonesia.

6. The Creation of Humankind

In Bible and Qur'an, the first human being was created from mud or dust and was therefore named after the Hebrew word for earth: Adam = Men. God breathing His spirit into man to make him come alive is also found in both books. The Qur'an relates how God gave man beautiful forms. According to Genesis, God blessed humankind and saw that what He had created was good.

In the Bible, both men and women are said to have been created in God's image. The concept of God in the Qur'an is more abstract. Nobody can be equal to or like God, although humans are destined to return to God after death.

In both books, man is appointed God's caretaker on earth. He is to rule wisely over creation. He has, regarding the rest of creation, both exceptional power and an exceptional responsibility.

In the Qur'an, God explains to the angels his plan to create man. They are shocked. They warn God that men will use their powers to shed blood. But God went ahead with his plan. (a story also found in Jewish Bible commentaries or Midrash) He even ordered the angels to bow down to Adam, which they did obediently. But one called 'Iblis', or Devil, who was created from fire, refused. Because of his disobedience to God, he was called 'the unbeliever' and driven from paradise. But he was temporarily given the power to seduce man to evil, a role he was eager to accept. A comparable story about angels and the devil does not appear in Genesis. Elsewhere in the Bible, there is mention of a Satan who fell from Heaven, a Satan who seduced human beings to stray from God's path.

A typical human trait that plays a role right from the start is the power of speech. In Genesis, it was the (first) man who gave names to all things. In the Qur'an, it was God who taught man the names of everything. Angels lack this power of language, as became clear when God put them to the test. So angels must bow down before man.

In the Qur'an, the diversity in languages and colors of peoples is a Divine gift, a stimulus to become acquainted with one other. But the colorful

variety in languages can also lead to confusion and discord, as shown by the story of the Tower of Babel further on in Genesis.
The story about the creation of humankind has implications for the relation between the sexes. Well-known from the Bible is the story of the woman, Eve, (mother of life) created from the rib of Adam, (man from earth), to be his helper. There is a second story of the creation in Genesis, related both before and after the rib version, in which men and women were created simultaneously and as equals, both in the image of God. In Genesis 5 both men and women were named Adam [(KJV),] or Mankind [(NKJV).]
The Qur'an emphatically denies that man resembles God. Nobody can be like Him for He is the creator of everything.
The story about the rib does not appear in the Qur'an. Man and woman were created as equals, from a single soul; as couples with kindred spirits. The Arabic verses in question are difficult to translate accurately. An example is verse 39 The Crowds, 6, in Abdullah Yusuf Ali's translation:

*He created you (all) from a single person: then created, of like nature, **his** mate;*

This issue centers on two Arabic words:
nafs = soul, female, at least grammatically;
and zawj = partner, male, at least grammatically.

Thus an alternative translation given by Dawood is:

*"He created you from a single soul, then from that soul He created **its** spouse."*

Likewise, Abdel Halleem translates as follows:

*He created you all from a single being from which He made **its** mate.*

This implies that men and women were created simultaneously and as equals. To both God grants soul mates, of whatever gender.
Behind this difference in translation lies a difference in interpretation. Some Qur'an exegetes hold that, in spite of its grammatical feminine

nature, *nafs* refers to Adam (the man) and *zawj* (partner) refers to his wife, even though it is grammatically masculine. They base their interpretation on Genesis 2, to show that the woman was created from Adam's left rib. Other Qur'an exegetes point to Genesis 1 to show that God created men and women simultaneously and as equals. (see also the Jewish Midrash, presenting the first human, Adam as androgynic)
The Qur'an differs from the Genesis story of the creation of humankind in its emphasis on continuity. The Divine creation of humans continues after the original creation from earth and spirit, but in a different way. Men and women are created from a drop of water – sperm; but first and foremost from a lump of blood. The child grows in the mother's womb. The continuous creation of people after the first creation is considered a sign that God will also re-create man after his death on the Last Day.

The Creation of Humankind

Bible

Creation from Dust and Breath
...the LORD God made the earth and the heavens...and there was no man to till the ground;
And the LORD God formed man *of* the dust of the ground, and breathed into his nostrils the breath of life; and man became a living being.
Genesis 2:4-5, 7

Then God saw everything that He had made, and indeed it was very good. Genesis 1: 31

Qur'an

Man Moulded from Mud and Spirit
Behold! Your Lord said to the angels:
"I am about to create man, from sounding clay from mud moulded into shape;
When I have fashioned him (in due proportion) and breathed into him of My spirit, you fall down in obeisance unto him.
15 The Rocky Tract, 28-29

We have indeed created man in the best of moulds... 95 The Fig, 4

Man in God's Image

Then God said, "Let Us make man in Our image, according to Our likeness; let them have dominion over the fish of the sea, over the birds of the air, and over the cattle, over all the earth …

While the ministering angels were arguing…the Holy One…created him. Said He to them: 'What can ye avail? Man has already been made! Midrash R. Huna the Elder of Sepphoris, Simon 1961

So God created man in His own image…male and female He created them. Then God blessed them, and God said to them, "Be fruitful and multiply; fill (replenish KJV) the earth and subdue it; have dominion over the fish of the sea, over the birds of the air, and over every living thing that moves on the earth." Genesis 1:26-28

Man as Vice-Regent

Say: He is Allah, the One…
And there is none like unto Him. 112 Purity (of faith), 1-4

Behold, your Lord said to the angels: "I will create a viceregent on earth." They said: "Will You place therein one who will make mischief therein and shed blood?- while we do celebrate Your praises and glorify Your holy (name)?"
He said: "I know what you do not know." 2 The Heifer,30
We did indeed offer the Trust to the Heavens and the Earth…but they refused to undertake it, being afraid thereof: but man undertook it… 33 The Confederates, 72

Satan Falling

In the Bible the story of Satan's fall and his role as a tempter of humankind is not associated with the creation of humankind. It does appear in other stories, notably the story of Job.

Below are some fragments from the New Testament showing Jesus referring to the fall of Satan and

Haughty Iblis (Devil)

And behold, We said to the angels: "Bow down to Adam" and they bowed down:

not so Iblis: he refused and was haughty: he was of those who reject Faith. 2 The Heifer, 34

(Allah) said: "What prevented you from bowing down when I

tempted by the devil.

And He (Jesus ed.) said to them, "I saw Satan fall like lightning from heaven." Luke 10:18

Then Jesus being filled with the Holy Spirit returned from the Jordan and was led by the Spirit into the wilderness, being tempted for forty days by the devil.

And the devil said to him, "If you are the Son of God, command this stone to become bread."

But Jesus answered him, saying, "It is written, 'Man shall not live by bread alone, but by every word of God.'"

Then the devil, taking Him up on a high mountain, showed Him all the kingdoms of the world in a moment of time. And the devil said to Him, "All this authority I will give You, and their glory; if You will worship before me, all will be Yours."

And Jesus answered and said to him, "Get behind Me, Satan!" Luke 4: 1-8

commanded you?"

He said: "I am better than he: you created me from fire, and him from clay."

(Allah) said: "... it is not for you to be arrogant here: get out, for you are of the meanest (of creatures)."

He said: "Give me respite till the day they are raised up."

(Allah) said: "Be you among those who have respite."

He said: "Because you have thrown me out of the Way, lo! I will lie in wait for them on Your Straight Way. Then will I assault them from before them and behind them, from their right and their left: nor will You find gratitude in most of them (for your mercies)."

(Allah) said: "Get out from this, disgraced and expelled. If any of them follow you - I will fill Hell with you all." 7 The Heights,12-18

Adam gives names

Out of the ground the LORD God formed every beast of the field, and every fowl of the air;

and brought them to Adam to see what he would call them. And

The Gift of Language

And He taught Adam the nature of all things; then He placed them before the angels, and said: "Tell me the nature of these if you are right."

They said: "Glory to You, of

whatever Adam called every living creature, that was its name.

So Adam gave names to all cattle, to the birds of the air, and to every beast of the field. Genesis 2:19-20

knowledge We have none, save what You have taught us: in truth it is You Who are perfect in knowledge and wisdom."
He said: "O Adam! Tell them their natures." When he had told them their names, Allah said: "Did I not tell you that I know the secrets of heaven and earth…"
And behold, We said to the angels: 'Bow down to Adam:' 2 The Heifer,31-34

The Tower of Babel - Confusion
Now the whole earth had one language, and one speech.
And they said, "Come, let us build ourselves a city, and a tower, whose top is in the heavens; let us make a name for ourselves, lest we be scattered abroad over the face of the whole earth."
But the LORD came down to see the city and the tower, which the sons of men had built.
And the LORD said, "Indeed the people are one, and they all have one language; and this is what they begin to do; now nothing that they propose (have imagined [KJV]) to do will be withheld from them.
Come, let Us go down and there confuse their language, that they may not understand one another's

Diverse Languages and Colors
And among His Signs is the creation… of the variations in your languages and your colors: verily in that are Signs for those who know. 30 The Roman Empire, 22

O mankind! We created you from a single (pair) of a male and a female, and made you into nations and tribes, that you may know each other. (Not that you may despise each other).

Verily, the most honored of you in the sight of Allah is (he who is) the most righteous of you...
49 The Inner Apartments, 13

If Allah had so willed, He would have made you a single people, but (His Plan is) to test you in what He

speech.
So the LORD scattered them abroad from there over the face of all the earth, and they ceased building the city. Therefore its name is called Babel, because there the LORD confused the language of all the earth; Genesis 11:1, 4-9

has given you: so strive as in a race in all virtues. 5 The Table Spread, 48

Creation of Men and Women

In the day that God created man, He made him in the likeness of God.
He created them male and female, and blessed them, and called them Mankind… (Adam, KJV) in the day when they were created. Genesis 5:1-2

R. Jeremiah b. Leazar said: When the Holy One…created Adam, He created him an herma- phrodite [bi-sexual], Simon, 1961

And the LORD God said, "It is not good that man should be alone; I will make him a helper comparable to him." Genesis 2:18
And the LORD God caused a deep sleep to fall on Adam, and he slept; and He took one of his ribs, and closed up the flesh in its place. Then the rib which the LORD God had taken from man, He made into a woman, and He brought her to the man.
And Adam said, "This is now bone

Creation of Pairs

Oh mankind! Reverence your Guardian-Lord, Who created you from a single Person, created, and of like nature, his (its, her ed.) mate, and from them twain scattered (like seeds) countless men and women… 4 The Women, 1

He created you (all) from a single Person: then created, of like nature, his (its ed.) mate… 39 The Crowds, 6
He has made for you pairs from among yourselves...by this means does He multiply you: there is nothing whatever like unto Him… 42 Consultation, 11

O mankind! We created you from a single (pair) of a male and a female… that you may know each other. (not that you may despise each other). Verily, the most honored of you in the sight of Allah is he (he {she ed.} who is) the most righteous of you... 49 The Inner Apartments, 13

of my bones, and flesh of my flesh. She shall be called Woman, because she was taken out of Man. Therefore a man shall leave his father and mother, and be joined to his wife and they shall become one flesh. Genesis 2: 21-24

And among His Signs is this, that He created for you mates from among yourselves, that you may dwell in tranquility with them, and He has put love and mercy between your (hearts). 30 The Roman Empire, 21

Continuous Creation

In the name of your Lord and Cherisher, Who created man, out of a clot of congealed blood. 96 Read!, 1-2

Then We placed him as (a drop of) sperm in a place of rest, firmly fixed; Then We made the sperm into a clot of congealed blood; then of that clot We made a (foetus) lump; then we made out of that lump bones and clothed the bones with flesh; then We developed out of it another creature. He Who created all things in the best way, and He began the creation of man with clay, And made his progeny from a quintessence of the nature of despised fluid:

23 The Believers; 13-14 32 Adoration ,8

He makes you, in the wombs of your mothers, in stages, one after another, in three veils of darkness.

39 The Crowds, 6

He knows you well when He brings you out of the earth, and when you are hidden in your mothers' wombs.

53 The Star, 32

iii. The Wife of Adam and the Biblical Eve

Gender issues in the interpretation of the Qur'an

Intermezzo by Barbara Freyer Stowasser

For the Qur'an interpreters of the classical age and their modern traditionalist descendants, the women of sacred Qur'anic history, like the prophetic figures with whom they are associated, belong into a special 'sacred' realm of past factual events. These were the events that marked humankind's historical evolution toward God's final message in human time, of which the Prophet Muhammad received knowledge by way of revelation. However even the most literalist interpreters past and present, have also recognized the symbolic, 'exemplary' didactic dimension of the Qur'anic message in relation to the women of the sacred past. Over time, Islamic scripturalist scholars molded the images of women figures in the Qur'an to enforce their own societies' prevailing value systems. In so doing they often changed the images' of these women of their nature and role, as first expressed in the Qur'an.

Classical Islamic interpretation of the notion of 'women's nature' as exemplified in the person of Adam's wife represents an example of this process. It shows how the medieval Qur'an interpreters brought about a paradigmatic alteration, a negation even of the Qur'anic theme of women's full humanity, spiritual freedom, and moral responsibility. This shift in understanding was achieved by way of adaptation of Bible-related lore *(isra'iliyyat)* available in the form of Hadith (traditions about the life and words of Muhammad)). Their chain of transmission often originated with an early Jewish or Christian convert to Islam. The *isra'iliyyat,* including their symbolic images of the female's defective nature, helped to enforce some of the sociopolitical foundations of the medieval Islamic world view; thus, they were seamlessly integrated into an Islamic framework.

The theme of 'woman's weakness' with its paradoxical twin, 'woman as threat to the male and society,' dominated the scripture-based paradigm on gender throughout the medieval period, and the *isra'iliyyat* played a major role in its formulation. The modern age, which in the Arab world had its first stirrings in the eighteenth century, required a different scripturalist canon on women. As the image of female spiritual, mental, and physical defectiveness were being replaced by those of female nurturing strength and women's importance in the struggle for cultural revival, the old Bible-derived legends ceased to be meaningful. It is, therefore, in nineteenth-century modernist tafsir that we first find a full-scale rejection of *isra'ilivvat* traditions. Nevertheless, Bible-related traditions of gender images survived in traditionalist interpretation into the twentieth century. Since the 1980's, there is now also a discernible feminist voice in Qur'anic interpretation that endeavors to separate and eliminate the Hadith-based classical interpretation from the Qur'an's gender-egalitarian message.

Classical Muslim interpretation of the Qur'anic story of the rebellion of Adam and his wife against their Lord departs from the scripturalist referent in numerous ways. When al-Tabari (d. 923) wrote his great Hadith-based Qur'an commentary in the late ninth and early tenth centuries, many traditions on the story were in circulation which the Muslim scholars - as Tabari repeatedly acknowledges - "had learned from the people of the Torah." While he quotes large numbers of these traditions, Tabari remains cautious as to their reliability; frequently he indicates mental reservations with the phrase "God knows best," or by expressing his hope that his sources "God willing" are right.

Tabari quotes numerous accounts to elucidate how and why the woman was created: Iblis had refused to prostrate himself before Adam and had been cursed and expelled from the Garden. Then Adam was allowed to dwell there, but he felt lonely without a mate.

God cast a slumber over him, took a rib from his left side, soldered its place with flesh, and from the rib created his wife Hawwa' .

This Biblical story does not appear in the Qur'an itself. It was however linked to the Qur'an by quoting "so that Adam would find rest in her" (cf. Qur'an 7:189, 30:12). When Adam awoke, he supposedly saw her at his side and said - according to what they allege, and God knows best - "my flesh, my blood, my wife," and he found rest in her. While, - according to this tradition, though not literally to be found in the Qur'an - the woman was thus created 'from' and 'after' the man, she also played a major role in the couple's disobedience and their expulsion from the Garden. Most of the traditions brought together by Tabari blame the woman for yielding to Satan's temptation. Indeed, it was the majority opinion of Muslim experts by Tabari's time that it was only through the woman's weakness and guile that Satan could bring about Adam's downfall. Satan entered the Garden, from which he had previously been expelled, in the belly (or the mouth, fangs, jaw) of a snake, again a biblical image not found in the Qur'an.

At that time, the snake was a four-legged, splendid riding animal resembling the Bactrian camel; some say that it wore clothes; it was also the only animal willing to heed Satan's request for transportation into the Garden. Satan then tempted the woman to eat of the Forbidden Tree. After she had succumbed, she tempted her husband using Satan's very words; or she commanded her husband to eat; or she refused to sleep with him unless he first ate of the Tree; or she gave him wine, and when he was drunk and his rational faculties had left him, she led him to the Tree and he ate. God then put His curse on the woman and the snake, but He did not curse the man, only the earth from which he had been created, and banished him to a life of want and toil.

According then to these Muslim traditions, God's curse on the woman was more severe; it involved the constitution and mental abilities, indeed the personhood of Hawwa' - the name given to the unnamed Qur'anic wife of Adam - and her daughters for all time to come. Because Hawwa' had tempted Adam, God's servant and had made the Tree bleed when she picked its fruit, she was condemned to bleed once a month. She was doomed to carry and deliver her children against her will, and to be often close to death at delivery.

God also made the woman foolish and stupid, while He had initially created her wise and intelligent. Tabari quotes a tradition which says that “were it not for the calamity that afflicted Hawwa", the women of this world would not menstruate, would be wise, and would bear their children with ease.

The snake in whose belly Iblis had entered the Garden was cursed to slither (naked} on its belly, to eat dust, and to be the eternal enemy of man, stinging his heel and having its head crushed by him whenever they would meet, wherefore the Prophet commanded the Muslims to "kill the snake wherever you find it." Again this is very much more recognizable as a Biblical than as a Qur’anic tale.

On the question of the human’s repentance after their disobedience, as described in the Qur’an, some traditions quoted by Tabari indicate that both man and woman acknowledged their sin and asked God's forgiveness and mercy; a larger number of reports specify that the prayer for forgiveness and God's promise for eternal life involved Adam alone. The later Qur'anic commentaries largely followed Tabari's reinterpretation of the Qur'anic story. In the Qur'an the wife of Adam is a participant in human error, repentance and God's challenge to recover the pristine innate nature of humankind (fitra) through struggle for righteousness on earth. In the tradition the woman had largely become Satan’s tool and was seen as afflicted through her own fault with the curse of moral, mental, and physical deficiency. Conversely the man, in the Qur'an her partner and spokesman, now alone embodied the human conscience. He alone was aware of his error, and repented; he was forgiven, and freed from God’s curse. Even the great rationalist exegete Fakhr ai-Din Razi (d. 1210) finds occasion to quote the widely circulated and still popular woman-as-rib-of-Adam hadith that reflects Hawwa's origin in Adam and thereby sums up female nature.

The hadith reflects Hawwa's (‘Eve's’) origin in Adam and also means to describe women's nature. On the authority of the Prophet it indicates that *"the woman was created from a crooked rib. If you set out to straighten her, you will break her, and if you leave her alone while there is crookedness in her, you will enjoy her."*

Even the rationalist Qur'anic exegete Fakhr al-Din al-Razi (d. 1210) quotes this hadith in his al-Tafsir al-Kabir (vol. IX, page 161), and it has remained a popular item in Islamic sermons and publications on women's issues.

The onslaught of modernity changed the interpretation of the Qur'anic story of Adam and his wife beyond recognition. The Egyptian theologian and jurist Muhammad Abduh (d. 1905) was Islamic modernism's most important early representative in the Arab world. He endeavored to 'renew' Muslim morality and reform the traditional social structures of his day and particularly his region, Egypt, by returning to the pristine and dynamic faith and morality of Islam's first generation. Reformation of Muslim society in that mold would bring about an Islamic modernism indigenous and righteous, internally dynamic and externally powerful. To this end, Abduh approached the Qur'anic text by emphasizing the literal meaning of the Qur'anic verses as well as their context, and largely deemphasizing the Hadith, most particularly the isra'iliyyat. By way of an interpretation "purified of foreign lore," Abduh sought to rediscover the original meaning of the Qur'an that had shaped the faith and ethics of the 'righteous forefathers' (al-salaf al-salih) in order to recapture a sense of their morality for infusion into his own society. Here, Abduh placed great importance on the notions of woman's full humanity and equality with the man before God, because they are Qur'anic in origin and, in his opinion, indispensible in shaping a truly moral society.

Traditionalist versions of the story of Adam and Eve, however, persevered. By the second half of the 20th century, even conservative voices had started to pick up on the notion of equality of the sexes in Islam.

However they based this equality ever more urgently on the divinely decreed, immutable, and complete differences of their natures.

God created the sexes as mutually complementary halves. To the man He gave decisive will, power of reason, and physical strength. The woman He created sensitive, emotional, supportive, and caring. Since this doctrine of the sexes' psychological and physical difference does not have a clear basis in the Qur'an, contemporary traditionalists once again make use of the Bible inspired Hadith. Thus the woman-as-rib- of Adam tradition reappears, but now it emerges in a new context and underlies a new purpose. In the hands of the Egyptian preacher Muhammad Mutawalli al-Sha'rawi, the 'crookedness' of the rib (from which the woman was created) defines her natural disposition and the preponderance of emotions over rationality . . . unlike the male in whom rationality surpasses emotion. Neither men nor women are inferior one to the other. The "crookedness" in the Hadith does not imply any corruption or imperfection in woman's nature but signifies the very quality that enables her to be a compassionate mother and wife. On this basis, her "crookedness" has become a laudatory attribute for the women, because this "crookedness" is in reality woman's "straightest" qualification for her task.

My students are often amazed at the difference in plot and tenor of the 'Eve' story in Bible and Qur'an. It is the Qur'anic 'wife of Adam' who is created in full equality with the man, while both are endowed with the gift of free will to choose obedience or rebellion (and then suffer exile and hardship, but not a fall from grace). According to my students, hers is one of the most egalitarian stories in the Qur'an.

Barbara Stowasser

7. Paradise Lost: Adam and Eve/Hawwa

The first human couple lived in the Garden of Eden. The Qur'an speaks of Adam and his wife, in Islamic tradition named Hawwa. The Bible talks in the abstract about man, who was later joined by the woman created from his rib. In this garden of paradise, they were allowed to enjoy the abundance. But the fruit of one tree was forbidden in both books. In the Bible, it was the tree of the knowledge of good and evil; in the Qur'an, it represented transgression.
Both books relate how the man and the woman ate from the tree. They were seduced to that deed of disobedience by a snake (Bible), by Satan (Qur'an). Thus, they lost paradise.
In the Bible, it was the woman who committed the first sin. The couple was driven from the garden of Eden. Angels with a flaming sword stood on guard by its forever closed gate. From then on man was burdened by sin. This is the source of the Christian concept of original sin with which every human being comes into the world. Redemption is brought by Jesus Christ; sin is washed away in baptism.
In the Qur'an, the human couple committed injustice together. Together, they repented. They were both forgiven. Thus, the children of men and women are born without knowledge of sin, expressed as follows:

It is He Who brought you forth from the wombs of your mothers when you knew nothing; [16 The Bee, 78]

In the Qur'an Adam and his wife were also forced to leave paradise, to make a living on earth, and return to it after death. However, by living a good life on earth, they might be resurrected and return to the paradisiacal Garden of Eden.

Bible Paradise Lost Qur'an

The Garden of Eden
The LORD God planted a garden eastward in Eden, and there He put the man whom He had formed. And out of the ground the LORD God made every tree grow that is pleasant to the sight and good for food. The tree of life was also in the midst of the garden, and the tree of the knowledge of good and evil.... a river went out of Eden to water the garden, and from there it...became four riverheads.
Genesis 2: 8-10

Adam and wife in the garden
We said: "O Adam! You and your wife dwell in the Garden; and eat of the bountiful things therein as...you will..." 2 The Heifer,35

...Gardens of Eternity, beneath which rivers flow...
98 The Clear Evidence, 8

"O Adam! You and your wife dwell in the Garden, and enjoy (its good things) as you wish... " 7 The Heights,19

Forbidden fruit
Then the LORD God took the man and put him in the garden of Eden to tend and keep it. And the LORD God commanded the man, saying, "Of every tree of the garden you may freely eat;
But of the tree of the knowledge of good and evil you shall not eat, for in the day that you eat of it you shall surely die." Genesis 2: 15-17

Tree of transgression
...but do not approach this tree, or you run into harm and transgression." 2 The Heifer, 35

...but do not approach this tree, or you run into harm and transgression." 7 The Heights,19

The snake seduces the woman
Now the serpent was more cunning than any beast of the field which the LORD God had made. And he said to the woman, "Has God

Satan seduces man and wife
Then We said: "O Adam! verily, this is an enemy to you and your wife: so let him not get you both out of the Garden, so that you are

indeed said, 'You shall not eat of every tree of the garden'?"
And the woman said to the serpent, "We may eat the fruit of the trees of the garden; but of the fruit of the tree which is in the midst of the garden, God has said, 'You shall not eat it, nor shall you touch it, lest you die.'"
Then the serpent said unto the woman, "You will not surely die. For God knows that in the day you eat of it your eyes will be opened, and you will be like God (as gods, kjv) knowing good and evil."
So when the woman saw that the tree was good for food, and that it was pleasant to the eyes, and a tree desirable to make one wise, she took of its fruit and ate. She also gave to her husband with her, and he ate. [Genesis 3: 1-6]

landed in misery. [20 Ta-Ha Mystic Letters, 117]

But Satan whispered evil to him: he said: "O Adam! shall I lead you to the Tree of Eternity and to a kingdom that never decays?"
20 Ta-Ha Mystic Letters,117; 120

Then began Satan to whisper suggestions to them, bringing openly before their minds all their shame that was hidden from them (before): he said: "Your Lord only forbade you this tree, lest you should become angels or such beings as live forever." [7 The Heights, 20]

In the result, they both ate of the tree…
20 Ta-Ha Mystic Letters,121

Eyes opened to nakedness

Then the eyes of them both were opened, and they knew that they were naked; and they sewed fig leaves together and made themselves coverings (aprons [KJV]).
And they heard the sound of the LORD God walking in the garden in the cool of the day, and Adam and his wife hid themselves from the presence of the LORD God

Covering with leaves

In the result, they both ate of the tree, and so their nakedness appeared to them: they began to sew together, for their covering, leaves from the Garden: thus Adam disobeyed his Lord and allowed himself to be seduced.
20 Ta Ha Mystic Letters,121

Then did Satan make them slip from the (Garden), and get them

among the trees of the garden.
Then the LORD God called to Adam and said to him, "Where are you?" Genesis 3: 7-9

Blaming the other

So he (Adam ed.) said, "I heard Your voice in the garden, and I was afraid because I was naked; and I hid myself."
And He said, "Who told you that you were naked? Have you eaten from the tree of which I commanded you that you should not eat?"
Then the man said, "The woman whom You gave to be with me, she gave me of the tree, and I ate."
And the LORD God said to the woman, "What is this that you have done?"
The woman said, "The serpent deceived (beguiled kjv) me, and I ate.
Genesis 3: 10-13

Driven out of Eden

So He drove out the man; and He placed cherubim at the east of the garden of Eden, and a flaming sword which turned every way, to guard the way to the tree of life.
Genesis 3:24

out of the state (of felicity) in which they had been. We said: "Get you down, all (you people), with enmity between yourselves.
2 The Heifer, 36

They both repent

...And their Lord called to them: "Did I not forbid you that tree, and tell you that Satan was an avowed enemy to you?"
They said: "Our Lord! We have wronged our own souls: If You do not forgive us and do not bestow on us Your Mercy, we shall certainly be lost." 7 The Heights, 22-23
Then Adam learnt from his Lord words of inspiration, and his Lord turned toward him; for He is Oft-Returning, Most Merciful.
2 The Heifer, 37

But his Lord chose him (for His Grace): He turned to him and gave him guidance. 20 Ta-Ha Mystic Letters,122

Paradise Lost

...We said: "Get you down, all (you people).... On earth will be your dwelling-place and your means of livelihood for a time."
2 The Heifer, 36

Sin and suffering

To the woman He said: "I will greatly multiply your sorrow and your conception; In pain you shall bring forth children; Your desire shall be for your husband, and he shall rule over you.

Then to Adam He said, "Because you have heeded the voice of your wife, and have eaten from the tree of which I commanded you, saying, 'You shall not eat of it': "cursed is the ground for your sake; in toil you shall eat of it all the days of your life; Both thorns and thistles it shall bring forth... In the sweat of your face you shall eat bread till you return to the ground…

For dust you are, and to dust you shall return." Genesis 3: 16-19

Behold, I was brought forth in iniquity; And in sin my mother conceived me. Psalm 51: 5

Another chance

We said: "Get you down all from here; and if, as is sure, there comes to you guidance from Me, whosoever follows My guidance, on them shall be no fear, nor shall they grieve. 2 The Heifer, 38

And Allah has produced you from the earth growing (gradually), and in the End, He will return you into the (earth) and raise you forth (again at the Resurrection).

71 Noah, 17-18

…Allah beckons by His Grace to the Gardens (of Bliss) and forgiveness… 2 The Heifer 221

…for the Righteous, is a beautiful place of (final) Return - Gardens of Eternity, whose doors will (ever) be open to them… therein can they call… for fruit in abundance…

38 Saad, 49-51

For such the reward is forgiveness from their Lord, and Gardens with rivers flowing underneath - an eternal dwelling… 3 'Imran,136

Life in Christ

For as in Adam all die, even so in Christ all shall be made alive. (Paul to the) 1 Corinthians 15: 22

For as by one man's disobedience (Adam ed.) many were made sinners, so also by one (Jesus' ed.) Man's obedience many will be made righteous. Romans 5: 19

Return to Eden

...Gardens...in which they shall abide forever: goodly mansions in the gardens of Eden... 9 Repentance, 72 (Dawood)

But those who repent...and do what is right shall enter paradise ...the gardens of Eden... 19 Mary, 61 (Dawood)

iv. Returning to dust

Intermezzo by Khaled Abou el Fadl

As the flowers awaken at the touch of the morning dew, I pace the skies. If it hadn't been for the muddied soil, these flowers would not reach for the Heavens, and if it hadn't been for this broken body, I would not have craved the embrace of the sky ... But in the end, and after all is said and done, it is this brain that has been the mind's throne and shelter—the brain returns to the mud from where it came, and the mind returns to God.

In Search of Beauty in Islam p.233

v. Longing for Brotherhood

intermezzo by Khaled Abou El Fadl

The wonder of brotherhood cannot be invented by genes or constructed by law. It is a magnificent state which is equal in worth to an escape from Hellfire or a gift from Heaven. For those who were on the brink of hellfire were saved by brotherhood.

"And hold fast, all together, by the Rope which Allah (stretches out for you), and be not divided among yourselves; and remember with gratitude Allah's favor on you; for you were enemies and He joined your hearts in love, so that by His Grace, you became brethren; and you were on the brink of the Pit of Fire, and He saved you from it." 3 Al-'Imran103

And those who attained Heaven were anointed with brotherhood.

"And We shall remove from their hearts any lurking sense of injury: (they will be) brothers (joyfully) facing each other on thrones (of dignity)." 15 The Rocky Tract 47

Brotherhood is a state, and not a status. As a blessing, it flows, bonding souls and hearts, but it cannot be legislated, quantified, or institutionalized.

The blessing of brotherhood is given by God to those whose piety is channeled into an unwavering sense of fidelity to all that is decent and beautiful. Ultimately, brotherhood is the just reward for those who are truly decent and truly beautiful.

The Search for Beauty in Islam p.76-77

8. Fratricide, Cain and Abel, sons of Adam

The story of the first murder, one brother killing the other, is told in both the Qur'an and the Bible. In Genesis, these sons of Adam and Eve are called Cain and Abel. In the Qur'an, they receive no name, but Islamic tradition has named them Qabil and Habil.
The root of evil here is jealousy in pleasing God. Abel's sacrifice is accepted, that of Cain is rejected. In the Bible the reason for this is unclear. The Qur'an refers to earlier crimes. The sacrifice of a righteous man will be accepted, but that of a criminal will not. The high moral standards of Habil shows in his refusal to retaliate. In the Qur'an, the first murder is the occasion to proclaim a general ban: you shall not murder! This corresponds with the sixth commandment received by Moses. The Qur'an recognizes that the Israelites were the first to receive this commandment and confirms its importance in a passage also found in a Jewish legal document from the end of the second century A.D.

vi. Saving one is saving all
intermezzo by Awraham Soetendorp

I had not noticed the beautiful passage in the Qur'an about the killing and especially the saving of one person, a familiar and moving passage for me.
Then during the first Gulf war a booklet with Qur'an quotes was given me at an interfaith meeting organized by the Dutch Minister of internal affairs. The idea was that religious leaders of all faiths should express their solidarity at a time of increasing anti-islam sentiment.
Later I found a friend in Achmed Kuftaro, the Grand Mufti of Syria. It was at a meeting in Japan that he recited this Qur'an passage to me. It was a moment of intense unity.

The story about the two sons of Adam ends in different ways.
In the Bible, the killer is punished with many hardships. He flees, but God finally protects him from revenge by a special sign. In the Qur'an, the killer shows remorse. A raven teaches him how to pay his brother his last respects.

Cain and Abel/ Qabil and Habil

Bible

Cain and Abel
Now Adam knew (slept with ed.) Eve his wife, and she conceived and bore Cain, and said,
"I have acquired a man from the LORD."
Then she bore again, this time his brother Abel. Genesis 4:1-2

Jealousy at harvest time
...Cain brought an offering of the fruit of the ground to the LORD. Abel also brought of the firstborn of his flock and of their fat.
And the LORD respected Abel and his offering, but He did not respect Cain and his offering. And Cain was very angry, and his countenance fell.
Genesis 4:3-5

Sin wants to destroy you

Qur'an

The sons of Adam
Recite to them the truth of the story of the two sons of Adam.
5 The table spread, 27

Sacrifice not accepted
Behold! they each presented a sacrifice (to Allah): It was accepted from one, but not from the other. Said the latter: "Be sure I will slay you." 5 The table spread, 27

Slay me

So the LORD said to Cain,

"Why are you angry? And why has your countenance fallen?

If you do well, will you not be accepted?

And if you do not do well, sin lies at the door." Genesis 4:6-7

"Surely," said the former: "Allah accepts of the sacrifice of those who are righteous. If you stretch your hand against me, to slay me, it is not for me to stretch my hand against you to slay you: for I do fear Allah, the Cherisher of the Worlds. For me, I intend to let you draw on yourself my sin as well as yours, for you will be among the Companions of the Fire, and that is the reward of those who do wrong."

5 The table spread, 28-29

The first murder

Now Cain talked with Abel his brother; and …when they were in the field …Cain rose up against Abel his brother and killed him.
Then the LORD said to Cain, "Where is Abel your brother?"
He said, "I do not know. Am I my brother's keeper?"
And He said, "What have you done? The voice of your brother's blood cries out to Me from the ground. So now you are cursed from the earth, which has opened its mouth to receive your brother's blood from your hand." Gencsis 4: 8-11

He murdered his brother

The (selfish) soul of the other led him to the murder of his brother:

He murdered him and became (himself) one of the lost ones.

5 The table spread, 30

Cain punished and protected

"When you till the ground, it shall no longer yield its strength to you. A

Criminal shows remorse

Then Allah sent a raven, who scratched the ground, to show him

fugitive and a vagabond you shall be on the earth."
And Cain said to the LORD, "My punishment is greater than I can bear…and it will happen that anyone who finds me will kill me."
And the LORD said to him, "…whoever kills Cain, vengeance shall be taken on him sevenfold."
And the LORD set a mark upon Cain, lest anyone finding him should kill him. Genesis, 4: 12-15

Sixth commandment
And God spoke all these words, saying…
"You shall not murder." Exodus 20: 1, 13

……………………………………………………

Therefore, the human being (*Adam*) was created alone, to teach you that anyone who destroys one soul from the sons of Man (*benei Adam*) is reckoned by scripture as if he destroyed the whole world; and anyone who saves one soul from the sons of Man, is reckoned by scripture as if he had saved the whole world…
Mishnah Sanhedrin, 4.5 about 200A.D.

how to hide the shame of his brother.

"Woe is me!" said he; "was I not even able to be as this raven, and to hide the shame of my brother?" Then he became full of regrets.
5 The table spread, 31

Killing one is as killing all

On that account:
We ordained for the Children of Israel that if anyone slew a person - unless it be for murder or for spreading mischief in the land – it would be as if he slew the whole people (humankind ed.): and if anyone saved a life, it would be as if he saved the life of the whole people (humankind ed.).
Then although there came to them Our Messengers with Clear Signs, yet, even after that, many of them continued to commit excesses in the land. 5 The Table Spread,32

9. Noah/Nuh and the great flood

In both the Hebrew Bible and the Qur'an, Noah/Nuh is instructed by God to build a ship, which allows a few members of humankind and two specimens of each species of animals to survive the great flood. There are subtle differences between the two versions of this story.

In the Bible, God is portrayed as extremely disappointed in humankind. Only Noah is worthy in his eyes. Noah and his family go on board and are saved, along with each species of animal. Animals are important, especially the dove, which Noah lets loose to see if the flood is receding. It returns with an olive branch, an image now used widely to represent peace. When they stepped on dry land once again, God concludes a covenant with Noah and all living creatures that such an all-destructive flood will never happen again. The rainbow is the symbol of that covenant.

In the Qur'an, it is Nuh who is disappointed in his people. He tries to warn them of the approaching disaster, but they make fun of him. God tells him to build a ship, but that again brings ridicule upon his head. In his anger Nuh asks God to destroy all unbelievers, a thing he will later regret. When the storm comes he is only allowed to bring other believers on board. Being one of Nuh's relatives is no guarantee for survival. His unbelieving wife drowns. The Qur'an compares Noah's wife to the wife of Lut. Both women meet disaster, in spite of their husbands' fame and piety. The idea expressed here is that each individual is responsible for the consequences of his or her own choice. The same holds for Nuh's obstinate son, who took refuge in the mountains. The scene in which Nuh takes leave of his son, begging God to spare him, is very moving. His son drowns. However, the Qur'an story ends on a positive note as does its biblical counterpart. Nuh is called a prophet and his issue is blessed.

In the Qur'an, surah 17 is named after Nuh, but he also figures in other surahs. The Bible story of Noah is found in Genesis.

Bible Noah/Nuh Qur'an

God plans destruction

Then the LORD saw that the wickedness of man was great in the earth, and that every intent of the thoughts of his heart was only evil continually. And the LORD was sorry that He had made man on the earth, and He was grieved in his heart.

So the LORD said, "I will destroy man whom I have created from the face of the earth, both man and beast, creeping thing and birds of the air, for I am sorry that I have made them."

The earth also was corrupt before God, and the earth was filled with violence. So God looked upon the earth, and indeed it was corrupt; for all flesh had corrupted their way on the earth.

And God said to Noah, "The end of all flesh is come before Me, for the earth is filled with violence through them; and behold, I will destroy them with the earth."

Genesis 6: 5-7, 11-13

Noah warns his people

We sent Noah to his People (with the Command): "Warn your People before there comes to them a grievous Penalty."

He said: "O my People! I am to you a Warner, clear and open: That you should worship Allah, fear Him and obey me: So He may forgive you your sins and give you respite for a stated Term:

...Ask forgiveness from your Lord; for He is Oft-Forgiving; He will...give you increase in wealth and sons; and bestow on you gardens and bestow on you rivers...What is the matter with you, that you do not place your hope for kindness and long-suffering in Allah?

Noah said: "O my Lord! Do not leave of the Unbelievers, a single one on earth! For, if You leave... them, they will but mislead Your devotees..." 71 Noah, 1-4, 10-13, 26

Except Noah
But Noah found grace in the eyes of the LORD. Noah was a just man… Noah walked with God. Genesis 6:8-9

By faith Noah, being divinely warned of things not yet seen, moved with godly fear, prepared an ark for the saving of his household, by which he…became heir of the righteousness... Hebrews 11:7
But as the days of Noah were, so also will the coming of the Son of Man be. For as in the days before the flood, they were eating and drinking, marrying and giving in marriage, until the day that Noah entered the ark, and did not know until the flood came and took them all away… Matthew 24:37-39

How to build the ark
And God said to Noah… "Make yourself an ark of gopherwood; make rooms in the ark, and cover it inside and outside with pitch. "
"And this is how you shall make it: The length of the ark shall be three hundred cubits, its width fifty cubits, and its height thirty cubits. "

"You shall make a window for the ark…and set the door of the ark in

Warnings in vain
The leaders of his people said: "Ah! we see you evidently wandering (in mind)."
…they rejected him… 7 The Heights,60,64

He said: "O my Lord!... I have spoken to them in public and secretly in private…
I have called to my People night and day: But my call only increases (their) flight (from the Right).
"And every time I have called to them, that You might forgive them, they have (only) thrust their fingers into their ears, covered themselves up with their garments, grown obstinate, and given themselves up to arrogance. 71 Noah, 5-7

Noah, construct an Ark!
It was revealed to Noah: "None of your People will believe except those who have believed already! So grieve no longer over their (evil) deeds. But construct an Ark under Our eyes and Our inspiration, and address Me no (further) on behalf of those who are in sin: for they are about to be overwhelmed (in the Flood)."
Forthwith he (starts) constructing

its side. You shall make it with lower, second and third decks."
Genesis 6: 13-16

The animals came two by two

"And of every living thing of all flesh you shall bring two of every sort into the ark, to keep them alive with you; they shall be male and female.

"Of the birds after their kind, of animals after their kind, and of every creeping thing of the earth after its kind, two of every kind will come to you to keep them alive."... two by two they went into the ark to Noah, male and female, as God had commanded Noah. Genesis 6:19-21,7:9

The flood

"And, behold, I Myself am bringing floodwaters on the earth, to destroy from under heaven all flesh in which is the breath of life; everything that is on the earth shall die." Genesis 6:17

And it came to pass after seven days that the waters of the flood were upon the earth. And the rain was on the earth forty days and forty nights. Now the flood was on the earth forty days. The waters increased and lifted up the ark, and it rose high above the earth, and moved about

the Ark: every time that the Chiefs of his People passed by him, they threw ridicule on him. 11 Hud, 36-38

Two of each, male and female

At length, behold! There came Our Command... We said: "Embark therein, of each kind two, male and female, and your family - except those (his son and wife ed.) against whom the Word has already gone forth – and the Believers."

But only a few believed with him. So he said: "You embark on the Ark, In the name of Allah, whether it move or be at rest! For my Lord is, be sure, Oft-Forgiving, Most Merciful!" 11 Hud, 40-41

Water from earth and heaven

So We opened the gates of heaven, with water pouring forth. And We caused the earth to gush forth with springs, so the waters met (and rose) to the extent decreed.

54 The Moon, 11-12

...but the Deluge overwhelmed them (Noah's people ed.) while they (persisted in) sin. 29 The Spider, 14

...We delivered him, and those with him, in the Ark: but We overwhelmed in the Flood those who rejected Our Signs. They were indeed a blind people! 7 The Heights, 64

on the surface of the waters… And all flesh died that moved on the earth… All in whose nostrils was the breath of the spirit life…died. So He destroyed all living things… Genesis 7: 10, 12, 17-19, 21-22

The dove

…Noah opened the window of the ark… and… He… sent out…a dove, to see if the waters had receded from the face of the ground. …Then the dove came to him in the evening, and behold, a freshly plucked olive leaf was in her mouth; and Noah knew that the waters had receded from the earth. Genesis 8:6,8,11

Noah's family saved

Only Noah and those who were with him in the ark remained alive. Genesis 7:23

…Noah, and Noah's sons …and Noah's wife and the three wives of his sons with them, entered the ark. Genesis 7:13

But We bore him on an (Ark) made of broad planks and caulked with palm-fiber: She floats under our eyes (and care): recompense to one who had been rejected (with scorn)! 54 The Moon, 13-14

Noah's wife and son lost

Allah sets forth, for an example to the Unbelievers, the wife of Noah and the wife of Lut: they were… under two of our righteous Servants, but they were false to their (husbands), and …were told: "You enter the Fire along with (others) that enter!" 66 The Holding, 10

So the Ark floated with them on the waves (towering) like mountains, and Noah called out to his son, who had separated himself (from the rest): "O my son! Embark with us, and be not with the Unbelievers!" The son replied: "I will betake myself to some mountain: it will

save me from the water…"
…And the waves came between them, and the son was among those overwhelmed in the Flood. And Noah called upon his Lord, and said: "O my Lord! Surely my son is of my family!..."
He (Allah ed.) said: "O Noah! He is not of your family: for his conduct is unrighteous." [11 Hud, 42-43,45-46]

Disembark with your family!
Then God spoke to Noah, saying, "Go out of the ark, you and your wife, and your sons and your sons' wives with you. Bring out with you every living thing of all flesh that is with you: birds and cattle and every creeping thing that creeps on the earth, so that they may abound on the earth, and be fruitful and multiply on the earth." [Genesis 8:16-17]

Noah leaves the ark
The word came:

"O Noah! come down (from the Ark) with Peace from Us, and Blessing on you and on some of the Peoples (who will spring) from those with you… [11 Hud, 48]

The rainbow, a promise
And God said: "I set My rainbow in the cloud, and it shall be for the sign of the covenant between Me and the earth… when I bring a cloud over the earth…the rainbow shall be seen in the cloud; and I will remember My covenant…the waters shall never again become a flood to destroy all flesh.
This is the sign of the covenant

Noah blessed
(In the days of old), Noah cried to Us, and We are the best to hear prayer.

And We delivered him and his people from the Great Calamity, And made his progeny to endure (on this earth);

And We left (this blessing) for him

which I make between Me and you and every living creature that is with you, for perpetual generations: I set my rainbow in the cloud, and it shall be for a token of a covenant between me and the earth.
It shall be, when I bring a cloud over the earth, that the rainbow shall be seen in the cloud. While the earth remains, Seedtime and harvest, Cold and heat, Winter and summer, And day and night Shall not cease."
Genesis 9:12-15; 8:22

among generations to come in later times:

"Peace and salutations to Noah among the nations!" Thus indeed do We reward those who do right. [37]
The Saffat, 75-80

10. Abraham/Ibrahim; Ishmael/ Ismail; Isaac/ Ishaq

In both Bible and Qur'an, Abraham/Ibrahim is an important figure. Via his first-born son Ishmael on one side and his son Isaac on the other, he is believed to be the patriarch of both Arabs and Israelites. The New Testament gives this kinship a symbolic meaning, as determined by faith rather than parentage.

In both books, Abraham breaks with the past and carves out new paths. In the Bible, he leaves his father and his people behind to make a covenant with God, in which the land of Canaan is promised to his progeny, on condition of good behavior. Thus, the Bible relates how God becomes the only God of this one people.

The Qur'an also refers to the land promised to the children of Israel with whom God had a covenant. But the concept of the Promised Land usually refers to the Paradise Gardens promised to all righteous people. This higher level of abstraction is also maintained in the story of Ibrahim. It is not so much about the relation of God to a specific people, as to a monotheism that is in principle valid for all humankind. In the Qur'an Ibrahim frees himself of false gods, realizing that what he and others adored - the sun, the moon, etc. - are only aspects of creation. God, the creator, is far superior to all that He created. Thus, monotheism is declared generally valid for all peoples in opposition to the polytheism of their (and Ibrahim's) forefathers. Ibrahim's people are angered by his destruction of idols; they throw him into a fire. But God saves him by making the fire cold. Abraham then leaves his father and his people to find his own way. The ban on carving and worshipping idols, emphasized in the story of Ibrahim is also important in the Bible, but is addressed primarily within the context of the story of Moses.

Both books relate the dramatic events involving the two sons of Abraham. According to the Bible, Ishmael, his first-born, was conceived by the Egyptian slave, Hagar, at the request of Sarah, Abraham's barren wife. The Biblical story is one of prejudice, exile and suffering. Hagar is forced to leave Abraham's tent and flee into the desert. God and his angels lend a helping hand. Thus, Hagar discovers a well (known in Islamic tradition as 'Zamzam') just in time to save Ishmail dying of thirst.

The few words that the Qur'an devotes to Ishmail are very positive. He is mentioned in one breath with the great prophets. The story of Hagar is told summarily, without naming her. The meaning of the phrase:

"I *have made some of my offspring to dwell by Your Sacred House*," [14] Abraham, 37 becomes clear against the backdrop of the tradition that Hagar and Ishmael were sent into the desert for a higher purpose. For it took them to the ruins of the Ka'aba, the holy house built near the Zamzam by Adam in the later Mecca. In that wild and arid place, Hagar runs back and forth seven times between two mountains, the as-Safa and al-Marwa, in her desperate search for water for her son. This running back and forth in honor of Hagar forms part of the ritual of the Hajj to Mecca; pilgrims still drink from the well (Zamzam) that eventually saved Hagar and Ishmael. Later Ibrahim and Ishmail are said to have rebuilt the Ka'aba , still the center of worship during the pilgrimage or Hadj.

The Qur'an also praises Abraham's second son Isaac. Both Bible and Qur'an describe the announcement of his birth by angelic messengers and the miracle of a child born from elderly parents.

The dramatic event of the near-sacrifice of Abraham's son Isaac is also mentioned in the Qur'an, but according to Islamic tradition, the intended victim is Ishmael. There are subtle distinctions between the two versions of the story. Unlike the Biblical Abraham, Ibrahim does not receive a command from God, but has a dream in which he sees himself sacrificing his son. Perhaps because Ishmael was older at the time, his father discusses the intended sacrifice with his son, which the Biblical Abraham does not. Noteworthy is the willingness of Ishmael to cooperate in the sacrifice. Ishmael, who is not mentioned by name in the story of the sacrifice, is explicitly mentioned in the story about (re)building the Ka'aba. The feast of Eid al-Adha in commemoration of the saving of Ibrahim's son, is still celebrated by Muslims every year.

According to the Bible, the two brothers meet once again at their father's funeral. Isaac receives God's blessing after the death of Abraham; Ishmael does not. Isaac's wife Rebekah later gives birth to Jacob, who, in turn, fathers Joseph.

The Biblical story of Jacob and the ladder and his fight with the angel do not figure in the Qur'an and are, therefore, not included in this anthology. The Qur'an only briefly mentions Jacob/Israel who, together with his father Isaac and grandfather Abraham, is held in high regard. They introduce the obligations of Salat (prayer) and Zakat (charity) and know of the heavenly reward for those who do good. The Qur'an refers to the Jewish people as the children of Israel.

In the Qur'an, surah 14 is named Ibrahim. In the Bible, his story is found in Genesis, with brief references to him elsewhere.

"We live in a globalized world
in which
the Children of Abraham
increasingly live side by side
in Muslim countries
and in Europe and America."

John L. Esposito

The Prince Alwaleed Center for
Muslim-Christian Understanding,
Georgetown University, Washington D.C.

Abraham, God's friend

"Abraham believed God, and it was accounted to him for righteousness." And he was called the friend of God. James, 2:23

...Abraham My friend. Isaiah 41:8

...know that only those who are of faith are sons of Abraham. Galatians 3: 6-7

Moses: ban on carved images

"You shall not make for yourself a carved image—any likeness of anything that is in heaven above, or that is in the earth beneath, or that is in the water under the earth; you shall not bow down to them nor serve them." Exodus 20:4-5

"Take careful heed to yourselves... lest you act corruptly and make for yourselves a carved image in the form of any figure: the likeness of male or female, the likeness of any animal that is on the earth or the likeness of any winged bird that flies in the air, the likeness of anything that creeps on the ground, or the likeness of any fish that is in the water beneath the earth. And

Ibrahim the righteous

For Allah took Abraham for a friend. 4 The Women, 125

And who turns away from the religion of Abraham but such as debase their souls with folly? Him We chose and rendered pure in this world: And he will be in the Hereafter in the ranks of the Righteous. 2 The Heifer, 130

Ibrahim: destruction of idols

Lo! Abraham said to his father Azar: "Do you take idols for gods? For I see you and your people in manifest error."

So also did We show Abraham the power and the laws of the heavens and the earth, that he might (with understanding) have certitude. When the night covered him over, he saw a star and he said: "This is my Lord." But when it set, he said: "I do not love those that set." When he saw the moon rising in splendor, he said: "This is my Lord." But when the moon set, he said: "Unless my Lord guide me, I shall surely be among those who go astray." When he saw the sun rising in splendor, he said:

take heed, lest you lift your eyes to heaven, and when you see the sun, the moon, and the stars, all the host of heaven, you feel driven to worship them and serve them…" Deuteronomy 4:15-19

"Take heed to yourselves, lest you forget the covenant of the LORD your God which He made with you, and make for yourselves a carved image in the form of anything which the LORD your God has forbidden you. For the LORD your God is a consuming fire, a jealous God." Deuteronomy 4: 23

"Take heed to yourself, lest you make a covenant with the inhabitants of the land where you are going, lest it be a snare in your midst. But you shall destroy their altars, break their sacred pillars, and cut down their wooden images." Exodus 34: 12-13

The covenant

… the LORD appeared to Abram and said to him, "I *am* Almighty God; walk before Me and be blameless. Then Abram fell on his

"This is my Lord; this is the greatest (of all)."
But when the sun set, he said: "O my people! I am indeed free from your (guilt) of giving partners to Allah. For me, I have set my face, firmly and truly, towards Him Who created the heavens and the earth, and never shall I give partners to Allah." His people disputed with him…
6 The Cattle, 74-80

Behold! he said to his father and his people: "What are these images, to which you are (so assiduously) devoted?" They said: "We found our fathers worshipping them." He said: "Indeed you have been in manifest error - you and your fathers."
21 The Prophets, 52-54

… your Lord is the Lord of the heavens and the earth, He Who created them (from nothing): and I am a witness to this (truth).
And by Allah, I have a plan for your idols -- after you go away and turn your backs." So he broke them to pieces, (all) but the biggest of them… 21 The Prophets, 56-58

The cool fire

They said: "Who has done this to our gods?
He must indeed be some man of impiety!" 21 The Prophets, 59

face, and God talked with him, saying: "…My covenant is with you…No longer shall your name be called Abram, but your name shall be Abraham[5]; for I have made you a father of many nations. I will make you exceedingly fruitful; and I will make nations of you, and kings shall come from you. And I will establish an everlasting covenant, to be God to you and your descendants after you."
This *is* My covenant which you shall keep, between Me and you and your descendants after you: Every male child among you shall be circumcised;
So Abraham took Ishmael his son…and …every male among the men of Abraham's house, and circumcised the flesh of their foreskins that very same day, as God had said to him.
Genesis 17:1-5,7, 9-11,23-26

They said: "Are you the one that did this with our gods, O Abraham?" He said: "Nay, this was done by -- this is their biggest one! Ask them, if they can speak intelligently!" So they turned to themselves and said… "You know full well that these (idols) do not speak!" (Abraham) said: "Do you then worship, besides Allah, things that can neither be of any good to you nor do you harm? Fie upon you, and upon the things that you worship besides Allah. Have you no sense?" They said: "Burn him and protect your gods, If you do (anything at all)!" We said: "O Fire! You be cool, and (a means of) safety for Abraham!" Then they sought a strategem against him: but We made them the ones that lost most!
21 The Prophets, 62-70

The Promised Land

Now the LORD had said to Abram: "Get out of your country, from your family and from your father's house, to a land that I will show you. I will make you a great nation; I will bless you and make your name great…" Genesis 12:1-2

The Land of Promise

O Children of Israel! call to mind the (special) favor which I bestowed upon you, and fulfill your Covenant with Me as I fulfill My Covenant with you, and fear none but Me. 2 The Heifer,40

And We said thereafter to the

[5] In Hebrew the word Abraham sounds like the word for 'Father of many Nations'.

"Also, I give to you and your descendants after you the land in which you are a stranger, all the land of Canaan, as an everlasting possession; and I will be their God." Genesis 17:8

"Lift your eyes now and look from the place where you are— northward, southward, eastward, and westward; for all the land which you see I give to you and your descendants forever. And I will make your descendants as the dust of the earth; so that if a man could number the dust of the earth, then your descendants also could be numbered." Genesis 13:14-16

Children of Israel , "Dwell securely in the land (of promise)": 17 The Children of Israel,104

The parable of the Garden which the righteous are promised - beneath it flow rivers: perpetual is the enjoyment thereof and the shade therein: such is the End of the Righteous; 13 The Thunder 35

Allah has promised to Believers, men and women, Gardens under which rivers flow…Gardens of everlasting bliss. 9 Repentance 72

Ishmael born of a slave girl

Now Sarai, Abram's wife, had borne him no children. And she had an Egyptian maidservant whose name was Hagar. So Sarai said to Abram, "See now, the LORD has restrained me from bearing children. Please, go in to my maid; perhaps I shall obtain children by her."

And Abram heeded the voice of Sarai. Then Sarai, Abram's wife, took Hagar, her maid, the Egyptian, and gave her to her husband Abram to be his wife…And when she saw

Ishmael, the firstborn son

(Abraham said: ed.) "O my Lord! Grant me a righteous (son)!" So We gave him the good news of a boy (Ishmael ed.) ready to suffer and forbear. 37 Those Ranged in Ranks, 100-101

Also mention in the Book (the story of) Ishmael: He was (strictly) true to what he promised, and he was a Messenger (and) a prophet... (a man) of constancy and patience;

We admitted them to Our Mercy: for they were of the righteous ones.

19 Mary, 54; 21 The Prophets, 85-86

that she had conceived, her mistress became despised in her eyes. And when Sarai dealt harshly with her, she fled from her presence. Now the Angel of the LORD found her by a spring of water in the wilderness, by the spring on the way to Shur. And He said, "Hagar, Sarai's maid, where have you come from, and where are you going?" She said, "I am fleeing from the presence of my mistress Sarai." The Angel of the LORD said to her, "Return to your mistress…I will multiply your descendants exceedingly, so that they shall not be counted for multitude. Behold, you are with child, and you shall bear a son. You shall call his name Ishmael, because the LORD has heard your affliction. He shall be a wild man; his hand shall be against every man, and every man's hand against him." Genesis 16: 1-4, 6-7, 9-12

And commemorate Ishmael… (He ed.) was of the company of the good. 38 Saad, 48

You say: "We believe in…the revelation given to Abraham, Ishmael, Isaac… and that given to Moses and Jesus…" 2 The Heifer, 136

"O our Lord! I (Ibrahim ed.) have made some of my offspring (Ishmael and his mother Hagar ed.) to dwell in a valley without cultivation, by Your Sacred House; in order, O our Lord, that they may establish regular Prayer: so fill the hearts of some among men with love towards them, and feed them with fruits: so that they may give thanks." 14 Ibrahim, 37

Behold! (the mountains ed.) Safa and Marwa are among the Symbols of Allah. So if those who visit the House (the Ka'aba ed.) in the Season or at other times, should compass them round, it is no sin in them. And if any one obeys his own impulse to Good-- be sure that Allah is He Who recognizes and knows. 2 The Heifer, 158

The birth of Isaac

(Abram ed.) …lifted his eyes and looked, and behold, three men were standing by him; and when he saw them, he ran from the tent door to meet them, and bowed himself to

Allah's messengers visit Ibrahim

There came Our Messengers to Abraham with glad tidings. They said: "Peace!"
He answered: "Peace!" and hastened to entertain them with a roasted calf.

the ground, and said…,
"Please let a little water be brought, and wash your feet, and rest yourselves under the tree. And I will bring a morsel of bread, that you may refresh your hearts."
So Abraham hurried into the tent to Sarah and said, "Quickly, make ready three measures of fine meal; knead it and make cakes."
And He (God or one of the men ed.) said, "…Sarah your wife shall have a son."

Now Abraham and Sarah were old, well advanced in age; and Sarah had passed the age of childbearing. Therefore Sarah laughed within herself, saying,
"After I have grown old, shall I have pleasure, my Lord being old also?"
And the LORD said to Abraham, "Why did Sarah laugh, saying, 'Shall I …bear a child, since I am old?'" Is anything too hard for the LORD? Genesis 18:2-6,10-15
And the LORD…did for Sarah as He had spoken. For Sarah conceived and bore Abraham a son in his old age…Isaac. Genesis 21:1-3
And Sarah saw the son of Hagar…she said to Abraham;

But when he saw their hands did not go toward the (meal), he felt some mistrust of them, and conceived a fear of them.
They said: "Fear not: We have been sent… (by Allah ed.) "
And his wife was standing (there), and she laughed: but We gave her glad tidings of Isaac…
She said: "Alas for me! shall I bear a child, seeing I am an old woman, and my husband here is an old man? That would indeed be a wonderful thing!"
They said: "Do you wonder at Allah's decree? The grace of Allah and His blessings on you, O you people of the house! For He is indeed worthy of all praise, full of all glory!" 11 Hud, 69-73

"Peace and salutation to Abraham!" Thus indeed do We reward those who do right. For he was one of Our believing Servants. And We gave him the good news of Isaac - a Prophet- one of the Righteous. We blessed him and Isaac: but of their progeny are (some) that do right, and (some) that obviously do wrong, to their own souls. 37 The Saffat, 109-113
"Praise be to Allah, Who has granted to me in old age Ishmael and Isaac:

“Cast out this bondswoman and her son…”
So Abraham…sent her away.
And the water …was used up. She said to herself; “Let me not see the death of the boy.”
Then the angel of God called to Hagar out of heaven...
Then God opened her eyes and she saw a well of water and she gave the lad to drink. And God was with the lad. Genesis 21:9-20

Isaac nearly sacrificed
God tested Abraham, and said to him, “Abraham! Take now your son, your only son Isaac, whom you love, and offer him… as a burnt offering on one of the mountains of which I shall tell you.”
So Abraham rose early in the morning and saddled his donkey, and took…with him…Isaac his son; and he split the wood for the burnt offering, and arose and went to the place of which God had told him.
So Abraham took the wood of the burnt offering and laid it on Isaac his son; and he took the fire in his hand, and a knife, and the two of them went together.

for truly my Lord is He, the Hearer of prayer! 14 Ibrahim, 39
And commemorate Our Servants Abraham, Isaac… possessors of Power and Vision. Verily We chose them for a special (purpose) - proclaiming the Message of the Hereafter. They were, in Our sight, truly, of the company of the Elect and the Good. And commemorate Ishmael… each of them was of the company of the Good. 38 Saad, 45-48

The near offering of Ishmael
Then, when (the son) (Ishmael ed.) reached (the age of) (serious) work with him (Abraham ed.), he said: “O my son! I see in vision that I offer you in sacrifice: Now see what is your view!” (The son) said: “O my father! Do as you are commanded: you will find me, if Allah so wills, one practicing patience and constancy!” So when they had both submitted their wills (to Allah), and he had laid him prostrate on his forehead (for sacrifice), We called out to him: “O Abraham! You have already fulfilled the vision!” - thus indeed do We reward those who do right. For this was obviously a trial. And We left (this blessing) for him among generations (to come) in later

But Isaac spoke to Abraham his father and said, "My father! Look, the fire and the wood, but where is the lamb for a burnt offering?"
And Abraham said, "My son, God will provide for Himself the lamb for a burnt offering."
Then they came to the place of which God had told him. And Abraham built an altar there and placed the wood in order; and he bound Isaac his son and laid him on the altar, upon the wood. And Abraham stretched out his hand and took the knife to slay his son.

But the Angel of the LORD called to him from heaven and said, "Abraham, Abraham! Do not lay your hand on the lad, or do anything to him; for now I know that you fear God, since you have not withheld your son, your only son, from Me."

Then Abraham lifted his eyes and looked, and there behind him was a ram caught in a thicket by its horns. So Abraham went and took the ram, and offered it up for a burnt offering instead of his son.

Genesis 22:1-3, 6-13

times: "Peace and salutation to Abraham!"

37 The Saffat, 102-109

And remember Abraham and Ishma'il raised the foundations of the House (the Ka'aba ed.) (with this prayer): "Our Lord! Accept (this service) from us: For You are the All-Hearing, the All-Knowing. Our Lord! make of us Muslims, bowing to Your (Will), and of our progeny a People Muslim, bowing to Your (Will); and show us our places for the celebration of (due) rites; and turn to us (in Mercy); for You are the Oft-Returning, Most Merciful."

2 The Heifer, 127-128

Remember We made the House (the Ka'aba ed.) a place of assembly for men and a place of safety… a place of prayer; and We covenanted with Abraham and Ishma'il, that they should sanctify My House for those who compass it round, or use it as a retreat, or bow, or prostrate themselves (therein in prayer).

2 The Heifer, 125

Allah made the Ka'ba, the Sacred House, an asylum of security for men, as also the Sacred Months, the animals for offerings, and the garlands that mark them…

5 The Table Spread, 97

Isaac blessed with a son: Jacob

Then Abraham… died in a good old age, an old man and full of years, and was gathered to his people. And his sons Isaac and Ishmael buried him in the cave of Machpelah … And it came to pass, after the death of Abraham, that God blessed his son Isaac. Genesis 25:8-11

Isaac… took Rebekah as wife… Isaac pleaded with the LORD for his wife, because she was barren; and the LORD granted his plea, and Rebekah his wife conceived.
And the first came out red. He was like a hairy garment all over; so they called his name Esau. Afterward his brother came out, and his hand took hold of Esau's heel; so his name was called Jacob. Genesis 25: 19-21, 24-26

Ishaq, Yaqoub, Allah's servants

And We bestowed on him (Abraham ed.) Isaac and, as an additional gift, (a grandson), Jacob, and We made righteous men of every one (of them). And We made them leaders, guiding (men) by Our Command, and We sent them inspiration to do good deeds, to establish regular prayers (Salat ed.), and to practice regular charity (Zakat ed.); and they constantly served Us (and Us only). 21 The Prophets, 72-73

And commemorate Our servants Abraham, Issac, and Jacob, possessors of Power and Vision. Verily We chose them for a special (purpose) – proclaiming the Message of the Hereafter. Gardens of Eternity, whose doors will (ever) be open to them. 38 Saad, 45-46, 50

11. Lot/Lut and the Destruction of Sodom

In addition to good tidings about the birth of Isaac, the angels also had some bad tidings for Abraham. They came to warn him about the destruction of Sodom, a city notorious for its many crimes. The Biblical Abraham could not understand how God could allow the innocent to suffer with the guilty. He negotiated with God and was promised that the city would be saved if 10 righteous people could be found inside its walls.

The story continues with Abraham's cousin Lot, a righteous man, who lived in the sinful city of Sodom. Just like other prophets, Lot attempted to warn his people of God's punishments for a godless life. The people of Sodom refused to listen and threatened to drive him and his followers out of the city.

Lot was also visited by the angels that Abraham had hosted. He welcomed them to his house. At that moment, a crowd of angry men came to his door, demanding he hand over his male guests for their sexual pleasure. Lot refused to do so but instead offered his two daughters to the men. Lot was afraid of the men, but the angels reassured him that the mob would not triumph.

This incident is open to various interpretations. It is about the importance of hospitality: guests take priority over everything else, especially when they are angels. It is also regarded as a rejection of (mass) rape, regardless of the genders involved.

In Christian and Islamic circles, the story of Lot and the lustful mob has been interpreted as a rejection of homosexual relations, even if they involve two loving adults. In the Bible, this interpretation is supported by an explicit ban on homosexual relations[Leviticus 20:13] and a rejection by Paul of Greek/Roman homosexual habits. Jude explains the destruction of Sodom and Gomorrah as a punishment for unnatural sex. Whether thes passages are to be taken as the word of God, or the opinion of writers in a specific historical context, is undecided. However, Christians and Jews now oppose capital punishment for homosexuals, as contradicting the concept of a loving God.

The story of Lot is the only context in which homosexuality is discussed in the Qur'an. The Prophet Lot describes men who are attracted to men instead of women as immoderate people. [7 The Heights, 80-81] Except for this type of statement by the prophet Lot, - in the context of a threatening situation - the Qur'an contains no explicit ban on homosexuality, whereas other aspects of sexual relations are explicitly dealt with. This very vacuum inspires some Muslims to reach out to the Bible for guidance. Thus, the killing of homosexuals, which occasionally takes place in one or two countries, seems ultimately based on the Bible rather than on the Qur'an. In spite of the lack of clear guidance in the Qur'an, many Muslims feel that homosexuality goes against the natural destiny of men, to whom God has given wives. Therefore, they respect the choice of others but will not make such a choice themselves. On the other hand, homosexual Muslims maintain that homosexual love relations between equals as such are not condemned in the Qur'an.

Another question open to interpretation is the meaning behind Lot's offer to give his daughters to the mob. The term 'daughters' is often interpreted figuratively in Islamic circles. Offering daughters in Arabic means offering in marriage, not for unmarried sex. Lot counsels the lewd men to return to the daughters of the people, in other words, to their own wives and to renounce sex with Lot's male guests. But the men insist on sex with Lot's male guests. The city is subsequently destroyed because of the idolatry and wrong-doings of its citizens, not, or at least not only, because of homosexuality.

Having been warned by angels, Lot escapes. But his wife hesitates. Genesis tells us she looked back and turned into a pillar of salt. In the Qur'an, Lot's wife remained behind in the sinful city. A comparison is made between the wives of Noah and Lot. Both are the wives of prophets, but in the end that does not save them. Ultimately, it is not ancestry or marrying into the right family that matters, but taking responsibility as an individual.

Ten righteous people?

Then the men (angels ed.)...looked toward Sodom, and Abraham went with them to send them on the way. And the LORD said, "Shall I hide from Abraham what I am doing?...the outcry against Sodom and Gomorrah is great, and because their sin is very grave..."

And Abraham came near and said, "Would You also destroy the righteous with the wicked? Suppose there were fifty righteous within the city; would You...not spare it for the fifty righteous that were in it? Far be it from You... to slay the righteous with the wicked... Shall not the Judge of all the earth do right?"

So the LORD said, "If I find in Sodom fifty righteous within the city, then I will spare all the place for their sakes."

And he spoke to Him yet again and said, "Suppose there should be forty found there?"

So He said, "I will not do it for the sake of forty."

Then he said, "Let not the Lord be angry, and I will speak but once more: Suppose ten should be found

Ibrahim's plea

Tell them about the guests of Abraham. When they entered his presence and said: "Peace!" He said: "We feel afraid of you!"

15 The Rocky Tract, 51-52

They said: "We give you glad tidings in truth: be not then in despair!" He said: "And who despairs of the mercy of his Lord, but such as go astray?" Abraham said: "What then is the business on which you (have come), O you messengers (of Allah)?"

They said: "We have been sent to a people (deep) in sin."

15 The Rocky Tract, 55-58

They said: "Fear not: we have been sent against the people of Lut."

11 Hud, 70

Excepting the adherents of Lut: we are certainly (charged) to save them (from harm), - all - "except his wife, who, We have ascertained, will be among those who will lag behind."

15 The Rocky Tract, 59-60

When fear had passed from (the mind of) Abraham... he began to plead with Us for Lut's people. For

there?"
And He said, "I will not destroy it for the sake of ten."
Genesis 18:16-17, 20, 23-26, 29, 32

Abraham was, without doubt, forbearing (of faults), compassionate, and given to look to Allah. O Abraham! Do not seek this. The decree of your Lord has gone forth: for them there comes a Penalty that cannot be turned back!
11 Hud, 74-76

Men who lie with men

Then the LORD spoke to Moses, saying… If a man lies with a male as he lies with a woman, both of them have committed an abomination. They shall surely be put to death.
Leviticus 20,13

Therefore, God also gave them (Greeks and Jews ed.) up to uncleanness, in the lusts of their hearts, to dishonor their bodies among themselves…
For even their women exchanged the natural use for what is against nature. Likewise also the men, leaving the natural use of the woman, burned in their lust for one another, men with men committing what is shameful, and receiving in themselves the penalty of their error which was due. (Letter of Paul to the)
Romans 1:24-27

…Sodom and Gomorrah, and the cities around them in a similar

Lut warns his people

Behold, their brother Lut said to them: "Will you not fear (Allah)? I am to you a Messenger worthy of all trust. So fear Allah and obey me. No reward do I ask of you for it: my reward is only from the Lord of the Worlds. Of all the creatures in the world, will you approach males, and leave those whom Allah has created for you to be your mates? Nay, you are a people transgressing (all limits)!"
They said: "If you desist not, O Lut! you will assuredly be cast out!"
26 The Poets, 161-167

(We also sent) Lut (as a Messenger): behold, he said to his people: "Do you do what is shameful though you see (its iniquity)? Would you really approach men in your lusts rather than women?"

manner to these, having given themselves over to sexual immorality and gone after strange flesh, are set forth as an example, suffering the vengeance of eternal fire. Jude 1:7

Angels arrive at Sodom

… the two angels came to Sodom in the evening… When Lot saw them, he rose to meet them, and he bowed himself with his face toward the ground. And he said, "Here now, my Lords, please turn in to your servant's house and spend the night, and wash your feet; then you may rise early and go on your way." …so they…entered his house. Then he made them a feast, and baked unleavened bread, and they ate. Now before they lay down, the men of Sodom, both old and young… surrounded the house. And they called to Lot and said to him, "Where are the men who came to you tonight? Bring them out to us that we may know them carnally." So Lot went out to them through the doorway, shut the door behind him, and said, "Please, my brethren, do not do so wickedly! See now, I have two daughters who have not known a man; please, let me bring them out

But his people gave no other answer but this: they said: "Drive out the followers of Lut from your city: these are indeed men who want to be clean and pure!"

27 The Ants, 54-56

Lut protects his guests

When Our messengers came to Lut, he was grieved on their account and felt himself powerless (to protect) them.
He said: "This is a distressful day." And his people came rushing towards him, and they had been long in the habit of practising abominations. 11 The Prophet Hud, 77-78

We also (sent) Lut: he said to his people: "Do you commit lewdness such as no people in creation (ever) committed before you? For you practise your lusts on men in preference to women: you are indeed a people transgressing beyond bounds." 7 The Heights, 80-81

He said: "O my people! Here are my daughters: they are purer for you (if you marry)! Now fear Allah, and do not cover me with shame about my guests! Isn't there among you a single right-minded man?"

to you, and you may do to them as you wish; only do nothing to these men, since this is the reason they have come under the shadow of my roof."

And they said, "Stand back! …They came near to break down the door. But the men (angels ed.) reached out their hands and pulled Lot into the house with them, and shut the door. And they struck the men who were at the doorway of the house with blindness… Genesis 19:1-11

Sodom destroyed

Then the men (angels ed.) said to Lot, "…we will destroy this place, because the outcry against them has grown great before the face of the LORD, and the LORD has sent us to destroy it."

When the morning dawned, the angels urged Lot to hurry, saying, "Arise, take your wife and your two daughters who are here, lest you be consumed in the punishment of the city." And while he lingered, the men took hold of his hand, his wife's hand, and the hands of his two daughters, the LORD being merciful to him, and they brought him out and set him outside the city.

They said: "You know well we have no need of your daughters: indeed you know quite well what we want!"

He said: "Would that I had power to suppress you or that I could betake myself to some powerful support."

(The angels ed.) said: "O Lut! We are Messengers from your Lord!

By no means they shall reach you!"

11 The Prophet Hud, 78-81

Lut escapes destruction

(The Angels ed.) said: "O Lut! We are Messengers from your Lord!..Now travel with your family while yet a part of the night remains, and let not any of you look back: but your wife (will remain behind): to her will happen what happens to the people. Morning is their appointed time: Is not the morning near?"

When Our decree issued, We turned (the cities) upside down, and rained down on them brimstones hard as baked clay, spread layer on layer. 11 Hud, 81-82

And We rained down on them a shower (of brimstone): then see what was the end of those who

So it came to pass, when they had brought them outside, that he (the angel ed.) said, "Escape for your life! Do not look behind you nor stay anywhere in the plain. Escape to the mountains, lest you be destroyed."
Then the LORD rained brimstone and fire on Sodom and Gomorrah…So He overthrew those cities, all the plain, all the inhabitants of the cities, and what grew on the ground.

But his wife looked back behind him, and she became a pillar of salt.

And Abraham…looked toward Sodom and Gomorrah, and… he saw… the smoke of the land which went up like the smoke of a furnace.

And it came to pass…that God remembered Abraham, and sent Lot out of the midst of the overthrow, when He overthrew the cities in which Lot had dwelt.
Genesis 19: 12-13, 15-17, 24-29

indulged in sin and crime! 7 The Heights, 84

But we saved him and his family, except his wife: she was of those who lagged behind. 7 The Heights, 83
Allah sets forth, for an example to the Unbelievers, the wife of Noah and the wife of Lut: they were (respectively) under two of our righteous Servants, but they were false to their (husbands), and they profited nothing before Allah on their account, but were told: "You enter the Fire along with (others) that enter!" 66 Forbidden, 10
And to Lut, too, We gave Judgment and Knowledge, and We saved him from the town which practised abominations: truly they were a people given to Evil, a rebellious people. And We admitted him to Our Mercy: for he was one of the Righteous. 21 The Prophets, 74-75
But We delivered him (Abraham ed.) and (his nephew) Lut (and directed them) to the land which We have blessed for the nations.
21 The Prophets, 71

12. Joseph / Yusuf in Egypt

Joseph was one of twelve sons of Jacob, a grandson of Abraham by Isaac. The story begins with a dream in which Joseph sees eleven stars, a sun and a moon bow before him. In the Qur'an, to avoid jealousy, his father Jacob advises him not to tell his brothers about his dream. For Joseph and his little brother Benjamin are their father's favorites, and the other brothers envy them.

The jealous brothers hatch a plan to get rid of Joseph by throwing him into a well. The Bible relates how the brothers – except for Benjamin and the well-meaning Rueben – sell him to passing traders for mere pennies. In the Qur'an, the traders are the ones who pull the abandoned child from the well and sell it. The brothers tell their father that his favorite son has been killed by wolves.

In both books, Joseph is sold as a slave to one of the Egyptian notables. He is extremely good-looking. As a young man, he is nearly seduced by the lady of the house, but he remains steadfast. When the rejected woman falsely accuses him, he is put in jail.

He is released after successfully interpreting a strange dream of the Pharaoh. The seven fat and the seven lean cows in the Pharaoh's dream represent seven years of great prosperity, followed by seven years of failed harvests and famines. Joseph is released and appointed advisor to the Pharaoh.

In the Qur'an Joseph refuses to be released until the issue of the lascivious woman is resolved. Justice is maintained with a torn garment as evidence. The king interrogates the ladies and they admit to their wicked scheme. After his name has been cleared and faith in him fully restored, Joseph is willing to accept responsibility for the country's economy.

Under the guidance of Joseph, Egypt successfully survives the lean years, with enough to export to less fortunate peoples. Others, including Joseph's brothers, who lived in luxury during the fat years, are now destitute and come to Egypt to buy grain. At first, they do not recognize their long lost brother. But later, the family is joyfully reunited, and Joseph forgives his

brothers. Father Jacob, who in Bible and Qur'an is also called Israel, also travels to Egypt. On his deathbed, he pronounces his blessing on his twelve sons and promises the return of his people to Canaan.
The story of Joseph is told in great length and detail in both books. The following version has been substantially abridged. Some scenes occurring in both books, (e.g., relating to Benjamin), have been left out for the sake of the storyline.
While most stories in the Qur'an are scattered over various surahs, Joseph's story is contained in a single chapter, which is named after its protagonist. The Biblical story is found in the final chapters of Genesis. Through its explanation of how the sons of Israel come to the land of Egypt, it creates a link with the next book, Exodus, which relates how Moses led his people out of Egypt to freedom.

Bible — Joseph /Yusuf — Qur'an

Joseph's dream

Now Joseph had a dream, and he told it to his brothers ..."Please hear this dream which I have dreamed: There we were, binding sheaves in the field. Then...my sheaf arose and...stood upright; and...your sheaves...bowed down to my sheaf."
And his brothers said to him, "Shall you indeed reign over us?"
Then he dreamed still another dream and told it to his brothers "|...the sun, the moon, and the eleven stars bowed down to me." ...His father rebuked him..."Shall your mother and I and your brothers indeed come

Stars and sun bow to Yusuf

... Joseph said to his father (Jacob ed.): "O my father! I saw eleven stars and the sun and the moon: I saw them prostrate themselves to me!"
Said (the father): "My (dear) little son! Do not relate your vision to your brothers, lest they concoct a plot against you!" [12 Yusuf, 4-5]

They (his brothers ed.) said: "Truly Joseph and his brother (Benjamin) are loved more by our father than we: But we are a goodly body! Really our father is obviously wandering (in his mind)! You slay

to bow down to the earth before you?"
And his brothers envied him, but his father kept the matter in mind.
Genesis 37:5-11

Joseph or cast him out to some (unknown) land, that so the favor of your father may be given to you alone: (there will be time enough) for you to be righteous after that!"
12 Yusuf, 4-5:8-9

Joseph thrown into a pit

They (His brothers ed.)...conspired against him to kill him. Then they said to one another, "Look, this dreamer is coming! Come therefore, let us now kill him and cast him into some pit; and we shall say, 'Some wild beast has devoured him.' We shall see what will become of his dreams!"
But Reuben heard it, and he delivered him out of their hands, and said, "Let us not kill him." And Reuben said to them, "Shed no blood, but cast him into this pit which is in the wilderness, and do not lay a hand on him"-that he might deliver him out of their hands, and bring him back to his father.
...when Joseph had come to his brothers...they stripped Joseph of the tunic of many colors that was on him. Then they took him and cast him into a pit. Genesis 37:18-24

Yusuf left in a well

Said one of them: "Do not slay not Joseph, but if you must do something, throw him down to the bottom of the well: he will be picked up by some caravan of travellers."

They said: "O our father! Why don´t you trust us with Joseph – seeing we are indeed his sincere well-wishers? Send him with us tomorrow to enjoy himself and play, and we shall take every care of him."
(Jacob) said: "Really it saddens me that you should take him away: I fear lest the wolf should devour him while you do not attend to him."
They said: "If the wolf were to devour him while we are (so large) a party, then we should indeed (first) have perished ourselves!" So they took him away, and they all agreed to throw him down to the bottom of the well... 12 Yusuf, 10-15

Joseph sold to Egypt, Jacob mourns

Then they…looked, and there was a company of Ishmaelites...bearing spices…on their way to carry them down to Egypt.

So Judah said to his brothers, "What profit is there if we kill our brother and conceal his blood? Come and let us sell him to the Ishmaelites, and let not our hand be upon him, for he is our brother and our flesh." And his brothers listened**…**so the brothers pulled Joseph up and lifted him out of the pit, and sold him to the Ishmaelites for twenty shekels of silver. And they took Joseph to Egypt…and sold him… to Potiphar, an officer of Pharaoh.

Then Reuben returned to the pit, and indeed Joseph was not in the pit; and he tore his clothes. And he returned to his brothers and said, "The lad is no more; and I, where shall I go?" Then…they took Joseph's tunic, killed a kid of the goats, and dipped the tunic in the blood…and they brought it to their father…And he recognized it and said, "It is my son's tunic. A wild beast has devoured him….Then Jacob tore his clothes, put sackcloth on his waist,

Yaqoub's sorrow, Yusuf sold

Then they came to their father in the early part of the night, weeping. They said: "O our father! We went racing with one another, and left Joseph with our things; and the wolf devoured him. But you will never believe us even though we tell the truth."

They stained his shirt with false blood.

He (the father ed.) said: "Nay, but your minds have made up a tale (that may pass) with you. (For me) patience is most fitting: against that which you assert, it is Allah (alone) Whose help can be sought"...

Then there came a caravan of travellers: they sent their water-carrier (for water), and he let down his bucket (into the well)...

He said: "Ah there! Good news! Here is a (fine) young man!" So they concealed him as a treasure!

The (Brethren) sold him for a miserable price,-for a few dirhams (pennies ed.) counted out: in such

and mourned for his son many days.
Genesis 37:25-36

low estimation did they hold him!
12 Yusuf, 16-20

Joseph's career in Egypt

Now Joseph had been taken down to Egypt. The Lord was with Joseph, and he was a successful man; and he was in the house of his master the Egyptian. And his master saw that the Lord was with him and that the Lord made all he did to prosper in his hand. So Joseph found favor in his sight, and served him. Then he made him overseer of his house, and all that he had he put under his authority… the Lord blessed the Egyptian's house for Joseph's sake; and the blessing of the Lord was on all that he had in the house and in the field. Thus he (the master ed.) left all that he had in Joseph's hand… Genesis 39:1-6

Yusuf rises to power in Egypt

The man in Egypt who bought him, said to his wife: "Make his stay (among us) honorable: maybe he will bring us much good, or we shall adopt him as a son."

Thus We established Joseph in the land, that We might teach him the interpretation of stories (and events).

When Joseph attained his full manhood, We gave him power and knowledge: thus do We reward those who do right. 12 Yusuf, 21

Joseph resists temptation

Now Joseph was handsome in form and appearance…his master's wife cast longing eyes on Joseph, and she said, "Lie with me."

But he refused and said to his master's wife, "Look, my master does not know what is with me in the house, and he has committed all that he has to my hand. There is no one greater in this house than I, nor has he kept back anything from me

Yusuf rejects seduction

But she in whose house he was, sought to seduce him from his (true) self: she fastened the doors, and said: "Now come, you (dear one)!"

He said: "Allah forbid! truly (your husband) is my Lord! he made my sojourn agreeable! Truly to no good come those who do wrong!"

And (with passion) she desired him, and he would have desired her, but

but you, because you are his wife. How then can I do this great wickedness, and sin against God?" So it was, as she spoke to Joseph day by day, that he did not heed her, to lie with her or to be with her.
But it happened …when Joseph went into the house to do his work, and none of the men of the house was inside, that she caught him by his garment, saying "Lie with me." But he left his garment in her hand, and fled and ran outside. Genesis 39: 6-12

Joseph imprisoned
So she kept his garment with her until his master came home. Then she spoke to him… saying,
"The Hebrew servant whom you brought to us came in to me to mock me; so it happened, as I lifted my voice and cried out, that he left his garment saying… "

So it was, when his master heard the words which his wife spoke to him…that his anger was aroused.

Then Joseph's master took him and put him into the prison, a place where the king's prisoners were confined. Genesis 39:16-20

that he saw the evidence of his Lord: thus (did We order) that We might turn away from him (all) evil and shameful deeds: for he was one of Our servants, sincere and purified. So they both raced each other to the door, and she tore his shirt from the back: they both found her lord near the door.
She said: "What is the fitting punishment for one who formed an evil design against your wife, but prison or a grievous chastisement?" 12 Yusuf, 23-25

Yusuf cast into prison
She said: "There before you is the man about whom you blamed me! I sought to seduce him from his (true) self but he firmly saved himself guiltless!
And now, if he does not my bidding, he shall certainly be cast into prison, and… be of the company of the vilest!"
He said: "O my Lord! The prison is more to my liking than that to which they invite me (forced sex with a married woman ed.); unless You turn away their snare from me, I should (in my youthful folly) feel inclined toward them and join the ranks of the ignorant. " Then it occurred to the men, after they had

Seven fat and seven lean cows

... at the end of two full years...Pharaoh had a dream; and behold, he stood by the river. Suddenly there came up out of the river seven cows, fine looking and fat; and they fed in the meadow. Then behold, seven other cows came up after them out of the river, ugly and gaunt, and stood by the other cows on the bank of the river. And the ugly and gaunt cows ate up the seven fine looking and fat cows. ...in the morning...his spirit was troubled, and he sent and called for all the magicians of Egypt and all its wise men. And Pharaoh told them his dreams, but there was no one who could interpret them for Pharaoh.

seen the Signs... to imprison him for a time. [12 Yusuf, 32-33,35]

Pharaoh's dreams

The king (of Egypt) said: "I do see (in a vision) seven fat kine (cows ed.) whom seven lean ones devour, and seven green ears of corn, and seven (others) withered. O you chiefs! expound to me my vision if it be that you can interpret visions." They said: "A confused medley of dreams: and we are not skilled in the interpretation of dreams." [12 Yusuf, 43-44]

But the man... (who had been in prison)...said: you send me (to prison) (to fetch Joseph who explained my dream ed.)'
So the king said: "Bring him to me and say ed.'."
"O Joseph! O man of truth! Expound to us (the dream) of seven fat kine (cows ed.) whom seven lean ones devour..." [12 Yusuf, 43-48, 50-51,54-56]

Joseph sent for

Then Pharaoh sent and called Joseph, and they brought him quickly out of the dungeon; and he shaved, changed his clothing, and came to Pharaoh. And Pharaoh said to Joseph,

Joseph's innocence proved

But when the messenger came to him, (Joseph) said: "Go you back to your Lord, and ask him, 'What is the state of mind of the ladies...'
For my Lord is certainly well aware of their snare."
And one of her household saw and

"I have had a dream, and there is no one who can interpret it."

bore witness: "If it be that his shirt is rent from the front then her tale is true, and he is a liar!"
" But if it be that his shirt is torn at the back…"Behold it is a snare of you women!"
So when he saw his shirt- that it was torn at the back- (her husband) said: "Behold, it is a snare of you women."[12 Yusuf, 23-26-28]
Said the wife: "Now is the truth manifest (to all): it was I who sought to seduce him from his (true) self: He is indeed of those who are (ever) true (and virtuous)." 12 Yusuf, 26-28

Joseph interprets dreams
Then Joseph said to Pharaoh, "The dreams of Pharaoh are one; God has shown Pharaoh what He is about to do: The seven good cows are seven years, and the seven good heads are seven years; the dreams are one. And the seven thin and ugly cows which came up after them are seven years, and the seven empty heads blighted by the east wind are seven years of famine.
"…let Pharaoh select a discerning and wise man to collect one-fifth of the produce of the land of Egypt in the seven plentiful years…as a

Joseph explains the dreams
(Joseph) said: "For seven years you shall diligently sow as is your wont: and the harvests that you reap, you shall leave them in the ear, – except a little, of which you shall eat. Then will come after that (period) seven dreadful (years), which will devour what you shall have laid by in advance for them – (all) except a little which you shall have (specially) guarded."

So the king said:.. "I will take him specially to serve about my own person." (Joseph) said: "Set me

reserve for the land for the seven years of famine which shall be in the land of Egypt...."

Then Pharaoh said to Joseph, "Inasmuch as God has shown you all this, there is no one as discerning and wise as you. You shall be over my house, and all my people shall be ruled according to your word."

Now in the seven plentiful years the ground brought forth abundantly. Joseph gathered very much grain, as the sand of the sea... Genesis 41: 1-4, 8, 14-15, 25-27, 29-30, 33-36, 39-40, 47, 49

over the store-houses of the land: I will indeed guard them, as one that knows (their importance)."

Thus We gave established power to Joseph in the land, to take possession therein as, when, or where he pleased.

Jacob sends to Egypt for grain

Then the seven years of plenty which were in the land of Egypt ended, and the seven years of famine began to come, as Joseph had said. The famine was in all lands, but in all the land of Egypt there was bread. Genesis 41: 53-54

When Jacob saw that there was grain in Egypt, Jacob said to his sons... I have heard that there is grain in Egypt; go down to that place and buy for us there, that we may live and not die." Genesis 42:1-2

And the sons of Israel went to buy grain among those who journeyed, for the famine was in the land of Canaan. Genesis 42: 1-2, 5

Jacob (Israel) moves to Egypt

Then... he provided a home for his parents... ...and they (his parents and eleven brothers ed.) fell down in prostration, (all' before him.

He said: "O my father! this is the fulfillment of my vision of old! He (Allah ed.) was indeed good to me when He took me out of prison and brought you (all) here out of the desert (even) after Satan had sown enmity between me and my brothers.

"O my Lord! You have indeed bestowed on me some power, and taught me something of the interpretation of dreams and events-" 12 Yusuf, 99-101

Joseph forgives his brothers

Now the famine was severe in the land. And it came to pass, when they had eaten up the grain which they had brought from Egypt, that their father said to them, "Go back, buy us a little food." But Judah spoke to him, saying, "The man solemnly warned us, saying, 'You shall not see my face unless your brother is with you.' "

So the men took that present and Benjamin, and they took double money in their hand, and arose and went down to Egypt; and they stood before Joseph. And when Joseph came home, they brought him the present... Genesis 43:1-3,15, 26

Then Joseph could not restrain himself...and he...made himself known to his brothers. And he wept aloud...

Then he said: "I am Joseph your brother, whom you sold into Egypt. But now, do not therefore be grieved or angry with yourselves because you sold me here; for God sent me before you to preserve life. So now it was not you who sent me here, but God;" Moreover he kissed all his brothers and wept over them, and after that his brothers talked with him. Genesis 45:1-2, 4-5, 8,15

Yusuf makes himself known

Then came Joseph's brethren: they entered his presence, and he knew them, but they did not know him.

12 Joseph, 58

Then, when they came into (Joseph's) presence they said: "O exalted one! distress has seized us and our family: we have (now) brought but scanty capital: so pay us full measure, (we pray you), and treat it as charity to us. For Allah rewards the charitable."

He said: "Do you know how you dealt with Joseph...not knowing (what you were doing)?"

They said: "Are you indeed Joseph?

He said: "I am Joseph... Allah has indeed been gracious to us (all): behold, he that is righteous and patient, – never will Allah suffer the reward to be lost, of those who do right."

They said: "By Allah! Indeed Allah has preferred you above us, and we certainly have been guilty of sin!"

He said: "This day let no reproach be (cast) on you: Allah will forgive you, and He is the Most Merciful of those who show mercy!"

12 Joseph, 88-90; 91-92

Jacob

And Pharaoh said to Joseph, "Say to your brothers, '...Load your animals and depart; go to the land of Canaan. Bring your father and your households and come to me; I will give you the best of the land of Egypt, and you will eat the fat of the land.'" Genesis 45:17-18

Then God spoke to Israel in the visions of the night, and said, "Jacob, Jacob!...I am God, the God of your father; do not fear to go down to Egypt, for I will make of you a great nation there."

So they...went to Egypt, Jacob and all his descendants with him. Genesis 46:2-3,6

And Jacob lived in the land of Egypt seventeen years. When the time drew near that Israel must die, he called his son Joseph... Genesis 47:28-29

Then Israel (Jacob ed.) said to Joseph, "Behold, I am dying, but God will be with you and bring you back to the land of your fathers."

All these are the twelve tribes of Israel, and...he blessed them; ... each one according to his own blessing. Genesis 48:21; 49: 28

Yaqoeb

They (Joseph's brothers ed.) said: "O our father (Jacob ed.)! Ask for us forgiveness for our sins, for we were truly at fault."

He said: "Soon will I ask my Lord for forgiveness for you: for He is indeed Oft-Forgiving, Most Merciful."

Were you witnesses when Death appeared before Jacob? Behold, he said to his sons: "What will you worship after me?" They said: "We shall worship your God (Allah) and the God (Allah) of your fathers, - of Abraham, Isma`il, and Isaac, - the One (True) God (Allah): to Him we bow (in Islam)." 2 The Heifer,133

And We made a people, considered weak (and of no account), inheritors of lands in both East and West, - lands whereon We sent down Our blessings. 7, The Heights, 137

Allah took a Covenant from the Children of Israel, and We appointed twelve captains among them. 5 The Table Spread,12

13. Moses/Musa

Moses is a very important figure in both Bible and Qur'an. He liberated his people, fought idolatry and received the Law, or Torah, from God. The stories run parallel from the moment the baby Moses is cast into the river, via the exodus from Egypt to the Promised Land. Both books describe Moses' struggle to release his people from Egyptian bondage. To this end, God brings down plagues upon Egypt, the last of which is very gruesome. In one night, the first-born of all humans and animals are killed. Only the first-born of the Israelites are miraculously passed over. The children of Israel escaped in such haste that there was no time for the bread to leaven. Jews celebrate these events each year during Pesach (derived from Pasach = pass over).

The story begins with the oppression of the Israelites by a new King or Pharaoh. The Qur'an story focuses not on the oppression of Israelites as such, but on his splitting up his people into different groups and oppressing a minority. In both cases, the Pharaoh orders all Hebrew baby boys to be killed. To save her baby, one mother hides him in a small boat on the river, watched over by his sister Miriam. In the Bible, the Pharaoh's daughter finds him. Miriam arranges for her mother to suckle the child. In the Qur'an, it is Pharaoh's wife who adopts the child. She is an exemplary woman, upright and independent, no slavish follower of her husband's cruel regime. The Qur'an describes the emotions of the Egyptian queen on the one hand and Moses' mother on the other. When Moses grows up, he kills one of the oppressors. The Bible relates how he kills an Egyptian and flees. The Qur'an states that he kills a man, pleads and gains forgiveness. In both books, God's voice from a burning bush gives Moses the inspiration to plead with the Pharaoh to let his people go. Both books tell of Moses' hesitation to take on this divine mission; of his brother Aaron, called upon to help him and his sister Miriam who accompanies him.

The Bible speaks of the God of the Hebrews; in Moses' encounter with God, He speaks of Himself as *Yahweh*, translated here almost literally as *I am Who I am*. A comparable abstract concept of God is also found in the

Qur'an, which speaks more generally of the Lord of the Worlds, rather than of one specific people. Allah is the God, who guides one and all and is, therefore, the Lord both of the children of Israel and of the Egyptians. Moses and Aaron go to the Pharaoh, showing God's power by a staff, which in both books turns into a snake. The Pharaoh relents only after a series of plagues, briefly mentioned in the Qur'an and described in detail in the Bible. The last plague is the death of all first-born. In both books, the children of Israel escape through a dry passage in the sea, leaving the Egyptian troops following them to drown. In the Qur'an the Pharaoh repents, but too late. His body remains as a mummy; a sign to all people. Moses goes up Mount Sinai to meet God. This meeting is of a mystical nature, described in images in both books. Then Moses receives commandments, or laws, from God, an event which is celebrated by Jews in the feast of Shavuot, or Pentecost, the name referring to the 50 days that had passed since the exodus. The Law which Moses received is repeatedly described in the Qur'an as the law of the Israelites, valid more generally, for Muslims as well.

Only three of the Ten Commandments are included below, those that are specifically linked to Moses in the Qur'an. Both books include many other, partly overlapping, commandments and interdictions.

When Moses returns from the mountain, he sees his people dancing around a golden calf. In the Bible, he gets so angry that he breaks the tablets. In the Qur'an, Moses puts the tablets down before speaking to his people. In both cases, forgiveness is asked.

After forty difficult years, the people enter the land of milk and honey. This image that returns in the description of the paradise gardens in the Qur'an, with the practical addition that, in paradise, milk never sours.

For the Biblical story of Moses, we draw mainly on the second book of the Bible, Exodus, named after the exodus from Egypt. We draw on several surahs for the Qur'anic story.

Hebrew boys killed
Now there arose a new king over Egypt, who did not know Joseph. And he said to his people, "Look, the people of the children of Israel are more and mightier than we; come, let us deal shrewdly with them, lest they multiply, and it happen, in the event of war, that they also join our enemies and fight against us…"
And they were in dread of the children of Israel. And they (the Egyptians ed.) made their lives bitter with hard bondage.
So Pharaoh commanded all his people, saying, "Every (Hebrew ed.) son who is born you shall cast into the river, and every daughter you shall save alive." Exodus 1: 8-10, 12-14, 22

Pharaoh oppresses a minority
We rehearse to you some of the story of Moses and Pharaoh in Truth, for people who believe.

Truly Pharaoh elated himself in the land and broke up its people into sections, depressing a small group among them: their sons he slew, but he kept alive their females: for he was indeed a maker of mischief.

And We wished to be gracious to those who were being depressed in the land, to make them leaders (in faith) and make them heirs, to establish a firm place for them in the land… 28 The Narration, 3-6

Moses in the bulrushes
So the (Hebrew ed.) woman conceived and bore a son... she hid him three months. But when she could no longer hide him, she took an ark of bulrushes for him…put the child in it, and laid it in the reeds by the river's bank. And his sister stood afar off, to know what would be done to him.

The baby cast into the river
So We sent this inspiration to the mother of Moses: "Suckle (your child), but when you have fears about him, cast him into the river, but fear not nor grieve: for We shall restore him to you, and We shall make him one of Our Messengers." Then the people of Pharaoh picked him up (from the river): (It was

Then the daughter of Pharaoh came down to bathe at the river. And her maidens walked along the riverside; and when she saw the ark among the reeds, she sent her maid to get it. And when she had opened it, she saw the child, and behold, the baby wept. So she had compassion on him, and said, "This is one of the Hebrews' children."
Then his sister said to Pharaoh's daughter, "Shall I go and call a nurse for you from the Hebrew women, that she may nurse the child for you?" And Pharaoh's daughter said to her, "Go."
So the maiden went and called the child's mother. Then Pharaoh's daughter said to her, "Take this child away and nurse him for me, and I will give you your wages." So the woman took the child and nursed him.

And the child grew, and she brought him to Pharaoh's daughter, and he became her son. So she called his name Moses, saying, "Because I drew him out of the water."
Exodus 2:2-10

intended) that (Moses) should be to them an adversary and a cause of sorrow…
The wife of Pharaoh said: "(Here is) a joy of the eye, for me and for you: do not slay him. It may be that he will be of use to us, or we may adopt him as a son."
And Allah sets forth, as an example…, the wife of Pharaoh: behold she said: "O my Lord! build for me, in nearness to You, a mansion in the Garden, and save me from Pharaoh and his doings, and save me from those that do wrong";
66 Holding, 11

But there came to be a void in the heart of the mother of Moses: she was going almost to disclose his (case), had We not strengthened her heart…so that she might remain…a believer. And she said to the sister of (Moses): "Follow him." So she (the sister) watched him in the character of a stranger. And they did not know. And we ordained that he refused suck at first, until (his sister came up and) said: "Shall I point out to you the people of a house that will nourish and bring him up for you and be sincerely attached to him?" Thus We restored him to his mother, that

her eye might be comforted, that she might not grieve...
When he reached full age, and was firmly established (in life), We bestowed on him wisdom and knowledge... [28The Narration, 7-14]

Moses kills an Egyptian
Now it came to pass in those days, when Moses was grown, that he went out to his brethren and looked at their burdens. And he saw an Egyptian beating a Hebrew, one of his brethren. So he looked this way and that way, and when he saw no one, he killed the Egyptian and hid him in the sand.
And when he went out the second day, behold, two Hebrew men were fighting, and he said to the one who did the wrong, "Why are you striking your companion?" Then he said, "Who made you a prince and a judge over us? Do you intend to kill me as you killed the Egyptian?" So Moses feared and said, "Surely this thing is known!"
When Pharaoh heard of this matter, he sought to kill Moses.But Moses fled from the face of Pharaoh and dwelt in the land of Midian; and he sat down by a well. [Exodus 2: 11-15]

Moses murders a man
...and he (Moses ed.) found there two men fighting -one of his own religion, and the other, of his foes. Now the man of his own religion appealed to him against his foe, and Moses struck him with his fist and made an end of him. He said: "This is the work of Evil (Satan) for he is an enemy that manifestly misleads!" He (Moses ed.) prayed: "O My Lord! I have indeed wronged my soul! You then forgive me!" So (Allah) forgave him: for He is the Oft-Forgiving, Most Merciful. And there came a man, running, from the furthest end of the City. He said: "O Moses! The Chiefs are taking counsel together about you, to slay you: so you get away..." He therefore got away therefrom, looking about, in a state of fear. He prayed: "O my Lord! save me from people given to wrong-doing." [28 The Narration,15-17,20-21]
"Then you slew a man, but We saved you from trouble... [20 Ta-Ha,40]

Moses and the burning bush

And the Angel of the Lord appeared to him in a flame of fire from the midst of a bush… but the bush was not consumed. …God called to him from the midst of the bush and said, "Moses, Moses!... Do not draw near this place. Take your sandals off your feet, for the place where you stand is holy ground. I am the God of your father-the God of Abraham, the God of Isaac, and the God of Jacob." And Moses hid his face, for he was afraid to look upon God.

And the Lord said: "I have surely seen the oppression of My people who are in Egypt, and have heard their cry because of their taskmasters, for I know their sorrows. So I have come down to deliver them out of the hand of the Egyptians, and to bring them up from that land to a good and large land, to a land flowing with milk and honey…Then Moses said to God: "when… they say to me 'What is his name?' what shall I say to them?" And God said to Moses,

"(YaHWeH)

I AM WHO I AM."

Exodus 3: 2, 4-8, 13-14

A voice in the fire

Has the story of Moses reached you? Behold, he saw a fire: so he said to his family: "You tarry; I perceive a fire; perhaps I can bring you some burning brand…, (charcoal that you may warm yourselves ed. 28:29) or find some guidance at the fire."

But when he came to the fire, a voice was heard: "O Moses! Verily I am your Lord! Therefore (in My presence) put off your shoes: you are in the sacred valley... I have chosen you: listen, then, to the inspiration (sent to you).

Verily, I am Allah: There is no god but I: So you serve Me (only), and establish regular prayer for celebrating My praise. Verily the Hour is coming- My design is to keep it hidden – for every soul to receive its reward by the measure of its endeavor. [20 Ta-Ha, 9-15]

But when he came to the (Fire) a voice was heard from the right bank of the valley, from a tree in hallowed ground: "O Moses, Verily I am Allah, the Lord of the Worlds... [28 The Narration, 30]

A divine mission

And the Lord said: "I have surely seen the oppression of My people who are in Egypt, and have heard their cry because of their taskmasters, for I know their sorrows.

"So I have come down to deliver them out of the hand of the Egyptians, and to bring them up from that land to a good and large land, to a land flowing with milk and honey…

"Come now, therefore, and I will send you to Pharaoh that you may bring My people, the children of Israel, out of Egypt." Exodus 3: 7-8, 10

Then Moses said to the Lord, "O my Lord, I am not eloquent, neither before nor since You have spoken to Your servant; but I am slow of speech and slow of tongue."

So…the Lord…said: "Is not Aaron…your brother? I know that he can speak well. And look, he is also coming out to meet you. When he sees you, he will be glad in his heart. Now you shall speak to him and put the words in his mouth. And I will be with your mouth and with his mouth, and I will teach you what you shall do." Exodus 4: 10, 13-15

Moses hesitates

"You go to Pharaoh, for he has indeed transgressed all bounds."

(Moses) said: "O my Lord! Expand me my breast; ease my task for me; and remove the impediment from my speech, so they may understand what I say: and give me a Minister from my family, Aaron, my brother; add to my strength through him, and make him share my task: That we may celebrate Your praise…"

(Allah) said: "Granted is your prayer, O Moses!" 20Ta-Ha,:24-36

(Moses ed.) said: "O my Lord! I have slain a man among them, (the Egyptians ed.) and I fear lest they slay me. And my brother Aaron – he is more eloquent in speech than I: so send him with me as a helper, to confirm…me; for I fear that they may accuse me of falsehood."

He (Allah ed.) said: "We will certainly strengthen your arm through your brother, and invest you both with authority, so they shall not be able to touch you: with Our Signs you shall triumph……"

28,The Narration,33-35

Let my people go!
Afterward Moses and Aaron went in and told Pharaoh, "Thus says the Lord God of Israel: 'Let My people go, that they may hold a feast to Me in the wilderness.' "

And Pharaoh said, "Who is the Lord, that I should obey His voice to let Israel go? I do not know the Lord, nor will I let Israel go."
So they said, "The God of the Hebrews has met with us. Please, let us go… Exodus 5: 1-3
And Aaron cast down his rod before Pharaoh and before his servants, and it became a serpent.
But Pharaoh also called… the magicians of Egypt…every man threw down his rod, and they became serpents. But Aaron's rod swallowed up their rods.

And Pharaoh's heart grew hard, and he did not heed them… Exodus 7: 10-13

Allah, Lord of Pharaoh
"So you both go to him (Pharaoh ed.), and say: 'Verily we are Messengers sent by your Lord: send forth, therefore, the Children of Israel with us, and afflict them not…And Peace to all who follow guidance!
…(Pharaoh) said: "Who, then, O Moses, is the Lord of you two?"
He said: "Our Lord is He Who gave to each (created) thing its form and nature, and further, gave (it) guidance." 20 Ta-Ha,47, 49-50
"Am I (Pharaoh ed.) not better than this (Moses), who is a contemptible wretch and can scarcely express himself clearly?" 43 Gold Adornments, 52
Pharaoh said: "O Chiefs! No god do I know for you but myself."
28,The Narration,38

So (Moses) threw his rod, and behold, it was a serpent… 26 The Poets,32,

…We sent Moses with Our Signs to Pharaoh and his chiefs, but they wrongfully rejected them.
7 The Heights,103

Plagues
And all the waters that were in the river were turned to blood. Exodus 7: 20
"So…frogs…shall…come into your house, into your bedroom, on your

Locusts, frogs and blood
Moses said to his people: "Pray for help from Allah, and (wait) in patience and constancy: for the earth is Allah's, to give as a heritage to

bed....into your ovens and into your kneading bowls. Exodus,8:3
Then they took ashes from the furnace and stood before Pharaoh, and Moses scattered them toward heaven. And they caused boils...on man and beast. [Exodus 9: 10]
And the locusts went up over all the land of Egypt and rested on all the territory of Egypt. Exodus 10:14
And the Lord said to Moses, "I will bring yet one more plague on Pharaoh and on Egypt.
About midnight I will go out into the midst of Egypt; and all the firstborn in the land of Egypt shall die, from the firstborn of Pharaoh... to the firstborn of the female servant... and all the firstborn of the animals.
But against none of the children of Israel shall a dog move its tongue, against man or beast, that you may know that the Lord does make a difference between the Egyptians and Israel." [Exodus 11: 1, 4-5, 7]

And... at midnight...the Lord struck all the firstborn in the land of Egypt, from the firstborn of Pharaoh who sat on his throne to the firstborn of the captive who was in the dungeon, and all the firstborn of livestock. So Pharaoh rose in the night, he, all his

such of His servants as He pleases; and the end is (best) for the righteous."
They said: "We have had (nothing but) trouble, both before and after you came to us."
He said: "It may be that your Lord will destroy your enemy and make you inheritors in the earth; that so He may try you by your deeds."

We punished the people of Pharaoh with years (of drought) and shortness of crops; that they might receive admonition. But when good (times) came, they said: "This is due to us;" when gripped by calamity, they ascribed it to evil omens connected with Moses and those with him! Behold! In truth the omens of evil are theirs in Allah's sight, but most of them do not understand. They said (to Moses) "Whatever be the Signs you bring, to work therewith your sorcery on us, we shall never believe in you."

So We sent (plagues) on them: wholesale Death, locusts, lice, frogs, and blood: Signs openly self-explained:
but they were steeped in arrogance–a people given to sin.

servants, and all the Egyptians; and there was a great cry in Egypt, for there was not a house where there was not one dead.

Then he (Pharaoh ed.) called for Moses and Aaron by night, and said, "Rise, go out from among my people, both you and the children of Israel. And go, serve the Lord as you have said."
So the people took their dough before it was leavened… (and ed.) went out from the land of Egypt.
This is that night of the Lord, a solemn observance for all the children of Israel throughout their generations. Exodus 12: 29, 31,34, 41-42

Every time the Penalty fell on them, they said: "O Moses! On our behalf call on your Lord in virtue of His promise to you: if you will remove the Penalty from us, we shall truly believe in you, and we shall send away the Children of Israel with you."
But every time We removed the Penalty from them according to a fixed term which they had to fulfill – behold! They broke their word!
7The Heights,128-135

O you Children of Israel, We delivered you from your enemy…
20 Ta-Ha,80

And remember, We delivered you from the people of Pharaoh:
2 The Heifer,49

Passage through the sea
Now it was told the king of Egypt that the people had fled…

So the Egyptians pursued them and overtook them camping by the sea… And the Lord said to Moses, "… lift up your rod, and stretch out your hand over the sea and divide it. And the children of Israel shall go on dry ground through the midst of the sea."

Pursuing Egyptians drown
We sent an inspiration to Moses: "Travel by night with My servants, and strike a dry path for them through the sea, without fear of being overtaken (by Pharaoh) and without (any other) fear."
Then Pharaoh pursued them with his forces, but the waters completely overwhelmed them and covered them up.

Then Moses stretched out his hand over the sea; and the Lord caused the sea to go back... So the children of Israel went into the midst of the sea on the dry ground, and the waters were a wall to them on their right hand and on their left. And the Egyptians pursued and went after them into the midst of the sea…

Then the Lord said to Moses, "Stretch out your hand over the sea, that the waters may come back upon the Egyptians…And Moses stretched out his hand over the sea; So the Lord overthrew the Egyptians in the midst of the sea.

Then the waters returned and covered the chariots, the horsemen, and all the army of Pharaoh that came into the sea after them. Not so much as one of them remained.
But the children of Israel had walked on dry land in the midst of the sea, and the waters were a wall to them on their right hand and on their left.
So the Lord saved Israel that day out of the hand of the Egyptians, and Israel saw the Egyptians dead on the seashore. Exodus 14: 5, 9,15-16 , 21-23, 26-30

Pharaoh led his people astray instead of leading them aright.
20 Ta-Ha, 77-79

We took the Children of Israel across the sea; Pharaoh and his hosts followed them in insolence and spite.
10 Yunus, 90

And remember We divided the Sea for you and saved you and drowned Pharaoh's people within your very sight. 2The Heifer,50

Pharaoh repents, too late
At length, when overwhelmed with the flood, he said: "I believe that there is no god except Him Whom the Children of Israel believe in: I am of those who submit (to Allah in Islam (obedience ed.)."

(It was said to him:) (Allah to Pharaoh ed.):
"Ah now! - But a little while before, you were in rebellion! - and you did mischief (and violence)!
This day shall We save you in your body, that you may be a Sign to those who come after you. But verily, many among mankind are heedless of our Signs!" 10 Yunus, 90-92

Journey through the desert

Then…the children of Israel set out on their journey…but there was no water…and the people complained against Moses…

"Why is it you have brought us up out of Egypt, to kill us and our children and our livestock with thirst?"

So Moses cried out to the Lord, saying, "What shall I do with this people? They are almost ready to stone me!" And the Lord said to Moses, "… take in your hand your rod…and strike the rock, and water will come out of it, that the people may drink."

Then…the children of Israel complained…"Oh, that we had died…in…Egypt…when we ate bread to the full! For you have brought us out into this wilderness to kill this whole assembly with hunger."

Then the Lord said to Moses, "Behold, I will rain bread from heaven for you. So it was that …in the morning…on the surface of the wilderness was a small round

Water and manna

And remember Moses prayed for water for his people. [2 The Heifer, 60]

We divided them into twelve Tribes or nations. We directed Moses by inspiration, when his (thirsty) people asked him for water: "Strike the rock with your staff": out of it there gushed forth twelve springs: each group knew its own place for water. We gave them the shade of clouds, and sent down to them manna…(saying): "Eat of the good things We have provided for you": (but they rebelled); to Us they did no harm, but they harmed their own souls. [7The Heights, 160]

And remember you (the people of Israel ed.) said:

"O Moses! We cannot endure one kind of food (always); so beseech your Lord for us to produce for us of what the earth grows, - its pot-herbs, and cucumbers, its garlic, lentils, and onions."

He said: "Will you exchange the better for the worse?"…They were covered with humiliation and misery.
2The Heifer, 61

substance, as fine as frost on the ground. And Moses said to them, "This is the bread which the Lord has given you to eat."

Exodus 17:1,3, 4-6; 16: 2-4, 13-15

God radiant on the mountain

And Moses went up to God, and the Lord called to him from the mountain, saying,

"…if you will indeed obey My voice…then you shall be a special treasure to Me above all people… And you shall be to Me a kingdom of priests and a holy nation."

Now Mount Sinai was completely in smoke, because the Lord descended upon it in fire.

And when the blast of the trumpet sounded long and became louder and louder, Moses spoke, and God answered him…

Then Moses went up…and saw the God of Israel. And there was under His feet…a paved work of sapphire stone, and it was like the very heavens in its clarity. And when He had made an end of speaking with him on Mount Sinai, He gave Moses two tablets of the Testimony, tablets of stone, written with the finger of God. Exodus 19:3,5-6, 18-19, 24:9-10, 31:18

Allah speaks with Moses

Also mention…Moses: for he was specially chosen, and he was a Messenger (and) a prophet. And we called him from the right side of Mount (Sinai), and made him draw near to Us, for mystic (converse)…(The people ed.) said: "O Moses! We shall never believe in you until we see Allah manifestly," but you were dazed with thunder and lightning even as you looked on. When Moses came to the place appointed by Us…he said: "O my Lord! show (Yourself) to me…" Allah said: "By no means can you see Me (direct) …When his Lord manifested His Glory on the mount…and Moses fell down in a swoon. And We ordained laws for him in the Tablets in all matters, both commanding and explaining all things, (and said): "Take and hold these with firmness, and enjoin your people to hold fast by the best in the precepts." 19 Maryam, 51-52; 2,The Heifer, 55; 7 The Heights ,143,14

The golden calf

And the Lord said to Moses, "Go, get down! For your people whom you brought out of the land of Egypt have corrupted themselves. They have turned aside quickly out of the way which I commanded them. They have made themselves a molded calf, and worshiped it…"

And Moses turned and went down from the mountain, and the two tablets of the Testimony were in his hands… and the writing was the writing of God…as soon as he came near the camp…he saw the calf and the dancing.
So Moses' anger became hot, and he cast the tablets out of his hands and broke them at the foot of the mountain. Then he took the calf which they had made, burned it in the fire, and ground it to powder; and he scattered it on the water and made the children of Israel drink it.

Then Moses returned to the Lord and said, "Oh, these people have committed a great sin, and have made for themselves a god of gold! Yet now, if You will forgive their sin-… Exodus 32: 7-9, 15-16, 19-20, 31-32

Musa grieved

The people of Moses made, in his absence, out of their ornaments, the image of a calf, (for worship): it seemed to low: did they not see that it could neither speak to them, nor show them the Way? They took it for worship and they did wrong.
When Moses came back to his people, angry and grieved, he said: "Evil it is that you have done…in my absence"… He put down the Tablets… 7 The Heights, 148,150
And remember Moses said to his people: "O my people! You have indeed wronged yourselves by your worship of the calf: so turn (in repentance) to your Maker… For He is Oft- Returning, Most Merciful.
2 The Heifer, 54

When they repented, and saw that they had erred, they said: "If our Lord have not mercy upon us and forgive us, we shall indeed be of those who perish." 7 The Heights, 149

Even then We did forgive you; there was a chance for you to be grateful.
2 The Heifer, 52

(Some of the) ten commandments
And the Lord said to Moses, "Cut two tablets of stone like the first ones, and I will write on these tablets the words that were on the first tablets which you broke."
Exodus 34:1

"I am the Lord your God…You shall have no other gods before Me." "Honor your father and your mother…" Exodus 20: 2-3 Exodus 20: 12

"Honor your father and mother."
Matthew *19:19*

"You shall not murder." Exodus 20:13

Laws in the tablets
When the anger of Moses was appeased, he took up the Tablets: in the writing thereon was Guidance and Mercy for such as fear their Lord.

And We ordained laws for him in the Tablets… 7 The Heights, 154, 145

Your Lord has decreed that you worship none but Him, and that you be kind to parents. 17 The Israelites, 23

We gave Moses the Book…Shed no blood amongst you…. 2 The Heifer, 87,84

Land of milk and honey
"…I will bring you…to a land flowing with milk and honey."
Exodus 3:17

So the Lord's anger was aroused against Israel, and He made them wander in the wilderness forty years until all the generation that had done evil in the sight of the Lord was gone. Numbers 32:13
Then Moses went up to…mount Nebo… And the Lord showed him all the land of Judah as far as the

Gardens for the righteous
Allah said: "Therefore the land will be out of their reach for forty years: in distraction they will wander through the land: but you do not grieve over these rebellious people. 5 The Table Spread, 26

We settled the Children of Israel in a beautiful dwelling-place, and provided for them sustenance of the best: 10 Yunus, 93

Western sea and the plain of the Valley of Jericho, the city of palm trees…and said to him:
"This is the land which I swore to give Abraham, Isaac and Jacob, saying 'I will give it to your descendants.'
I have caused you to see it with your own eyes, but you shall not cross over there." Deuteronomy 34:4
After the death of Moses…the Lord spoke to Joshua… "go over this (river ed.) Jordan, you and all this people, to the land which I am giving to the children of Israel." Joshua,1:1-2
..a land flowing with milk and honey Exodus 3:17

And We said thereafter to the Children of Israel, "Dwell securely in the land (of promise). [17,The Israelites,104]

…the Garden which the righteous are promised:
in it are…rivers of milk of which the taste never changes;
rivers of wine, a joy to those who drink;
and rivers of honey pure and clear. [47]
The Prophet,15

14. David / Dawood; shepherd, poet, king

David is a favorite hero, both in the Hebrew Bible and the Qur'an.
As a youngster, he slew the 'giant' Goliath, using only sling and stone. According to the Qur'an, God later helped him to manufacture iron armor. However, he was not just a great warrior, but also a musician and the successor of King Saul.
The Bible attributes to David many psalms, in which deep despair alternates with exuberance. The Qur'an speaks of God giving David the *Zabur,* meaning text written on wood or stone. The (Arabic) Qur'an mentions the 'Mazamiru Dawud', zamir*(un),* as the Arabic equivalent of *zimra* in Hebrew, which means singing, music or songs. The Qur'an does not dwell on the fluctuating mood of David, but it does note and praise David's sense of guilt: repentance is becoming to a king. It also stresses his exuberance, with mountains and the birds sharing his joyful song. Both books promise that the virtuous, righteous or meek will inherit the earth.
In the Bible, the story of David is told in the first book of Samuel, and his psalms are numbered. In the Qur'an, David's story is found in various surahs.

Bible David /Dawood Qur'an

King Saul fears the giant
And Saul and the men of Israel…drew up in battle array against the Philistines. And a champion went out from the camp of the Philistines, named Goliath…whose height was six cubits and a span.…he stood and cried out to the armies of Israel, and said to them, "Why have you come

David slays Goliath
When Talut (Saul ed.) set forth with the armies… he and the faithful ones with him – they said: "This day we cannot cope with Goliath and his forces."
But those who were convinced that they must meet Allah, said: "How oft, by Allah's will, has a small force vanquished a big one? Allah

out to line up for battle? Am I not a Philistine, and you the servants of Saul? Choose a man for yourselves, and let him come down to me. If he is able to…kill me, then we will be your servants. But if I…kill him, then you shall be our servants..."

Then David said to Saul, "Let no man's heart fail because of him; your servant will go and fight with this Philistine."

And Saul said to David, "You are not able to go against this Philistine to fight with him; for you are a youth…"

…David prevailed over the Philistine with a sling and a stone, and struck the Philistine and killed him… David ran and stood over the Philistine, took his sword and drew it out of its sheath and killed him, and cut off his head with it. And when the Philistines saw that their champion was dead, they fled.

1 Samuel 17: 2,4, 8-9, 32-33, 50-51

is with those who steadfastly persevere."

When they advanced to meet Goliath and his forces, they prayed: "Our Lord! Pour out constancy on us and make our steps firm: Help us against those that reject faith."

By Allah's will they routed them; and David slew Goliath; and Allah gave him power and wisdom and taught him whatever… He willed.

And did not Allah check one set of people by means of another, the earth would indeed be full of mischief: But Allah is full of bounty to all the worlds.

2 The Heifer, 249-251

…And We made the iron soft for him; - (commanding): "You make coats of mail, balancing well the rings of chain armour, and you work righteousness."

34 The City of Saba, 10-11

David's sense of sin and despair

Behold, I was brought forth in iniquity, and in sin my mother conceived me. Psalm 51: 5

My God, My God, why have You forsaken Me? But I am a worm, and no man; A reproach of men, and

David asks forgiveness

Have patience at what they say, and remember Our Servant David, the man of strength: for he ever turned (to Allah). 38 Saad, 17

…And David gathered that We had tried him: he asked forgiveness of

despised by the people. Psalm 22:1,6

…my life is spent with grief, and my years with sighing; My strength fails because of my iniquity, and my bones waste away. Psalm 31:10-11

Blot out my transgressions. Wash me thoroughly from my iniquity. And cleanse me from my sin. Psalm 51:1-2

Psalms of joy

Sing to Him a new song; Play skillfully with a shout of joy. Psalm 33:3

O Lord… You have lifted me up…O Lord my God, I cried out to You,

And You healed me. O Lord, You brought my soul up from the grave. Psalm 30: 1-3

Praise the Lord from the earth…mountains and all hills, fruitful trees and all cedars, beasts and all cattle; creeping things and flying fowl. Psalm 148:7,9-10

The righteous shall inherit the land, and dwell in it forever… Psalm 148:29

Blessed are the meek, For they shall inherit the earth. Matthew 5: 5

his Lord, fell down, bowing (in prostration), and turned (to Allah in repentance). So We forgave him this (lapse):

O David! We did indeed make you a vice-regent on earth: so you judge between men in truth (and justice): nor do you follow the lusts (of your heart), for they will mislead you from the Path of Allah. 38 Saad, 24-26

The Zabur, a gift for Dawood

And it is your Lord that knows best all beings that are in the heavens and on earth: We bestowed on some prophets more (and other) gifts than on others: and We gave to David (the gift of) the Psalms.
17 The Children of Israel, 55

We bestowed Grace aforetime on David from Ourselves: "O you Mountains! you sing back the Praises of Allah with him! and you birds (also)! 34 The City of Saba, 10

...it was Our power that made the hills and the birds celebrate Our praises, with David: 21 The Prophets, 79

Before this We wrote in the Psalms…: "My servants, the righteous, shall inherit the earth."
21 The Prophets, 105

15. Solomon/Sulaiman ...Queen of Sheba/Saba

Solomon inherited his father David's kingdom. He was also a sovereign with a sense of guilt and a willingness to apologize for his mistakes. In the Qur'an, he repented for being carried away by a lust for material possessions like beautiful racehorses. In the Bible, Solomon realizes that all his achievements are only wind, and striving for them mere vanity. Solomon did indeed achieve a great deal. God bestowed special powers on him. In the Qur'an he understands the language of animals. Surah 27 is named ants, who Solomon heard warning one another to avoid being trampled on by his army. The king also has a special power over the forces of nature, over Satan and Jinns (fiery spirits), which he was able to utilize in such projects as the laying out of beautiful gardens. The word *jinn* is found in English words such as ***engin**eer* and **gen**ius. Solomon is similarly famous in the Bible for his prowess as a builder, which had its zenith in his palace and the temple in Jerusalem.
The story of the queen of Sheba/Saba is told in both books. It relates of a king and queen preferring diplomacy above warfare. Intrigued by the rumors of the king's wisdom and the luxury of his court, the queen (called Bilqis in Islam tradition), travels from afar to visit him. In the Bible, the queen takes her leave, profoundly impressed by everything she has seen, and laden with princely gifts. In the Qur'an, the queen ultimately converts to the faith of Solomon, the belief in the one God.

Bible Solomon /Sulaiman Qur'an

King Solomon the brilliant
Then Solomon sat on the throne of his father David; and his kingdom was firmly established. [1 Kings 2:12]
And God gave Solomon wisdom

Solomon asks for forgiveness
And Solomon was David's heir.
27 The Ants, 16

To David We gave Solomon (for a son) – how excellent in Our service!

and exceedingly great understanding, and largeness of heart...[1 Kings 4: 29]
...in the fourth year of Solomon's reign over Israel ...he began to build the house of the Lord. [1 Kings 6:1]
And it came to pass, when Solomon had finished building the house of the Lord and the king's house, and all Solomon's desire which he wanted to do, that the Lord appeared to Solomon... and...said to him: "I have consecrated this house which you have built...and My eyes and My heart will be there perpetually." [1 Kings 9:1-3]
I (Solomon ed.) communed with my heart saying, "Look, I have attained greatness, and have gained more wisdom that all who were before me in Jerusalem. My heart has understood great wisdom and knowledge." [Ecclesiastes 1: 16]

I made my works great. I built myself houses, and planted myself vineyards. I made myself gardens and orchards...I made myself water pools from which to water the growing trees of the grove. I also gathered for myself silver and gold...So I became great and excelled more than all who were ever did he turn (to Us)! Behold, there were brought before him, at eventide, coursers (horses ed.) of the highest breeding, and swift of foot;
And he said: "Truly do I love the love of Good, with a view to the glory of my Lord..."
And We did try Solomon... but he turned (to Us in true devotion): He said: "O my Lord! Forgive me...
38 Saad, 30-32, 34-35

...and there were Jinns (spirits ed.). that worked in front of him, by the leave of his Lord... They worked for him as he desired, (making) Arches, Images, Basins as large as Reservoirs, and (cooking) Cauldrons fixed (in their places).
34 The City of Saba,12-13

Then We subjected the wind to his power, to flow gently to his order, whithersoever he willed – As also the evil ones, (including) every kind of builder and diver – As also others bound together in fetters. [38 Saad, 36-38]

And Solomon...said:
"O you people! We have been taught the speech of Birds... this is indeed Grace manifest."
And before Solomon were

before me in Jerusalem. Also my wisdom remained with me.
Then I looked on all the works that my hands had done… There was no profit under the sun. Therefore I hated life…for all is vanity and grasping for the wind.
Ecclesiastes 2: 4-6, 8-9, 11,17

marshaled his hosts – of Jinns and men and birds, and they were all kept in order and ranks. At length, when they came to a (lowly) valley of ants, one of the ants said: "O you ants, get into your habitations, lest Solomon and his hosts crush you (under foot) without knowing it." So he smiled, amused at her speech…
27 The Ants,17-19

The Queen of Sheba

But Solomon took thirteen years to build his own house…Then he made a hall for the throne, the Hall of Judgment, where he might judge…And the house… had another court inside the hall of like workmanship. [1 Kings 7:1, 7-8]
Now when the queen of Sheba heard of the fame of Solomon… she came to test him with hard questions. She came to Jerusalem with a very great retinue, with camels that bore spices, very much gold, and precious stones; and…she spoke with him about all that was in her heart.
So Solomon answered all her questions; there was nothing so difficult for the king that he could not explain it to her.
And when the queen of Sheba had

A Queen converted

And he took a muster of the Birds; and he said: "Why is it I do not see the Hoopoe (a desert bird ed.) ? Or is he among the absentees? But the Hoopoe did not tarry far: he (came up and) said: "…I have come to you from Saba with true tidings. I found (there) a woman ruling over them…she has a magnificent throne. I found her and her people worshipping the sun... Satan has made their deeds seem pleasing in their eyes, and has kept them away from the Path, - so they receive no guidance."
(Solomon) said… "You go, with this letter of mine, and deliver it to them: then…(wait to) see what answer they return"...
(The Queen) said: "You chiefs! Here is - delivered to me - a letter

seen all the wisdom of Solomon, the house that he had built, the food on his table… there was no more spirit in her. Then she said to the king: "It was a true report which I heard in my own land about your words and your wisdom. However I did not believe the words until I came and saw with my own eyes; and indeed the half was not told me. Your wisdom and prosperity exceed the fame of which I heard.
Blessed be the Lord your God, who delighted in you, setting you on the throne of Israel!"
Then she gave the king one hundred and twenty talents of gold, spices in great quantity, and precious stones.

Before the throne there was a sea of glass, like crystal. Revelation 4: 6

Now King Solomon gave the queen of Sheba all she desired, whatever she asked, besides what Solomon had given her according to the royal generosity. So she turned and went to her own country…
1 Kings 10: 1-7, 9-10,13

worthy of respect. It is from Solomon, and is (as follows):
…'come to me in submission (to the true Religion).'
She said: " You Chiefs…Kings when they enter a country, despoil it and make the noblest of its people the meanest…But I am going to send him a present, and (wait) to see with what (answer) (my) ambassadors return."
Now when (the embassy) came to Solomon, he said: "Will you give me abundance in wealth? But that which Allah has given me is better than that which He has given you! "

So when she arrived, she was asked to enter the lofty Palace: but when she saw it, she thought it was a lake of water, and she (tucked up her skirts), uncovering her legs.
He said: "This is but a palace paved smooth with slabs of glass."
She said: "O my Lord! I have indeed wronged my soul: I do (now) submit…with Solomon, to the Lord of the Worlds."
27 The Ants, 20, 22-24, 27-31,35-36, 43-44

16. The Sorrow of Job/Ayyub

The story of Job appears in both books, but in the Qur'an, it is much shorter than in the Bible, and is rather difficult to follow. For this reason, the Qur'an text is supplemented here with quotes from *The Stories of the Prophets* by Al Imam Ibn Kathir 701 -774 AH or 1301 -1372 AD.

These quotes are shaded to distinguish them from those from the Qur'an itself.

The story is about a wealthy man with a large family, who leads an exemplary life. The Qur'an numbers him among the prophets. Job is struck by great misfortune. His children die, and his wealth disappears overnight. Then, he becomes seriously ill. The question raised by this story is how God, who is both Almighty and Righteous, can allow such a high-standing man to fall into ruin. In both books, the devil (Iblis or Satan) is the culprit, but he does act with God's permission.

In the Bible, Job suffers great tragedies. The loss of his wealth and his children does not make him turn away from God as the devil had assumed. But when he contracts a kind of leprosy, leading to social isolation, he becomes desperate. He vents his anger on God, whom he blames for his misfortune. Why does God allow such an upright man to suffer, while rewarding the ungodly with health, wealth and ample offspring? His friends treat him to extensive philosophical monologues, exploring the causes of his misfortune. Elihu and Bildad blame Job for his own downfall. This is the way, they argue, that God deals with sinners. But Job refuses to accept his suffering as a punishment for wrongdoings. The Almighty addresses Job personally, and he realizes that he is only a tiny part of God's creation. He understands that to the limited human mind God's ways are inexplicable. That gives him peace of mind.

In the Qur'an, Job remains patient throughout his suffering. When his wife becomes desperate and presses him to beg Allah for relief, he persists in his gratitude for all the years of health and wealth that had been granted to

him, before he became ill. He asks her to leave him alone, promising to whip her if he regains health.
Finally, Job is rewarded:
- in the Qur'an for his continuing patience,
-in the Bible, due to his returning peace of mind (after bouts of anger and bitterness)
His health and wealth are restored, as are his children. The Qur'an mentions medicinal waters. Tradition sees Job as a patron of leprosy cures. Job and his wife reach reconciliation, marked by a whipping with grass. In this way Job keeps his promise without hurting his wife. Thus the concept of symbolic punishment by gentle whipping is introduced.
In the Bible Job resumes relationships with those who had shunned him during his illness. His children and his wealth are restored to him. He lives happily for another 140 years.

Job a truly good person
There was a man… whose name was Job and that man was blameless and upright, and one who feared God and shunned evil.
And seven sons and daughters were born to him.
Also his possessions were seven thousand sheep, three thousand camels, five hundred yoke of oxen, five hundred female donkeys, and a very large household, so that this man was the greatest of all the people of the East. [Job 1:1-3]

Satan meets the Lord
Now there was a day when the sons of God (angels ed.) came to present themselves before the Lord, and Satan also came among them. And the Lord said to Satan, "From where do you come?"
So Satan answered the Lord and said, "From going to and fro on the earth, and from walking back and forth on it."

Then the Lord said to Satan, "Have you considered My servant Job, that there is none like him on the earth, a blameless and upright man, one who fears God and shuns evil?"

Job as one of the prophets
We have sent you inspiration as We sent it to Noah and the Messengers after him: We sent inspiration to Abraham, Ismail, Isaac, Jacob and the Tribes, to Jesus, Job, Jonah…and Solomon, and to David We gave the Psalms. [4 The Women,163]
…We guided Noah, and among his progeny, David, Solomon, Job, Joseph, Moses, and Aaron… We chose them, and We guided them to a Straight Way. [6 The Cattle,84,87]

Iblis to seduce humankind
And behold, We said to the angels: "Bow down to Adam" and they bowed down:
not so Iblis (the devil ed.): he refused and was haughty: He was of those who reject Faith. [2 The Heifer, 34]
(Allah) said: "What prevented you from bowing down when I commanded you?"
He said: "I am better than he: You created me from fire, and him from clay."
(Allah) said: "… it is not for you to be arrogant here: get out, for you are of the meanest (of creatures)."
He (Satan ed.) said "Give me respite

So Satan answered the Lord and said, "Does Job fear God for nothing? Have You not made a hedge around him, around his household, and around all that he has on every side? You have blessed the work of his hands, and his possessions have increased in the land. But now, stretch out Your hand and touch all that he has, and he will surely curse You to Your face!"
And the Lord said to Satan, "Behold, all that he has is in your power; only do not lay a hand on his person.

Job 1: 6-12

till the day they (humankind ed.) are raised up."
(Allah) said: "Be you among those who have respite."
He (Satan ed.) said: "Because You have thrown me out of the Way, lo! I will lie in wait for them on Your Straight Way. Then I will assault them from before them and behind them, from their right and their left: Nor will You find gratitude in most of them, (for Your mercies)."

7 The Heights,12-17

Job loses wealth and children

...and suddenly a great wind came from across the wilderness and struck the four corners of the house, and it fell on the young people (Job's children ed.), and they are dead;
Then Job…fell to the ground and worshiped. And he said: "Naked I came from my mother's womb, And naked shall I return there. The Lord gave, and the Lord has taken away; Blessed be the name of the Lord."
In all this Job did not sin nor charge God with wrong.

Job 1: 19-22

Job in Distress

Commemorate Our Servant Job.
Behold he cried to his Lord:
" The Evil One (Satan ed.) has afflicted me with distress and suffering!" 38 Saad,41
And (remember) Job, when he cried to his Lord:
"Truly distress has seized me, but You are the Most Merciful of those that are Merciful." 21 The Prophets, 83

Job becomes a leper

So Satan answered the Lord and said, "...all that a man has he will give for his life...stretch out Your hand now, and touch his bone and his flesh, and he will surely curse You to Your face!"
And the Lord said to Satan, "Behold, he is in your hand, but spare his life."
So Satan went out from the presence of the Lord, and struck Job with painful boils from the sole of his foot to the crown of his head. [Job 2:4-7]

The devil ruins Job's health

Iblis (Satan or the Devil ed.) began to take revenge on Job's body and filled it with disease until it was reduced to mere skin and bone and he suffered severe pain.
(He was ed.) an almost lifeless form crumpled on the bed...suspended between life and death.
But through all the suffering Job remained strong in his faith, patiently bearing all the hardships without complaining. Ibn Kathir

Job's despair and anger

(Job to God ed.) "You have made desolate...You have shriveled me up...He tears me in His wrath, and hates me; He gnashes at me with His teeth... They gape at me with their mouth, they strike me reproachfully on the cheek, they gather together against me. God has delivered me to the ungodly, and turned me over to the hands of the wicked. [Job 16: 7-11]
Then Job...said: "Why do the wicked live and become old, Yes, become mighty in power? Their descendants are established with them in their sight, and their offspring before their eyes. Their houses are safe from fear, Neither is the rod of God upon them. [Job 21:1,7-9]

Job remains patient

Truly! We found him full of patience and constancy. How excellent is Our service! ever did he turn (to Us). [38 Saad,44]

... when he cried to his Lord, "Truly distress has seized me, but You are the most Merciful of those that are Merciful." [21 The Prophets,83]

Job's friends give him the blame

Elihu…said "Behold, God is mighty…He does not preserve the life of the wicked, but gives justice to the oppressed. He does not withdraw his eyes from the righteous, but they are on the throne with kings, for He has seated them forever…and if they are bound in fetters, held in cords of affliction, then He tells them …their transgressions – that they have acted defiantly. Job 36:1,5-9

Then Bildad the Shuhite (Job's friend ed.) answered and said: "You who tear yourself in anger…The light of the wicked indeed goes out, and the flame of his fire does not shine. The light is dark in his tent and his lamp beside him is put out. The steps of his strength are shortened …he is cast into a net by his own feet…Terrors frighten him on every side…His strength is starved, and destruction is ready at his side. It devours patches of his skin. He is uprooted from shelter of his tent, and they parade him before the king of terrors. His roots are dried out below, and his branches wither above, the memory of him

Job's wife dissatisfied

Iblis went to Job's wife… reminded her of the days when Job had good health, wealth and children. Suddenly, the painful memory of years of hardship overcame her, and she burst into tears. She said to Job:

"How long are you going to bear this torture from our Lord? Why don't you call upon Allah to remove this suffering?"

Job sighed, and in a soft voice replied:

"Iblis must have whispered to you and made you dissatisfied. Tell me, how long did I enjoy good health and riches?"

She replied, "For eighty years"

Then Job asked, "How long am I suffering like this?"

She said, "for seven years"

Then Job told her:

"In that case I am ashamed to call on my Lord to remove the hardship, for I have not suffered longer than the years of good health and plenty.

It seems your faith has weakened and you are dissatisfied with the fate of Allah. If I ever regain health, I swear I will punish you with a hundred strokes! From this day

perishes from the earth. He is driven from light into darkness. And chased out of the world. He has neither son nor posterity among his people. Nor any remaining in his dwellings. Surely such are the dwellings of the wicked, and this is the place of him who does not know God.

Job 18:1, 4-7, 11-21

God all-powerful

God says (ed.) "Who…is able to stand against me?...Who has preceded Me, that I should pay him? Everything under heaven is mine."
Job 41:10-11

Then Job answered the Lord and said: "I know that You can do everything…I have uttered what I did not understand. Things too wonderful for me, which I did not know. I have heard of you…but now my eye sees You. Therefore I …repent.

Job 42: 2-3, 5-6

Job blessed more than ever

Then all his brothers, all his sisters, and all those who had been his acquaintances before, camc to him and ate food with him in his house; and they consoled him and comforted him for all the adversity that the Lord had brought upon him.

onward, I forbid myself to eat or drink anything from your hand. Leave me alone and let my Lord do with me as He pleases."
Crying bitterly and with a heavy heart, she had no choice but to leave him.

Ibn Kathir

Water therapy heals Job

Truly We found him full of patience and constancy. How excellent in Our service! ever did he turn (to Us)! 38 Saad,44

…when he cried to his Lord, "Truly distress has seized me, but You are the most Merciful of those that are Merciful."
So We listened to him: We removed the distress that was on him…Strike with your foot: here is (water) wherein to wash, cool and refreshing, and (water) to drink."

21 The Prophets,83-84; 38 Saad,42

Allah restores Job's family

And We gave him (back) his people, and doubled their number… 38 Saad: 43

Meanwhile, his faithful wife could no longer bear to be parted from her husband and returned to beg his forgiveness, desiring to serve him.

Now the Lord blessed the latter days of Job more than his beginning; for he had fourteen thousand sheep, six thousand camels, one thousand yoke of oxen, and one thousand female donkeys.
He also had seven sons and three daughters. In all the land were found no women so beautiful as the daughters of Job; and their father gave them an inheritance among their brothers. After this Job lived one hundred and forty years, and saw his children and grandchildren for four generations. So Job died, old and full of days. [Job 42:11-13, 15-17]

On entering the house, she was amazed at the sudden change: Job was again healthy! She embraced him and thanked Allah for His mercy. Job was now worried, for he had taken an oath to punish her with a hundred strokes if he regained health, but he had no desire to hurt her. He knew if he did not fulfill the oath, he would be guilty of breaking a promise to Allah. Therefore, in His wisdom and mercy, Allah came to the assistance of His faithful servant, and advised him:

"And take in your hand a little grass (in a bundle ed.) and strike therewith (your wife ed.) and break not your oath. [38 Saad,44]

17. Jonah/Yunus in the Great Fish

Jonah is an unwilling prophet who tries to get out of the difficult task God put on his shoulders: warning the people of Nineveh (Bible) or his own people (Qur'an) about the pending disaster.
Jonah flees from his responsibility by boarding a ship going in another direction. But a storm arises, and after drawing lots, the crew throws him overboard to lighten the ship's load. He is swallowed by a fish. From its belly, he calls to God for help. He repents his ways and is reconciled with God. Three days later, the fish spits him out onto a beach. God causes a plant to grow to shelter him from the sun. When he recovers, he returns to his people (Qur'an) or to Nineveh, (Bible) who have unexpectedly mended their ways. The impending disaster is averted.
The Bible story continues with Jonah extremely irritated that Nineveh is not destroyed, as he had been forced to foretell. He fusses about the plant shriveling. He is in short a very human prophet, full of his own ego.
The Qur'an story ends with a plea for religious tolerance. The story shows that it is in the power only of God, not of humans, to bring others onto the right path. There can be no human compulsion in religion.
The beginning of the story of Jonah is similar to those of other prophets, such as Noah, in that it warns of impending disaster. However, the end is very different. Jonah's people (Qur'an) or the inhabitants of Nineveh (Bible) repent before God visits his wrath upon them. God forgives them and allows them a period of earthly happiness.

It is this theme of repentance and forgiveness, of reconciliation between God and Jonah, God and the people (of Nineveh), which is celebrated on the Jewish Day of Atonement, or Yom Kippur. On this yearly occasion, the story of Jonah is recited.

For Christians, Jonah's fate foretells that of Jesus' resurrection after three days.

...the prophet Jonah...was in the stomach of a big fish for three days and nights, just as the Son of Man will be deep in the earth for three days and nights. Matthew 12:40

Jonah is numbered among the list of prophets, and the Qur'an has a chapter named after him, although the story is also found elsewhere. The Bible also gives Jonah his own chapter.

Bible Jonah/Yunus Qur'an

Jonah sent to Nineveh

Now the word of the Lord came to Jonah…saying, "Arise, go to Nineveh, that great city, and cry out against it; for their wickedness has come up before Me." Jonah 1:1-2

Jonah flees to sea

But Jonah arose to flee…from the presence of the Lord. He…found a ship…to go with them …from the presence of the Lord.

But the Lord sent out a great wind on the sea, and there was a mighty tempest on the sea, so that the ship was about to be broken up. Then the mariners were afraid …they said to one another, "Come, let us cast lots, that we may know for whose cause this trouble has come upon us." So they cast lots, and the lot fell on Jonah. Then they said to him, "What shall we do to you that the sea may be calm for us?" - for the sea was growing more tempestuous. And he said to them, "Pick me up and throw me into the sea; then the sea will become calm for you. For I know that this great tempest is because of me."

God sends Yunus

So also was Jonah among those sent (by Us). 37, The Saffat,139

Jonah runs away to the ship

When he ran away (like a slave from captivity) to the ship (fully) laden;

he (agreed to) cast lots, and he was condemned. 37, The Saffat, 140-141

And remember Zun-nun (the man of the fish ed.), when he departed in wrath: he imagined that We had no power over him! 21 The Prophets, 87

So they picked up Jonah and threw him into the sea, and the sea ceased from its raging.
Jonah 1: 3-5,7,11-12,15

In the fish three days and nights

Now the Lord had prepared a great fish to swallow Jonah. And Jonah was in the belly of the fish three days and three nights. Jonah 1:17

Then Jonah prayed to the Lord his God from the fish's belly. And he said: "I cried out to the Lord because of my affliction, And He answered me. For You cast me into the deep, into the heart of the seas; The waters surrounded me, even to my soul; The deep closed around me; Weeds were wrapped around my head; The earth with its bars closed behind me forever; Yet You have brought up my life from the pit, O Lord, my God. Jonah 2:1-6

Jonah warns Nineveh

So the Lord spoke to the fish, and it vomited Jonah onto dry land. Jonah 2:10

Now the word of the Lord came to Jonah the second time, saying, "Arise, go to Nineveh, that great city, and preach to it the message that I tell you." So Jonah arose and went to Nineveh…

The big fish swallowed Yunus

Then the big fish swallowed him, and he had done acts worthy of blame. 37, the Saffat, 142

But he cried through the depths of darkness: “There is no god but You: glory to You: I was indeed wrong!” So We listened to him: and delivered him from distress: and thus do We deliver those who have faith. 21 The Prophets, 87-88

Had it not been that he (repented and) glorified Allah, he would certainly have remained inside the Fish till the Day of Resurrection.
37, The Saffat,143-144

The shore and the plant

But We cast him forth on the naked shore in a state of sickness…
37 The Saffat,145

Then he cried out and said, "Yet forty days, and Nineveh shall be overthrown!"

Jonah 3: 1-4

Nineveh saved

So the people of Nineveh believed God, proclaimed a fast, and put on sackcloth, from the greatest to the least of them. Then word came to the king of Nineveh; and he arose from his throne and laid aside his robe, covered himself with sackcloth and sat in ashes. And he caused it to be…published throughout Nineveh…let every one turn from his evil way and from the violence that is in his hands.

Then God saw their works, that they turned from their evil way; and God relented from the disaster that He had said He would bring upon them… Jonah 3: 5-8,10

Jonah's people saved

And We sent him (on a mission) to a hundred thousand (men) or more. And they believed; so We permitted them to enjoy (their life) for a while.

37 The Saffat, 145,147-148

Why was there not a single township (among those We warned), which believed – so its Faith should have profited it – except the People of Jonah? When they believed, We removed from them the Penalty of Ignominy in the life of the Present, and permitted them to enjoy (their life) for a while. 10 Jonah, 98

If it had been your Lord's Will, they would all have believed– all who are on earth! Will you then compel mankind, against their will, to believe! No soul can believe, except by the Will of Allah. 10 Yunus, 99-100

The vine grows and shrivels

But it displeased Jonah exceedingly, and he became angry.

And the Lord God prepared a plant and made it come up over Jonah, that it might be shade for his head to deliver him from his misery. So Jonah was very grateful for the plant. But as morning dawned the next day God prepared a worm, and it so damaged the plant that it withered…God prepared a vehement east wind; and the sun beat on Jonah's head, so that he grew faint. Then he wished death for himself… Then God said to Jonah, "You have had pity on the plant… which came up in a night and perished in a night. And should I not pity Nineveh, that great city, in which are more than one hundred and twenty thousand persons…? [Jonah, 4:1,6-11]

A spreading plant

(A plant is given to Yunus when he was cast ashore, before he returns to warn his people. The gourd is a multifunctional plant akin to the pumpkin, useful as a water carrier, the earliest plant to be domesticated ed.)

And We caused to grow, over him, a spreading plant of the gourd kind. [37 The Saffat,146]

So wait with patience for the Command of your Lord, and be not like the Companion of the Fish – when he cried out in agony. Had not Grace from his Lord reached him, he would indeed have been cast off on the naked shore, in disgrace. Thus did his Lord choose him and make him of the company of the Righteous. [68 The Pen, 48-50]

vii. Sharing the Prophets

intermezzo by Awraham Soetendorp

Jonah is the last prophet in this anthology. In my view a prophet is a person who sharply analyses his society, critically pointing to major faults and showing a way out. He refuses to say what people want to hear, listening to a whisper in his own heart, the truth, the word of God. This makes him unpopular with public opinion and the powers that be. As Jesus said, and Muhammad experienced, no prophet is accepted in his own country. Being a prophet requires enormous courage.

Prophets are human beings. They experience fear. Prophets like Moses were reluctant to take on their task. Jonah flatly refused.
An interesting difference between the prophets in the Hebrew Bible and the Qur'an is that whereas in the Qur'an prophets are moral examples, Hebrew prophets often have complex human traits. Jonah was angry that God had liberated the people without his help. Job was furious about the grave misfortunes he had suffered. Moses was so mad with rage with his people dancing around the golden calf that he smashed the tablets with God's commandments. In the Qur'an these human frailties are much less clear. The prophets seem to be somewhat polished, compared with the Hebrew counterparts. There Moses carefully puts down the tablets before he starts scolding his people.
There is a lot to say in favor of prophets who control their temper as an example for mankind. However I personally feel more in touch with the imperfect prophets of the Hebrew Bible. There humanity is shown in all its nakedness.

I am satisfied that if God loves even imperfect people, such as the great prophets, granting them significant tasks, he will surely love even me, with my irritable moods and all my other frailties.

The Hebrew Bible also speaks of female prophets, notably Miriam, whose very name means 'lady prophet'. She saved her baby brother Moses and accompanied Moses and Aaron, as the whisper of love, keeping her moody brother Moses on the right track until she died in the desert. It was at that very spot that water appeared for the thirsty Israelites.

Therefore modern Jews honor Miriam as the prophetess of the life bringing water.

Interestingly, Mary the mother of Jesus is scolded by her family in the Qur'an as 'the sister of Aaron'. Perhaps in a symbolic sense she was a female prophet of whispering love, like her predecessor Miriam.

Part Three

Stories in the Qur'an

and

the New Testament

18. Zacharias, John, Mary/ Zakariya, Yahya, Maryam

The Qur'an and the Bible also come together in the story of Zacharias/Zakariya. Both books describe the wonder of the elderly woman, - (in the Bible, she is called Elizabeth, few women are named in the Qur'an), who becomes pregnant with John/ Yahya. In the Bible this John is called 'the Baptist' because he baptized Jesus, and to distinguish him from other Johns such as the writer of one of the Gospels. In the Qur'an there is no baptism for there is no original sin from which people must be cleansed. In the Qur'an the only John is the son of Zakariya. In both books his birth is announced by an angel, who tells Zacharias that he will be struck dumb as a sign. In the Bible, this dumbness is a punishment for not believing the angel. In the Qur'an, Zakariya himself asks for a sign. The Bible and the Qur'an complement each other regarding the relationship of the Zacharias family to Mary, who comes to prominence as the mother of Jesus. Maryam is the daughter of the prophet Imran. When her mother is pregnant with her, her father Imran dies. His wife promises her child (whom she presumed would be a son) to God. When the child turns out to be a girl, she keeps her promise, even though women in those days were not allowed to be educated in the temple. Maryam's uncle Zakariya agrees to take care of the child and build her a private house within the temple precincts. He is amazed when the little girl is mysteriously provided with food and drink.

This background gives the Biblical story of the meeting between Elizabeth and Mary more depth. The Qur'an identifies the elderly lady as Mary's aunt, married to the priest who had raised and educated her. The unborn John recognizes Jesus as his Lord. The meeting is full of joy. Here the stories complement each other.

The Biblical story of the life and death of John the Baptist and his meeting Jesus to baptize him is no related in the Qur'an. There is no baptism in the Qur'an because there is no original sin which has to be washed away. However Islamic tradition does have Jesus and John meeting, as shown in the miniature.

In the Bible, John is important for preparing the way of the Lord, and for baptizing Jesus. During his baptism Jesus sees a dove and hears a voice proclaiming him to be the Son of God.

This idea is explicitly countered in the Qur'an, in which no-one is seen as the son of God. The Qur'an does, however, accord both Jesus and John great importance. They are included in the list of distinguished prophets. Both books describe John as a peace-loving and ascetic man.

Zacharias, John, Mary/ Zakariya, Yahya, Maryam

Bible

Elizabeth's pregnancy

There was in the days of Herod, the king of Judea, a certain priest named Zacharias… His wife was of the daughters of Aaron, and her name was Elizabeth. And they were both righteous before God…But they had no child, because Elizabeth was barren, and they were both well advanced in years.

Then an angel of the Lord appeared to him…And when Zacharias saw him, he was troubled, and fear fell upon him.

But the angel said to him, "Do not be afraid, Zacharias, for your prayer is heard; and your wife Elizabeth will bear you a son, and you shall call his name John.

For he will be great in the sight of the Lord, and shall drink neither wine nor strong drink. He will also be filled with the Holy Spirit, even from his mother's womb. And he will turn many of the children of Israel to the Lord their God.

Qur'an

Zakariya and his son Yahya

(This is) a recital of the Mercy of your Lord to His servant Zakariya. Behold! he cried to his Lord in secret, praying: "O my Lord! Infirm indeed are my bones, and the hair of my head glistens with grey: but never am I unblest, O my Lord, in my prayer to You! Now I fear (what) my relatives… (will do) after me: but my wife is barren: so give me an heir as from Yourself – (One that) will (truly) represent me, and represent the posterity of Jacob; (Israel ed.) and make him, O my Lord! one with whom You are well-pleased!"

(His prayer was answered): "O Zakariya! We give you good news of a son: his name shall be Yahya: on none by that name We have conferred distinction before."

19 Maryam, 2-7

While he was standing in prayer in the chamber, the angels called unto him: "Allah gives you the glad

And Zacharias said to the angel, "How shall I know this? For I am an old man, and my wife is well advanced in years."
And the angel answered and said to him,
"I am Gabriel, who stands in the presence of God, and was sent to speak to you and bring you these glad tidings. But behold, you will be mute and not able to speak until the day these things take place, because you did not believe my words which will be fulfilled in their own time."
And the people waited for Zacharias, and marveled that he lingered so long in the temple. But when he came out, he could not speak to them; and they perceived that he had seen a vision in the temple, for he beckoned to them and remained speechless.
Now after those days his wife Elizabeth conceived; and she hid herself five months, saying, "Thus the Lord has dealt with me…"
Luke 1: 5-7, 11-13, 15-16, 18-22, 24-25

tidings of Yahya, witnessing the truth of a Word from Allah, and (be besides) noble, chaste, and a Prophet – of the (goodly) company of the righteous." 3 Al-'Imran,39
He (Zakariya ed.) said: "O my Lord! how shall I have a son, when my wife is barren and I have grown quite decrepit from old age?"
He (the angel ed.) said: "So (it will be) your Lord says, 'That is easy for Me: I indeed created you before, when you had been nothing!'"
(Zakariya) said: "O my Lord! give me a Sign."
"Your Sign," was the answer, "shall be that you shall speak to no man for three nights, although you are not dumb."
So Zakariya came out to his people from him chamber: He told them by signs to celebrate Allah's praises in the morning and in the evening.
19 Maryam, 8-11

So We listened to him: and We granted him Yahya: We cured his wife's (barrenness) for him.
21 The Prophets, 90

Elizabeth and Mary

Now in the sixth month the angel Gabriel was sent to… to a virgin…whose name was…

Zakariya and the child Maryam

Behold! A woman of 'Imran said: "O my Lord! I do dedicate unto You what is in my womb for Your

Mary…the angel said to her "… behold, you will conceive in your womb and bring forth a Son, and shall call His name Jesus."
Then Mary said to the angel, "How can this be…?"
…The angel answered, "Elizabeth your relative has also conceived a son in her old age…For with God nothing will be impossible."
Now Mary…went…with haste, to a city of Judah, and entered the house of Zacharias and greeted Elizabeth. And it happened, when Elizabeth heard the greeting of Mary, that the babe leaped in her womb; and Elizabeth was filled with the Holy Spirit. Then she spoke out with a loud voice and said, "Blessed are you among women, and blessed is the fruit of your womb!"
And Mary said: "My soul magnifies the Lord…for He has regarded the lowly state of His maidservant;
Luke 1: 26-27, 30-31, 34-37 39-42 46, 48

special service: So accept this of me: for You hear and know all things."
When she was delivered, she said: "O my Lord! Behold! I am delivered of a female child!"
Allah knew best what she brought forth - And nowise is the male like the female.
"I have named her Mary, and I commend her and her offspring to Your protection from the Evil One, the Rejected."
Right graciously did her Lord accept her: He made her grow in purity and beauty: she was assigned to the care of Zakariya. Every time that he entered (her) chamber to see her, he found her supplied with sustenance.
He said: "O Mary! Whence (comes) this to you?" She said: "From Allah: for Allah provides sustenance to whom He pleases without measure."
3 Al-'Imran: 35-37

A baby for Elizabeth

Now Elizabeth's full time came for her to be delivered, and she brought forth a son… and they would have called him by the name of his father, Zacharias. His mother answered and said,

His name is John

…" O Zakariya! We give you good news of a son: His name shall be Yahya: on none by that name We have conferred distinction before."
19 Maryam, 7

"No; he shall be called John."
Now his father Zacharias was filled with the Holy Spirit, and prophesied, saying:
"And you, child, will be called the prophet of the Highest; For you will go before the face of the Lord to prepare His ways… Luke 1: 57,59-60,67,76

John the Baptist – life and death

So the child grew and became strong in spirit, and was in the deserts till the day of his manifestation to Israel. Luke 1:80
In those days John the Baptist came preaching in the wilderness of Judea, and saying, "Repent, for the kingdom of heaven is at hand!" Now John himself was clothed in camel's hair, with a leather belt around his waist; and his food was locusts and wild honey. Then Jerusalem, all Judea, and all the region around the Jordan went out to him and were baptized by him in the Jordan, confessing their sins.
Matthew 3:1-2,4-6

John, a righteous prophet

We gave him Isaac and Jacob: all (three) We guided: and before him, We guided Noah, and among his progeny, David, Solomon, Job, Joseph, Moses, and Aaron: thus We reward those who do good: And Zakariya and John, and Jesus and Elias all in the ranks of the Righteous:…and to all We gave favor above the nations: We chose them, and WE guided them to a straight Way. This is the guidance of Allah: These were the men to whom We gave the Book, and Authority, and Prophethood:
6 The Cattle, 84-89

And he preached, saying, "There comes One after me who is mightier than I…I indeed baptized you with water, but He will baptize you with the Holy Spirit."
…Jesus came from Nazareth of

(To his (Zakarkariya ed.) son came the command). "O Yahya! Take hold of the Book with might": and We gave him Wisdom even as a youth, and pity (for all creatures) as from Us, and purity: he was devout,

Galilee, and was baptized by John in the Jordan. And…He saw the heavens parting and the Spirit descending upon Him like a dove. Then a voice came from heaven, "You are My beloved Son, in whom I am well pleased." Mark 1:7-11

…she, (a successful royal dancer ed.), having been prompted by her mother, said,

"Give me John the Baptist's head here on a platter." (as a reward ed.) So he (King Herod ed.) sent and had John beheaded in prison. And his head was brought on a platter and given to the girl… Matthew 14: 8-11

and kind to his parents, and he was not overbearing or rebellious.

19 Maryam, 12-14

Christ Jesus the son of Mary was (no more than) a Messenger of Allah and His Word… 4 The Women,171

It is not befitting to the (majesty of) Allah that He should beget a son.

19 Maryam,35

…Yahya, witnessing the truth of a Word from Allah, and… noble, chaste, and a Prophet – of the (goodly) company of the righteous."

3 Al-'Imran: 39

So peace on him the day he was born, the day that he dies, and the day that he will be raised up to life (again)! 19 Maryam,15

viii. Sharing Mary

Intermezzo by Marlies ter Borg

My favorite Bible story is about the meeting between Mary and Elizabeth, a young and an elderly woman, both pregnant. Mary was visited by the angel Gabriel and became with child although she had never 'known' a man. Elizabeth's pregnancy was also a miracle. Her husband Zacharias was told by the angel that his wife would become pregnant, in spite of her age. What is the truth of these stories? Well, the factual truth doesn't interest me. That is about biology, about rape, perhaps, about lost virginity. Who cares? It's the spiritual truth that counts. The celebration of a wonder. Isn't any pregnancy a wonder? I like the way the Qur'an celebrates pregnancy with beautiful words, showing the careful attention God gives to pregnant women.

"And no female conceives, or lays down (her load), but with His knowledge."

35 The Originator of Creation, 11

A desired pregnancy really can fill you with joy, with feeling special, as if you are personally receiving Divine attention. In the Qur'an God calls for respect for the mother in whose womb we were created.

"He makes you, in the wombs of your mothers, in stages, one after another, in three veils of darkness." 39 The Crowds, 6

So the story about Maria and Elizabeth gives me that sense of wonder about creation, that I had lost in the rat race of life. It fills me with pride because of the special role we women play in creation. I'm from a Christian background which I left behind me in my late teens.
It was less than ten years ago that I discovered that Mary and her son Jesus also figured prominently in the Qur'an.

When I really began to study the texts for this book, I made another discovery. The Qur'an tells us the story of Mary's childhood, of how she grew up as an orphan fostered by Zacharias and Elizabeth. So the meeting between Mary and Elizabeth was no coincidence. Mary went straight to her foster mother with the news.
What is more, the Qur'an suggests that Mary had received an excellent education from the hands of Zacharias. When her own mother lost her husband, while already pregnant, she pledged the fruit of her womb to God. She expecting to have a son, a boy who would become a priest just like his father 'Imran. But the child turned out to be a girl. In Mary's time girls were not allowed into the temple let alone receive a priestly education. In Muhammad's time baby girls were frowned upon, sometimes even buried alive.
But Mary's mother had the courage to take her little girl to the temple.

"Right graciously did her Lord accept her: He made her grow in purity and beauty: she was assigned to the care of Zakariya" [3 Al-'Imran, 37]

The Qur'an gave me a completely new image of Mary. I had always imagined her merely as a beautiful, sweet and loving mother. According to the Christmas carol, she was a 'lowly maid'. And here she reappears, as the best educated woman of her day! Be it by 'coincidence' or Divine Will, this special girl, the future mother of Jesus, was brought up in the temple for special reasons.

She was being prepared to become a Lady of the Book, ready to receive God's word in her flesh and to educate her precocious son for his historic role. This is a startling new image. The mother who knew the Hebrew Bible, the Law, the psalms, the stories of Genesis, and who read it all to and discussed it with her precocious son. How else would Jesus have known all these things, brought up by the wife of a carpenter, as the Bible tells us? How could he have appeared so learned when visiting the temple at the age of twelve if his mother had not taught him?

The Qur'an paints a picture of Maria as a highly intelligent and well educated woman, bearing and bringing up her child alone and preparing him to receive the Gospel, God's word.

Looking again at pictures of the Madonna and child, painted by artists from the early Christian renaissance like Fra Angelico I suddenly realized that Mary was often painted with a book on her lap. I had seen and admired these paintings before. But I had never really focused on the book, dismissing it as a rather odd way of showing Mary's lowliness and holiness, not for one moment assuming that she could read, let alone enjoyed reading from the Hebrew Bible.
Now suddenly, thanks to the Qur'an, I realized that Medieval artists, such as Fra Angelico, were depicting Mary as an intelligent, highly-educated woman. Being familiar with the power and grace of words, she was able to receive the word of God in het whole being. Angelico paints the words flowing from the angel to Mary.
As for her lowliness, that should be understood in the way Nur Moch Ichwan understands muslim(a) with a small m. Mary's learning did not lead to arrogance but to submissiveness to the divine, rather than to fleeting human truth. In this vein she educated her son.

A painting from 15th century literally depicts Mary teaching Jesus to read.

In reading Qur'an and Bible stories side by side, there is often a surprise just around the corner, a new insight an enriching moment.

A beautiful story hidden in an early Christian text, - giving a learned woman a pivotal role in history – is excluded from the canon of the Bible, but revealed in the Qur'an, to be retold centuries later, and painted as contacts between the Christian and Islamic world intensified.* It fills me with a sense of humility and wonder, that we humans never know the whole story.

* the Infancy gospel of James, 145 AD, Gospel of pseudo-Matthew. 600 AD

19. Mary/Maryam and the birth of Jesus/'Isa

The stories of the birth of Jesus demonstrate that He is a major figure in Bible and Qur'an. In both books, his mother Mary becomes pregnant while still a virgin. Her pregnancy is a miracle. The birth of Jesus is announced by the angel Gabriel in the Bible; the name of the divine messenger is not specified in the Qur'an, but presumably it was the same angel Gabriel who brought Muhammad the Qur'an.

In the Bible, Joseph marries Mary and cares for her child. Angels tell of its birth. Shepherds adore the baby, and Wise Kings travel from afar to visit it. In later stories, an adoring ox and ass are added to the nativity scene.

In the Qur'an, the pregnant Mary remains alone, taking refuge in the desert. Hovering on the brink of despair, she hears a voice – was it the angel (Gabriel) or the newborn baby? – giving her fresh heart. Later, when Mary faces severe criticism from her family, the infant speaks up for her.

In the Bible, Jesus is called the Messiah, the Christ. This title derives from the Hebrew for 'God's anointed', a titled reserved for a king or savior. The Greek term used in the Bible is *Christos*. The birth of Jesus is celebrated by Christians at Christmas.

In the Qur'an, Jesus is also called Messiah or Christ. He is God's prophet and the messenger of His Word, receiver of the Gospel.

An important difference is the status of Jesus. In the Gospels according to John and Luke, He is called the 'son of God', giving Him a special status above the children of God. Jesus is God incarnate. He is part of the Divine Trinity, together with The Father and the Holy Spirit.

The Qur'an emphatically rejects the Trinity and the special status for Jesus. He is the son of Mary, not of God. God has no sons. No persons can acquire divine status. No one can be like God. The Qur'an does speak of the Word and the Spirit in connection with Jesus, but they are attributes of God, not of parts of a Trinity.

The birth of Jesus is described mainly in Surah 19, named after Mary. The Biblical story can be read in the Gospels according to Mathew and Luke, with John giving relevant statements about the status of Jesus.

Bible Mary- Jesus / Maryam - 'Isa Qur'an

The angel Gabriel visits Mary

...the angel Gabriel was sent by God to a city of Galilee named Nazareth, to a virgin betrothed to a man whose name was Joseph, of the house of David. The virgin's name was Mary. And…the angel said to her, "Rejoice, highly favored one, the Lord is with you; blessed are you among women!" But when she saw him, she was troubled at his saying, and considered what manner of greeting this was.

Then the angel said to her, "Do not be afraid, Mary, for you have found favor with God. And behold, you will conceive in your womb and bring forth a Son, and shall call His name Jesus. He will be great, and will be called the Son of the Highest; and the Lord God will give Him the throne of His father David."

Then Mary said to the angel, "How can this be, since I do not know a man?"

And the angel answered and said to her, "The Holy Spirit will come upon you, and the power of the Highest will overshadow you; therefore, also, that Holy One who is to be born will

Christ Jesus promised to Mary

Relate in the Book (the story of) Mary, when she withdrew from her family to a place in the East. She placed a screen (to screen herself) from them; then We sent to her Our angel (Gabriel ed.?), and he appeared before her as a man in all respects.

She said: "I seek refuge from you to (Allah) Most Gracious: (come not near) if you fear Allah."

He said: "Nay, I am only a messenger from your Lord, (to announce) to you the gift of a holy son.

She said: "How shall I have a son, seeing that no man has touched me, and I am not unchaste?"

He said: "So (it will be): Your Lord says, 'That is easy for Me: and (We wish) to appoint him as a Sign to men and a Mercy from Us': it is a matter (so) decreed."

So she conceived him ('Isa ed.) and she retired with him to a remote place. [19 Maryam, 16-22]

Behold! The angels said: "O Mary! Allah gives you glad tidings of a Word from Him: his name will be Christ Jesus, the son of Mary, held in honor in this world and the Hereafter

be called the Son of God. For with God nothing will be impossible." Then Mary said, "Behold the maidservant of the Lord! Let it be to me according to your word."
Luke 1: 26-32, 34-35, 37-38

…the virgin shall… bear a Son, and they shall call His name Immanuel …God with us. Matthew,1:23; Isaiah 7:14

…you may believe that Jesus is the Christ, the Son of God, and that believing you may have life in His name. John 20:31

and of (the company of) those nearest to Allah. He shall speak to the people in childhood and in maturity. And he shall be (of the company) of the righteous." She said: "O my Lord! how shall I have a son when no man has touched me?"
He said: "Even so: Allah creates what He wills: when He has decreed a Plan, He but says to it, 'Be,' and it is!"
3 Al-'Imran, 45-47

God's Son, Word Incarnate, Trinity

"…in the name of the Father (God ed.) and of the Son (Jesus ed.) and of the Holy Spirit." Matthew 28:19
...our fellowship is with the Father and His Son Jesus Christ. 1 John 1:3
In the beginning was the Word, and the Word was with God, and the Word was God. He was in the beginning with God. All things were made through Him, and without Him nothing was made that was made. In Him was life, and the life was the light of men. And the light shines in the darkness, and the darkness did not comprehend it.

But as many as received Him, to

Jesus son of Mary

Christ Jesus the son of Mary was (no more than) a Messenger of Allah, and

His Word, which He bestowed on Mary,
and a Spirit proceeding from Him: so believe in Allah and His Messengers. Do not say 'Trinity'. 4 The Women, 171

We gave Jesus the son of Mary clear (Signs) and strengthened him with the holy spirit. 2 The Heifer, 87
It is not befitting to (the majesty of) Allah that He should beget a son.
19 Maryam, 35

He begets not, nor is He begotten; And there is none like unto Him. 112 The Purity of Faith, 3-4

them He gave the right to become children of God, to those who believe in His name: who were born, not of blood, nor of the will of the flesh, nor of the will of man, but of God.

And the Word became flesh and dwelt among us, and we beheld His glory, the glory as of the only begotten of the Father, full of grace and truth. John 1-5, 12-14

Glory be to Him! When He determines a matter, He only says to it: “Be”, and it is. 19 Maryam, 35

The Holy Family

...a decree went out from Caesar Augustus that all the world should be registered …everyone to his own city. Joseph…went into… Bethlehem… to be registered with Mary, his betrothed wife, who was with child.

So it was, that while they were there, the days were completed for her to be delivered. And she brought forth her firstborn Son, and wrapped Him in swaddling cloths, and laid Him in a manger, because there was no room for them in the inn. Luke 2:1, 3-7

Mary, entering a stable, placed the child in a manger, and an ox and an ass adored him. Infancy Gospel of the seudo – Matthew Gospel, 8th century ; see Isaiah 1:3

Mary gives birth alone

So she conceived him (Jesus ed.) and she retired with him to a remote place.

And the pains of childbirth drove her to the trunk of a palm-tree: she cried (in her anguish): “Ah! would that I had died before this! would that I had been a thing forgotten and out of sight!”

But (a voice) cried to her from beneath the (palm-tree): “Do not grieve ! for your Lord has provided a rivulet beneath you; and shake toward yourself the trunk of the palm-tree: It will let fall fresh ripe dates upon you. So eat and drink and cool (your) eye.” 19 Maryam, 22-26

Angels and adoring shepherds

Now there were in the same country shepherds living out in the fields, keeping watch over their flock by night. And behold, an angel of the Lord stood before them, and the glory of the Lord shone around them, and they were greatly afraid.

Then the angel said to them, "Do not be afraid, for behold, I bring you good tidings of great joy which will be to all people. For there is born to you this day in the city of David a Savior, who is Christ the Lord. And this will be the sign to you: You will find a Babe wrapped in swaddling cloths, lying in a manger."

And suddenly there was with the angel a multitude of the heavenly host praising God and saying: "Glory to God in the highest, And on earth peace, goodwill toward men!"
Luke 2: 8-14

Wise men in adoration

...wise men from the East came to Jerusalem, saying,
"Where is He who has been born King of the Jews? For we have seen His star in the East and have come to worship Him."

The baby defends Mary

At length she brought the (babe) to her people, carrying him (in her arms).
They said: "O Mary! truly an amazing thing you have brought!

O sister of Aaron! your father was not a man of evil, nor your mother an unchaste woman!"
But she pointed to the babe.
They said: "How can we talk to one who is a child in the cradle?"
He (the baby Jesus ed.) said: "I am indeed a servant of Allah. He has given me Revelation and made me a prophet; And He has made me blessed wheresoever I be, and has enjoined on me Prayer and Charity as long as I live; "(He) has made me kind to my mother, and not overbearing or miserable; So Peace is on me the day I was born, the day that I die, and the day that I shall be raised up to life (again)"! 19 Maryam, 27-33

Mary not a goddess

And behold! Allah will say:
"O Jesus the son of Mary! Did you say to men, 'worship me and my mother as gods in derogation of Allah?'"

… the star…went before them, till it came and stood over where the young Child was. …they saw the young Child with Mary His mother, and fell down and worshiped Him. And when they had opened their treasures, they presented gifts to Him: gold, frankincense, and myrrh.

Matthew 2:1-2,9,11

He (Jesus ed.) will say: "Glory to You! Never could I say what I had no right (to say). Had I said such a thing, You would indeed have known it. You know what is in my heart, though I do not know what is in Yours. Never said I to them anything except what You commanded me to say, to wit, 'worship Allah, my Lord and your Lord'…"

5 The Table Spread, 116-117

20. Jesus/'Isa: His Life and Teachings

Jesus is the major figure in the New Testament, where he appears as the savior of humankind. He is also a major prophet in the Qur'an, named together with Abraham, David, Isaac, Ismail and Jacob and placed on equal footing with Moses and Muhammad. In both books, Jesus continues building on the Law of Moses, the Torah, introducing a number of important innovations. In both books Jesus cures the blind and lepers and raises the dead. The Qur'an and the Bible both portray Jesus surrounded by his disciples. Special meals play a role in both books. The teachings of Jesus are not fully expounded in the Qur'an, but there are many phrases in other contexts that are similar in content. (see values and virtues, ch. 29)

There are also important differences. The Gospels call Jesus the Son of God. The Qur'an says that God has no sons. He creates without the need to procreate. God has no one beside him. According to the Qur'an, Jesus was not divine and could perform miracles only with the help of God. Jesus was one of God's Messengers. In the Qur'an Jesus is not divine; he is a mortal just like Muhammad, but he is a Messenger, a particularly eminent prophet, because he received the Gospel as Muhammad did the Qur'an, and Moses the Law.

In the Bible, Jesus himself sometimes refers to the Gospel, implying His teaching. However the four gospels in the Bible are not understood by Christians as direct messages from God, but as reports written by (more or less divinely inspired) humans – the evangelists. Jesus is the central figure in the gospels, and also in letters from various apostles. The handful of verses in the Qur'an that tell of the life, work and message of Jesus are dispersed over a number of surahs.

xi. Jesus, my great Jewish brother

Intermezzo by Awraham Soetendorp

I was surprised to be invited to Moscow in 1989, because I had made no secret of my negative views on the Soviet attitude towards Jews. The second time I was even invited to give a lecture at the Moscow public library. The subject was: Jesus. I was able to convince my audience that Jesus was a Jew, but Mary as well? No way. That this lady, greatly loved and venerated in Russia, was in actual fact Jewish, was hard to accept.

For me of course Jesus is not my savior and I do not believe that he was himself divine. However I greatly admire him for who he was. He is, as Martin Buber wrote, my great Jewish brother. His greatness lay in his humility and his courage. I remember the story about the leper, the untouchable living in social isolation because of this very contagious illness. Jesus did what others shrank from doing. He looked at this man, he touched him. It is good to read about Jesus healing lepers in the Qur'an as well.

Jesus' - life and teachings of - 'Isa

Bible

The genealogy of Jesus Christ

...the genealogy of Jesus Christ, The Son of David, the Son of Abraham: Abraham begot Isaac, Isaac begot Jacob...and...David the king begot Solomon...and ...begot Joseph the husband of Mary, of whom was born Jesus who is called Christ.

Matthew 1: 1-2,6,16

Moses' Law and the Gospel

Do not think that I (Jesus ed.) came to destroy the Law or (the preaching of ed.) the Prophets. I did not come to destroy but to fulfill. Matthew 5:17

For the law was given through Moses, but grace and truth came through Jesus Christ. John 1:17

For whoever loses his life for My sake and the gospel's will save it.

Mark 8:35

The sermon on the mount

And seeing the multitudes, He went up on a mountain...and...His disciples came to Him... and He... taught them, saying:

Qur'an

Jesus Christ in the line of Abraham

You (Muhammad ed.) say: "We believe in Allah, and the revelation given to us, and to Abraham, Isma'il, Isaac, Jacob...and that given to Moses and Jesus...we make no difference between one and another of them: and we bow to Allah (in Islam; obedience ed.)." 2 The Heifer, 136

The Law of Musa and the Gospel

Then will Allah say: "O Jesus the son of Mary! Behold! I taught you the Book and Wisdom, the Law and the Gospel." 5 The Table Spread, 110

He (Jesus) said: "I am indeed a servant of Allah: He hath given9 me Revelation and made me a Prophet;

19 Maryam, 30

And Allah will teach him the Book and Wisdom, the Law and the Gospel.

3 Al- 'Imran: 48

Charity and forgiveness

And He has made me blessed wheresoever I be, and has enjoined on me Prayer and Charity as long as I live. 19 Maryam, 31

"Blessed are those who hunger and thirst for righteousness, for they shall be filled. Blessed are the merciful, for they shall obtain mercy. Blessed are the peacemakers, for they shall be called sons of God." Matthew 5: 1-2, 6-7, 9

"Love your enemies, do good to those who hate you, bless those who curse you, and pray for those who spitefully use you. To him who strikes you on the one cheek, offer the other also." Luke 6: 27-29

"In this manner, therefore, pray: 'Our Father in heaven…forgive us our debts, as we forgive our debtors…'" Matthew 6: 9, 12

Nor can Goodness and Evil be equal. Repel (Evil) with what is better; then will he between whom and you was hatred, become as it were your friend and intimate! 41 Fussilat, 34

…We ordained in the hearts of those who followed him (Jesus ed.) compassion and mercy. 57 The Iron, 27

…(Allah) will bestow on you a double portion of His Mercy: He will provide for you a Light by which you shall walk… and He will forgive you:.. for Allah is oft-Forgiving, Most Merciful. 57 The Iron, 28

Jesus heals and raises the dead

Now as Jesus passed by, He saw a man who was blind from birth. He spat on the ground and made clay with the saliva; and He anointed the eyes of the blind man with the clay.

And He said to him, "Go, wash... So he went and washed, and came back seeing. John 9: 1, 6-7

And behold a leper came and worshiped Him, saying: "Lord, if you are willing, You can make me clean." Then Jesus put his hand out and touched him, saying: " I am willing: be cleansed." Immediately the leprosy was cleansed. Matthew 8:2-4

Jesus' miracles by Allah's leave

"And (appoint him) (Jesus ed.) a Messenger to the Children of Israel, (with this message):

'I have come to you, with a Sign from your Lord, in that I make for you out of clay, as it were, the figure of a bird, and breathe into it, and it becomes a bird by Allah's leave:

And I heal those born blind, and the lepers, and

I quicken the dead, by Allah's leave;.. Surely therein is a Sign for you if you did believe. It is Allah Who is my

…when Jesus came, He found that he had already been in the tomb four days. He cried with a loud voice, "Lazarus, come forth!"
And he who had died came out bound hand and foot with grave clothes, and his face was wrapped with a cloth.
John 11: 17, 43-44

Lord and your Lord; then worship Him. This is a Way that is straight.'"
3 Al-'Imran 49, 51

Then Allah will say: "O Jesus, son of Mary…behold you brought forth th e dead by my leave.[5 The Table Spread, 110]

The disciples
…He called His disciples to Himself; and from them He chose twelve whom He also named apostles. [Luke 6: 13]
Then He appointed twelve, that they might be with Him and that He might send them out to preach, and to have power to heal sicknesses and to cast out demons. [Mark 3: 14-15]

The helpers
…Jesus…said: "Who will be my helpers to (the work of) Allah?"
Said the Disciples: "We are Allah's helpers: We believe in Allah, and you bear witness that we are Muslims. (obedient to Allah ed.)Our Lord! We believe in what You have revealed…[3 Al-'Imran: 52-53]

Bread and wine and fish
"Give us day by day our daily bread."
Luke 11:3

(Jesus ed.) took the five loaves and the two fish, and looking up to heaven, He blessed and broke and gave the loaves to the disciples; and the disciples gave to the multitudes. So they all ate and were filled… Now those who had eaten were about five thousand men, besides women and children. [Matthew 14:19-21]
And as they were eating, Jesus took bread, blessed and broke it, and gave

The table from Heaven
Behold! The Disciples, said: "O Jesus the son of Mary! can your Lord send down to us a Table set (with viands) from heaven? We only wish to eat thereof and satisfy our hearts, and to know that you have indeed told us the truth; and that we ourselves may be witnesses to the miracle."
Jesus the son of Mary said: "O Allah our Lord! Send us from heaven a Table set (with viands), that there may be for us - for the first and the last of us - a solemn festival and a Sign from

it to the disciples and said, "Take, eat; this is My body." Then He took the cup, and gave thanks, and gave it to them, saying, "Drink from it, all of you. For this is My blood of the new covenant, which is shed for many for the remission of sins." Matthew 26: 26-28

Jesus Christ the Son of God

The…gospel of Jesus Christ, the Son of God. Mark 1:1

…and behold, the heavens were opened to Him, and He saw the Spirit of God descending like a dove and alighting upon Him. Matthew 3: 16

Then a voice came from heaven, "You are my beloved Son, in whom I am well pleased." Mark 1: 11

… Peter (disciple of Jesus ed.)…said: "You are the Christ, the Son of the living God."
Matthew 16: 16

Grace, mercy and peace will be with you from God the Father and from Jesus Christ, the son of the Father, in truth and love. 2nd Epistle of John 1: 3

You; and provide for our sustenance, for You are the best Sustainer (of our needs)."

Allah said: "I will send it down unto you…" 5 The Table Spread, : 112-115

Jesus Christ son of Mary

Those Messengers We endowed with gifts, some above others: To one of them Allah spoke; others He raised to degrees (of honor); to Jesus the son of Mary We gave Clear (Signs), and strengthened him with the holy Spirit.
2 The Heifer, 253

O People of the Book! Christ Jesus the son of Mary was (no more than) a Messenger of Allah, and His Word …and a Spirit proceeding from Him:.. Do not say 'Trinity':.. for Allah is one God. glory be to Him: (far Exalted is He) above having a son. Say: He is Allah, the One and Only; He begets not, nor is He begotten; And there is none like unto Him. For it is not consonant with the majesty of (Allah) Most Gracious that He should beget a son. Not one of the beings in the heavens and the earth but must come to (God) Most Gracious as a servant.
4 The Women,171;112, Purity of Faith, 1, 3, 419;

Maryam, 92-93

21. Jesus/'Isa : Death, Resurrection, Ascension

The suffering and death of Jesus on the cross is of essential importance to the New Testament as is his resurrection from the dead (after three days). Together, they embody the idea of redemptive suffering. By taking his undeserved suffering upon himself, Jesus saved humankind from the burden of sin it had laid upon itself (through Adam and Eve) in the Garden of Eden. This event marking the salvation of humankind is commemorated every year on Good Friday, followed by Easter Sunday. In the New Testament, the ascension of Jesus is a separate event, remembered on Ascension Day. The Last Day will see the second coming of Jesus, when He will judge the living and the dead.

In the Qur'an, the suffering of Jesus figures barely if at all. The Qur'an dismisses outright the idea that the Jews crucified Jesus. God would not allow such a thing. If someone was crucified, as historians contend, Islamic tradition has it that it was someone else on whom God had bestowed the likeness of Jesus. God took Jesus to himself and did not let his beloved prophet be crucified. Another interpretation holds that Jesus was nailed to the cross, but survived, taken from the cross in a coma to regain consciousness after three days. He escaped to the East with his mother to preach the gospel of peace, travelling to high ground (India and Pakistan?) watered by many springs.

This does not imply that the concept of redemptive suffering is alien to the Qur'an. Almost all the prophets do come up against the resistance of their people; Noah and Moses are examples, and Muhammad himself met with much suffering and frustration. But in the Qur'an, their difficulties lead neither to the cross, nor to the salvation of humankind. In the Qur'an God lifts Jesus up to be close to him. He will act not as judge but as witness on the Last Day.

Jesus: death, resurrection and ascension: ΄Isa

Bible

Jesus crucified

He (Jesus ed.) said, "Assuredly…no prophet is accepted in his own country." But they shouted "Crucify Him, crucify Him!"

Luke 4: 24 Luke 23: 21

Then the soldiers of the governor …stripped Him and put a scarlet robe on Him. When they had twisted a crown of thorns, they put it on His head, and a reed in His right hand. And they bowed the knee before Him and mocked Him, saying, "Hail, King of the Jews!" Then they spat on Him… and they took the robe off Him… and led Him away to be crucified.
Now…there was darkness over all the land. And…Jesus cried out with a loud voice, saying…
"My God, My God, why have You forsaken Me?"
And Jesus cried out again with a loud voice, and yielded up His spirit. Then, behold, the veil of the temple was torn in two from top to bottom; and the earth quaked, and the rocks were split…
Matthew 27: 27-31, 45-46, 50-51

Qur'an

They killed him not

Is it that whenever there comes to you a Messenger with what you yourselves do not desire, you are puffed up with pride? - some you called impostors, and others you slay! 2 The Heifer, 87

And (the unbelievers) plotted and planned, (against Jesus ed.) and Allah too planned, and the best of planners is Allah. 3 Al-'Imran, 54

That they (Jews ed.) said (in boast): "We killed Christ Jesus the son of Mary, the Messenger of Allah.- but they did not kill him, nor crucify him,
but so it was made to appear to them,
and those who differ therein are full of doubts, with no (certain) knowledge, but only conjecture to follow,
for of a surety they did not kill him.
4 The Women,157

And We made the son of Mary and his mother as a Sign: We gave them both shelter on high ground,

Then he took it down, wrapped it in linen, and laid it (the corpse of Jesus ed.) in a tomb that was hewn out of the rock, where no one had ever lain before. Luke 23: 53

affording rest and security and furnished with springs.
23, The Believers, 50

... and gave them refuge on an elevated land of green valleys and springs of running water. 23, The Believers, 50 Trans:Maulawim Sher Ali

Resurrection and ascension

Now after the Sabbath...Mary Magdalene and the other Mary came to see the tomb. And behold an angel...came and rolled back the stone from the door, and sat on it. ...the angel...said to the women, "Do not be afraid, for I know that you seek Jesus who was crucified. He is not here; for He is risen..." Matthew 28: 1-2, 5-6

...He...presented Himself alive after his suffering by many infallible proofs...during forty days... ...while they (the disciples ed.) watched, He was taken up, and a cloud received Him out of their sight. And while they looked steadfastly toward heaven as He went up, behold, two men stood by them in white apparel, who... said, "...why do you stand gazing up into heaven? This same Jesus, who was taken up from you into heaven, will so come in like manner as you saw Him go into heaven." Acts 1: 3,9-11

Jesus raised up unto God

Nay, Allah raised him (Jesus ed.) up unto Himself; and Allah is Exalted in Power, Wise. 4 The Women, 158

Behold! Allah said: "O Jesus! I will take you and raise you to Myself and clear you (of the falsehoods) of those who blaspheme; I will make those who follow you superior to those who reject faith, to the Day of Resurrection:...and I will judge between you of the matters wherein you dispute." 3 Al-'Imran,55

22. Jesus/'Isa and Muhammad

Jesus is seen in the Qur'an as confirming the Law of Moses and as having received the Gospel. Muhammad explicitly builds on the work of Jesus. Obviously, the Bible makes no direct mention of Muhammad: it was completed centuries before his birth. The Qur'an does mention very general predictions of Muhammad, based on specific interpretations of certain Bible passages which of course are interpreted by Christians in a totally different way. An example of such differing interpretations is given below.

The Qur'an holds that Jesus announced the coming of a famous Messenger called Ahmad. Reference is made to the Gospel of John, in which the Greek word 'parakleitos' is used.

'Parakleitos' has a variety of meanings, such as comforter, helper, healer, spirit of Truth.

But there is another Greek word 'periklutos: famous' or, in Arabic, *Ahmad.* It is claimed that the word in question in John's gospel/manuscript should be read as periklutos, rather than as parakleitos. Ahmad, the renowned, the celebrated, is another name for Muhammad.

Such Biblical passages are held by Muslims to refer to Muhammad, the uneducated prophet, who is also known as Ahmad, the Renowned.

According to a generally (but not universally) accepted interpretation/translation of Qur´an verse. Muhammad was not able to read or write:

"And you were not (able) to recite a Book before this (Book came), nor are you able to transcribe it with thy right hand." [29The Spider ,48]

The Muslim interpretation of the texts of the Gospel according to John is rejected by Christian scholars. They argue that the Messenger, or Comforter (parakleitos), whose coming Jesus prophesied, is the Holy Spirit who descended on the apostles during the Jewish feast of Pentecost. This gave the disciples of Jesus the courage to spread his message to the world, even after his death. The descent of the Holy Spirit is seen as the beginning of the Christian Church and is celebrated at the annual Christian feast of Pentecost, or Whitsun.

Holy Spirit /Paraclete

Bible

The Holy Spirit
"But when the Helper (Paraclete ed.) comes, whom I shall send to you from the Father, the Spirit of truth who proceeds from the Father, He will testify of Me. John 15: 26

"It is to your advantage that I go away; for if I do not go away, the Helper will not come to you; but if I depart, I will send Him to you." John 16: 7

"And I will pray the Father, and He will give you another Helper, (Paraclete ed.) that He may abide with you forever- the Spirit of truth…" John 14: 16-17
(Jesus said to them ed.) "But you shall receive power when the Holy Spirit has come upon you; and you shall be witnesses to Me… to the end of the earth." Acts 1: 8

Muhammad

Qur'an

Ahmad the successor of Jesus
Then, in their wake, (of Noah and Abraham ed.) We followed them up with (others of) Our Messengers:

We sent after them Jesus the son of Mary, and bestowed on him the Gospel; and We ordained in the hearts of those who followed him compassion and mercy. 57 The Iron, 27

And remember, Jesus, the son of Mary, said: "O Children of Israel! I am the Messenger of Allah (sent) to you, confirming the Law (which came) before me, and giving Glad Tidings of a Messenger to come after me, whose name shall be Ahmad." 61The Battle Array, 6

When the Day of Pentecost had fully come, they were all…in one place. And suddenly there came a sound from heaven, as of a rushing mighty wind, and it filled the whole house where they were sitting. Then there appeared to them divided tongues, as of fire, and one sat upon each of them. And they were all filled with the Holy Spirit and began to speak with other tongues, as the Spirit gave them utterance. Acts 2: 1-4

He (God) said: "Those (of the People of the Book ed.) who follow the Messenger, the unlettered Prophet, whom they find mentioned in their own (Scriptures), - in the Law and the Gospel… he releases them from their heavy burdens and from the yokes that are upon them. So it is those who believe in him (Muhammad ed.), honor him, help him, and follow the Light which is sent down with him– it is they who will prosper." 7 The Heights,157

Part Four

The Afterlife

Life after death

23. The Last Day, the Last Judgment

Bible and Qur'an contain very similar images of the dreadful Last Day, the end of earthly times, when the universe as we know it will collapse. Both books speak of trumpets and angels heralding catastrophes: earthquakes, falling stars and a darkened sun. In both books, the sky is rolled up like a scroll. Conflict abounds. There will be natural disasters, such as the contamination of the seas, sicknesses and plagues, described in the Bible in gruesome detail. The Qur'an hardly mentions disease except in more general terms; people can cause their own moral disease.

Both books describe people awakened from death. For the Qur'an, the resurrection is a natural progression from the creation of Adam and that of all children in the womb. It is the third creation.

The Last Day leads to the Last Judgment of every human being's beliefs and deeds during earthly life. The judgment will not be arbitrary, but based on written evidence. People will be separated like sheep/goats: those on the right deserve heavenly bliss; those on the left the fire of hell. In the Bible, the function of judge devolves upon Jesus, on whose grace and forgiveness sinners can rely. In the Qur'an, Jesus is witness, God the Judge.

The story of the Last Day can be found in both the Hebrew Bible, e.g Isaiah and Daniel, and in the New Testament. The relevant passages in the gospels are prophetic words ascribed to Jesus. The story reaches its climax in the expressive language of Revelation, the final book of the Bible, the result of the visionary experience of a certain John.

The Last Day is mentioned many times in the Qur'an, with certain surahs describing various aspects, such as *The Day of Noise, and Clamor, The Convulsion,* and *The Folding* Up (of the heavens). Thus believers are warned time and again to start living in submission to Allah before it is too late.

Bible Judgment Day Qur'an

The Angel blew his trumpet
And I (John ed.) saw the seven angels who stand before God, and to them were given seven trumpets. The first angel sounded: And hail and fire followed, mingled with blood, and they were thrown to the earth. And a third of the trees were burned up, and all green grass was burned up.
And I looked, and I heard an angel flying through the midst of heaven, saying with a loud voice, "Woe, woe, woe to the inhabitants of the earth, because of the remaining blasts of the trumpet of the three angels who are about to sound!" Revelation 8:2,7,13

The day the trumpet is blown
And the Trumpet shall be blown; that will be the Day whereof Warning (had been given). 50 Qaf, 20
Then, when one blast is sounded on the Trumpet,– On that Day shall the (Great) Event come to pass. 69 The Sure Reality, 13,15

What is the (Day) of Noise and Clamor? (It is) a Day whereon men will be like moths scattered about, and the mountains will be like carded wool. 101 The Day of Noise and Clamor, 2, 4-5
The Day the heaven shall be rent asunder with clouds, and angels shall be sent down, descending (in ranks). 25 The Criterion, 25

Destruction
Wail, for the day of the Lord is at hand! It will come as destruction from the Almighty. Therefore all hands will be limp, Every man's heart will melt, And they will be afraid. Pangs and sorrows will take hold of them; They will be in pain as a woman in childbirth;
Behold, the day of the Lord comes,

Convulsion
When the sky is rent asunder, and hearkens to (the Command of) its Lord…And when the Earth is flattened out… 84 The Rending Asunder:1-3
O Mankind! Fear your Lord! for the convulsion of the Hour (of Judgment) will be a thing terrible! The Day you shall see it, every mother giving suck shall forget her

Cruel, with both wrath and fierce anger, to lay the land desolate; Isaiah 13: 6-9

But woe to those who are pregnant and to those who are nursing babies in those days! For there will be great distress in the land and wrath upon this people. Luke 21: 23

suckling- babe, and every pregnant female shall drop her load (unformed): you shall see mankind as in a drunken riot... 22 The Pilgrimage, 1-2

Plagues and sores

So the first (angel ed.)...poured out his bowl upon the earth, and a foul and loathsome sore came upon the men...Then the fourth angel poured out his bowl on the sun, and power was given to him to scorch men with fire. Revelation 16: 2, 8

Then out of the smoke locusts came upon the earth. They were commanded...to harm only those men who do not have the seal of God on their foreheads. And they were not given authority to kill them, but to torment them for five months. In those days men will seek death and will not find it; they will desire to die, and death will flee from them. Revelation 9:3-6

If anyone adds to these things, God will add to him the plagues that are written in this book. Revelation 22:18

A grievous penalty

But those who strive against Our Signs, to frustrate them – for such will be a penalty – a punishment most humiliating. 34 The City of Saba, 5

Is it that there is a disease in their hearts? Or do they doubt, or are they in fear, that Allah and His Messenger will deal unjustly with them? Nay, it is they themselves who do wrong. 24 The Light, 50

In their hearts is a disease; and Allah has increased their disease: and grievous is the penalty they (incur), because they are false (to themselves). 2 The Heifer,10

But the transgressors changed the word from that which had been given them; so We sent on the transgressors a plague from heaven, for that they infringed (Our command) repeatedly. 2 The Heifer, 59

Sun and moon darkened

Then the sky receded as a scroll when it is rolled up... Revelation 6:14

Therefore I will shake the heavens...the stars of heaven and their constellations will not give their light; The sun will be darkened in its going forth, And the moon will not cause its light to shine. Isaiah 13:13,10

...the sun will be darkened, and the moon will not give its light; the stars will fall from heaven... Matthew 24: 29

...and the sun became black as sackcloth of hair, and the moon became like blood. And the stars of heaven fell to the earth, as a fig tree drops its late figs when it is shaken by a mighty wind. Revelation 6:12-13

Earthquakes and famines

And the earth will move out of her place...in the wrath of the Lord... Isaiah 13:13

And Jesus...began to say: "And there will be earthquakes in various places... These are the beginnings of sorrows. For in those days there will be tribulation, such as has not

Heavens rolled up

The Day that We roll up the heavens like a scroll rolled up for books... 21 The Prophets, 104

On the Day when the firmament will be in dreadful commotion. 52 The Mount, 9

The Day that the sky will be like molten brass... 70 The Ways of Ascent, 8

At length, when the sight is dazed, and the moon is buried in darkness. And the sun and moon are joined together... 75 The Resurrection, 7-9

When the sun (with its spacious light) is folded up; When the stars fall, losing their lustre; 81 The Folding Up, 1-2

When the Sky is cleft asunder; When the Stars are scattered. 82 The Cleaving Asunder. 1-2

The Earth pulverized

When the earth is shaken to her (utmost) convulsion, and the earth throws up her burdens (from within), and man cries (distressed): 'What is the matter with her?' - On that Day will she declare her tidings: For that your Lord will have given her inspiration. 99 The Convulsion, 1-5 been since the beginning of the creation… Mark13:5, 8, 19

…and behold there was a great earthquake; …and every mountain and island was moved out of its place. Revelation 6:12,14

Nay! When the earth is pounded to powder… 89 The Break of Day, 21

When the mountains vanish (like a mirage). 81 The Folding Up, 3

Warriors of the Lord

Do you suppose that I (Jesus ed.) came to give peace on earth?... not at all, but rather division…from now on five in one house will be divided: Father will be divided against son and son against father…"

"Nation will rise against nation, and kingdom against kingdom."

Luke 12: 51-53; 21:10

Division and enmity

That Day shall a man flee from his own brother, and from his mother and his father, and from his wife and his children. 80 He Frowned, 34-36

Friends on that Day will be foes, one to another - except the Righteous.

43 The Gold Adornments, 67

And war broke out in heaven: Michael and his angels fought with the dragon; and the dragon and his angels fought, but they did not prevail… Revelation 12:7-8

Another horse, fiery red, went out. And it was granted to the one who sat on it to take peace from the earth, and that people should kill one another; and there was given to him a great sword. Revelation 6: 4

By the (Steeds) that run, with panting (breath), and strike sparks of fire, and push home the charge in the morning, and raise the dust in clouds the while, and penetrate forthwith into the midst (of the foe) en masse; Truly man is to his Lord ungrateful;

100 Those that Run,1-6

The graves open

Thus says the Lord God: "Behold, O My people, I will open your graves and cause you to come up from your graves... Ezekiel 37: 12

And many of those who sleep in the dust of the earth shall awake, Some to everlasting life, Some to shame and everlasting contempt. Daniel 12: 2

The sea gave up the dead who were in it, and Death and Hades delivered up the dead who were in them.

And they were judged, each one according to his works. Revelation 20: 13

The dead are raised

When we are (actually) dust, shall we indeed then be in a renewed creation?" 13 The Thunder, 5

Does man think that We cannot assemble his bones? Nay, We are able to put together in perfect order the very tips of his fingers. 75 The Resurrection, 3-4

From the (earth) We created you, and into it We shall return you, and from it We shall bring you out once again. 20 Ta-Ha 55

And when the graves are turned upside down; (Then) shall each soul know what it has sent forward and (what it has) kept back. 82 The Cleaving Asunder,4-5

The return of Jesus as judge

...for He (the Lord ed.) is coming to judge the earth. 1 Chronicles 16: 33

Then they will see the Son of Man coming in the clouds with great power and glory. Mark 13: 26

For as the lightning comes from the east and flashes to the west, so also will the coming of the Son of Man be. Matthew 24: 27

...the Lord Jesus Christ, who will judge the living and the dead at His appearing and His kingdom: 2 Timothy 4:1

God is Judge, Jesus witness

Will they wait until Allah comes to them in canopies of clouds, with angels (in His train)... 2 The Heifer, 210

...on the Day of Judgment He (Jesus ed.) will be a witness against them. 4 The Women, 141, 159

...Allah will judge. Betwixt you on the Day of Judgment.

Praise be to Allah... Master of the Day of Judgment. 1 The Opening, 2, 4

The dead judged

...He (The Lord ed.) is coming to judge the earth. With righteousness He shall judge the world, And the peoples with equity. Psalms 98:9

For we must all appear before the judgment seat of Christ, that each one may receive the things done in the body, according to what he has done, whether good or bad. 2 Corinthians 5:10

Then I saw a great white throne and Him who sat on it...I saw the dead, small and great, standing before God.... And the dead were judged according to their works... Revelation 20: 11-12

The Day of Judgment

That will be a Day of Sorting out! We shall gather you together and those before (you)! 77 Those Sent Forth 38

Then, he whose balance (of good deeds) will be (found) heavy, will be in a Life of good pleasure and satisfaction. But he whose balance (of good deeds) will be (found) light– will have his home in a (bottomless) Pit. 101The Day of Noise and Clamor, 6-9

Then anyone who has done an atom's weight of good, shall see it! And anyone who has done an atom's weight of evil, shall see it. 99 The Convulsion, 7-8

For us (is the responsibility for) our deeds, and for you for your deeds... 42 Consultation,15

The Book of life

Then those who feared the Lord spoke to one another, And the Lord listened and heard them; So a book of remembrance was written before Him for those who fear the Lord and who meditate on His name. Malachi 3:16

And at that time your people shall be delivered, Every one who is found written in the book. And

The record of deeds

And all things have We preserved on record. 78 The Great News, 29

Every man's fate We have fastened on his own neck: On the Day of Judgment We shall bring out for him a scroll, which he will see spread open. (It will be said to him:) "Read your (own) record: sufficient is your soul this day to make out an account against you." 17 The Israelites, 13-14

many of those who sleep in the dust of the earth shall awake, some to everlasting life, some to shame and everlasting contempt. Daniel 12:1-2

And another book was opened, which is the Book of Life. And the dead were judged according to their works, by the things which were written in the books.
Revelation 20:12

And anyone not found written in the Book of Life was cast into the lake of fire. Revelation 20:15

And the Book (of Deeds) will be placed (before you); and you will see the sinful in great terror because of what is (recorded) therein; they will say: "Ah! woe to us! What a book is this! It leaves out nothing small or great, but takes account thereof!" They will find all that they did, placed before them: and not one will your Lord treat with injustice. 18 The Cave, 49

Sheep and goats

Then you shall again discern
Between the righteous and the wicked... Malachi 3:18

All the nations will be gathered before Him, and He will separate them one from another, as a shepherd divides his sheep from the goats. And He will set the sheep on His right hand, but the goats on the left. Matthew 25: 32-33

The Right and the left

When the Inevitable Event comes to pass... you shall be sorted out into three classes. Then (there will be) the Companions of the Right Hand...
56 The Inevitable Event, 1, 7-8

But those who reject Our Signs, they are the (unhappy) Companions of the Left Hand. On them will be Fire vaulted over (all round).
90 The City, 19-20

Reward or punishment

And many of those who sleep in the dust of the earth shall awake, Some to everlasting life, Some to shame and everlasting contempt.

So it will be at the end of the age. The angels will come forth, separate the wicked from among the just, and cast them into the furnace of fire. There will be wailing and gnashing of teeth." Matthew 13: 49-50

And that You should reward Your servants small and great, And should destroy those who destroy the earth." Revelation11:18

Those who are wise shall shine like the brightness of the firmament, and those who turn many to righteousness like the stars forever and ever. Daniel 12:2-3

Hell or Paradise

When the Blazing Fire is kindled to fierce heat; And when the Garden is brought near; (Then) shall each soul know what it has put forward.
81 The Folding Up, 12-14

The Day when Man shall remember (all) that he strove for, and Hell-Fire shall be placed in full view for (all) to see-

Then, for such as had transgressed all bounds, and had preferred the life of this world, their Abode will be Hell-Fire; 79 Those Who Tear Out 35-39

Some faces that Day will be beaming, laughing, rejoicing. And other faces that Day will be dust-stained; Blackness will cover them.
80 He Frowned, 38-41

Violent images of the Last Day and Hell

A question from Marlies ter Borg

Being confronted with these violent images of the Last day and of the Hell to which sinners are driven makes one wonders if these words should be taken literally, or understood in a figurative sense.

For centuries the images concerning the Life after death played a great role in Christianity. The Book of Revelation, the Last Bible book was often recited. Images of the Divine Judge were carved into churches. Painters pictured the lost souls falling to the left and the redeemed souls rising to heaven. Composers reproduced the sounds of trumpets heralding the Dies Irae, the day of God's wrath.
Recently these images seem to have faded. The Last Day is something many Christians don't talk about, don't know about even. An example is the excellent book by Wimmer and Leimgruber: *Von Adam bis Muhammad. Bibel und Koran im Vergleich.* However it ends befóre the Last Day; which to Muslims means they are missing the whole point. For Muslims the concept of the Afterlife retains the central place it used to have for Christians. The Qur'an even offers Jews and Christians a shining future if they believe in the Last Day.

"Those who believe and those who follow the Jewish (Scriptures,) and the Christians ...who believe in Allah and the Last Day, and work righteousness, shall have their reward with the Lord; on them shall be no fear, nor shall they grieve." 2 The Heifer, 62

So what can it mean, to believe in the Last Day and the real possibility of Hell? I put this question to Mehmet Pacaci, expert in Eschatological Beliefs in the Qur'an and the Bible, and a fore fighter of figurative or symbolic Qur'an interpretation.

x. Individual responsibility and the Afterlife in the Qur'an

intermezzo by Mehmet Pacaci

Afterlife is one of the main themes of the Qur'an. The abode in which one will face the retribution of worldly deeds is called *akhira*. It is the opposite of the prevailing but transient life on earth (*al-hayat al-dunya*). *Akhira* is the future and unending period starting after the end of man's worldly life, (eschaton). For a Muslim, faith in life after death is concomitant with the faith in Almighty God manifested in his creative power. The *eschaton* is closely related to God's creative power. God has the absolute power over creation, death and resurrection or recreation; over the beginning and the end.

The description of what happens in the Afterlife is full of dramatic images. A strong figurative language is used to describe it. The point is that human beings will ultimately be judged by God in terms of their thoughts and deeds. This is a centerpiece of the Qur'an. Men and women are responsible creatures. God blew his breath into the humans (Adam) made of clay, and thus made them come alive. He allowed them to live on earth for a limited period of time, as vice-regents. Human beings have the intelligence and the freedom to make a choice between good and bad. This is an honor that other creatures and even the angels lack.

"We did indeed offer the trust to the Heavens and the Earth...but they refused to undertake it, being afraid thereof; but man undertook it..."

33 The Confederates, 72

The credit given to man is the source of his individual responsibility. Human beings will be held responsible for the choices they make. Earthly life is a test for men and women. Their task is

"to strive as in a race in all virtues." 5 The Table Spread, 48

Will men and women utilize the blessings bestowed onto them in a good way? Or will they waste their blessings? Or even use them for immoral or superficial goals? God will judge each individual fairly and on the basis of his or her deeds. Ultimately, God is the only and final authority. He will weigh men and women on the Last Day, the Day of Reckoning. This is the day that human beings return to God. On that Day nothing of what they tried to hide during their lives will remain hidden. Those whose good deeds outweigh their bad ones will be rewarded. Those who failed to live up to their task will be punished. For a Muslim the ultimate source of good deeds is submitting oneself to God. To refuse believing in God is bad *per se*. It is the source of all evil. Men and women should be constantly striving to act in the morally right way, and to recognize and shun what is wrong. They should obey God's morally guiding commands, and persevere on the Right Way.

This holds not only for Muslims but also for Jews and Christians. In the Bible the Last Day is described with images which are very similar to those in the Qur'an. The main difference is that whereas in the New Testament Jesus acts as judge, in the Qur'an it is only God who judges. There Jesus acts as witness, focusing specially on Christians. Have they acted against the rules Jesus gave them? Or have they lived a life of love and charity as Jesus demanded? In that case they are welcome in paradise.

So Jews, Christians and Muslims, indeed the whole of humankind, must be ready to face God for a final reckoning. Of course it is always possible to show remorse and ask for forgiveness, and God is Forgiving. But there is a point of no return. A Day when it is too late to mend one's ways.

"...to every People a term is appointed: when their term is reached, not an hour can they cause neither delay, nor (an hour) can they advance."

7 The Heights, 34

When will this Day of Judgment come? How much time do humans have? Nobody knows. The Last Day is something humans have no control over whatsoever. The time (*al-sa'ah*) determined for individuals as well as societies could be at any moment, and is sure to be unexpected.

Only the all-knowing, omniscient God knows when our last hour will strike. 33 The Confederates 63 All we human beings know is that the Day of reckoning is getting closer and closer every hour, every day. The reckoning is inescapable, inevitable (akhira) and human beings should keep that constantly in mind.

The signal for the final hour, the Last Day, is the blowing of the first trumpet. Then life on earth ends. The order of the universe will collapse with catastrophic events. On this Day of Verdict many will be filled with regret. They will try to escape, but in vain. They will get no support from their friends or relatives.

The trumpet will sound again to herald the Day of Resurrection. All men and women will awaken from the dead to face judgment. On this Day God establishes his court. The records of each individual will be opened and each individual will receive the book of his or her own life. Witnesses will be heard. Even the tiniest deeds of the earthly life will be weighed on scales as it were. Those whose life's deeds weigh heavily are redeemed; they will be welcomed in Paradise. Those who are shown up to be too light are the losers; they will be driven to Hell.

xi. Interpreting hell in an interfaith context

Intermezzo by Mehmet Pacaci

In 2009 I gave a course on eschatology in Bible and Qur'an at a Christian seminary in America. Of course we couldn't avoid the concept of hell, which occurs both in the Bible and in the Qur'an. Suddenly I felt that the immensity of the topic fell upon the classroom and smothered us all. My students, from a wide variety of ages, sat shrouded in a sad silence. They apparently could not admit this perception of terrible punishment by God. I understood from their later responses that they followed a figurative interpretation of the lake of fire in the New Testament, as is common in Christian circles in modern times. They understood 'hell' to mean 'eternal separation from God', as described in the Hebrew Bible.

"But your iniquities have separated you from your God;" Isaiah, 59:2

The sense of being forsaken by God is expressed in the psalms and even by Jesus in the depth of despair. In the Qur'an, God's ceasing His relation with the "hypocrites, both men and women", and with "those who barter away their bond with God and their own pledges for a trifling gain" is manifested in that "He has forgotten them" and "will not speak unto them " on the day of Resurrection.[9:67;2:174;3:77]

Later, when I was alone, I pondered on the subject. I think that a Muslim Sufi would simply prefer being in God's Hell with its punishments rather than to be eternally separated from God. That for a Sufi would mean eternal nothingness. Sufis consider it a joy when Allah is present even in the midst of 'Hell', and a loss when Allah is absent even in the bosom of 'Paradise'. The ultimate bliss for a Sufi, recognizable perhaps for Christian mystics is expressed as follows:

"By the Glorious Morning Light, And by the Night when it is still, - Your Guardian Lord has not forsaken you, nor is He displeased"

93: The Glorious Morning Light, 1-3

24. The Fires of Hell

The continuity and development of the concept of hell in Bible and Qur'an can be understood from the underlying Greek word 'Gehenna', used in the Septuagint, the Greek translation of the Hebrew Bible to refer to the valley of Hinnom, near Jerusalem, where children were sacrificed to the heathen god Moloch. The practice was outlawed by Joshua, but much later Jeremiah still had to warn the people of Judah to refrain from burning their children in Hinnom valley.

In the Hebrew Bible God can destroy with fire, but this refers to the living. The idea of hellfire as a punishment after death, as mentioned in the New Testament and elaborated in the Qur'an, is foreign to the Tenach.

In the New Testament the word 'Gehenna' acquires the broader meaning of the fiery place where the evildoers are punished after death. It is translated below as *hell.*

According to Jesus, he who refuses to help others deserves hellish punishment. Verbal aggression is also rewarded by fire.

The same word, *Jahannam* in Arabic, is also translated as *hell*. The Qur'anic version of hell is far more detailed than that of the New Testament and is described in many surahs.

In the Qur'an Iblis, the Devil or Satan, and his demons lead people astray until they finally join them in hell's flames. It is the *sinister* (Latin for left) ones who go to hell. The Qur'an speaks of the seven gates of hell, each for a different class of sins.

The Qur'an specifies killing oneself in injustice as a direct way to hell. Other sins relate to wealth. Usurping an orphan's wealth as well as cheating in trade and refraining from a good investment in the way of God lead to hell. Money that is buried produces the heat of hell.

Simply proclaiming one's faith is not enough to keep out of hell. Both books relegate hypocrites to the flames. Unbelievers also deserve hell. What does it take to belong to this category? In the Qur'an, the word 'unbeliever' has a strong ethical meaning. Satan/Iblis was the first and foremost 'unbeliever'. He does not deny the existence of God; he even talks to him. However, he disobeys God and strives against divine justice. Satan/Iblis is the enemy of humankind. He tempts people, Muslims and non-Muslims alike, and leads them to hell. In Revelation, Satan and his followers are thrown into the pit of fire. In the Qur'an, the devil and his friends undergo the same fate.

According to the Qur'an, on the other hand, Jews and Christians can escape from hell if they act in accordance with the Law of Moses and the Gospel. That is, if they take their own monotheism seriously.

In the New Testament Jesus holds up the Good Samaritan, a non-Jew, as an example to his fellow Jews, who far surpassing the Jewish priests in his charity.

So believer/unbeliever is not a black and white category in either book. The Qur'an indicates that the oppressed who have not been shown the true way can hope for forgiveness.

Both the New Testament and the Qur'an present the threat of hell to the wrongdoer but they also hold out the promise of forgiveness to those who repent.

Only one deed is exempt from forgiveness: in the New Testament, the blasphemy against the Holy Spirit, in the Qur'an, the setting up of partner gods besides Allah. In all other cases, man can repent and God forgives.

In the Hebrew Bible and in the Qur'an, God's forgiveness after showing remorse is a recurring theme. In the New Testament, redemption comes through the Grace of God and Jesus his Son.

Hinnom, Hell, Gehenna, Jahannam

Bible

Hinnom Valley and Hell
And (the King Josiah ed.)...defiled Topheth...in the Valley of the Son of Hinnom, that no man might make his son or his daughter pass through the fire to Molech. [2 Kings: 23:10]

"For the children of Judah have done evil in My sight," says the Lord. "...they have built the high places of Tophet, which is in the Valley of the Son of Hinnom, to burn their sons and their daughters in the fire, which I did not command, nor did it come into My heart." [Jeremiah 7:30-31]

(The Lord said ed.) "For a fire is kindled in My anger, And shall burn to the lowest hell; It shall consume the earth with her increase, And set on fire the foundations of the mountains." [Deuteronomy 32:22]

Fear Him who...has power to cast into hell; [Luke 12:5]

Qur'an

Jahannam, the blazing hell
In order that Allah may separate the impure from the pure, put the impure, one on another, heap them together, and cast them into Hell. [8 The Spoils of War, 37]

(They will be) in the midst of a fierce Blast of Fire and in Boiling Water, and in the shades of Black Smoke. [56 The Inevitable Event, 42-43]

Those who are wretched shall be in the Fire: there will be for them therein (nothing but) the heaving of sighs and sobs. [11 Hud,106]

And you will see the Sinners that day bound together in fetters- Their garments of liquid pitch, and their faces covered with Fire; That Allah may requite each soul according to its deserts; and verily Allah is swift in calling to account. [14 Ibrahim, 49-51]

...their abode will be Hell: every time it shows abatement, We shall increase from them the fierceness of

…Jesus said: "…if your eye causes you to sin, pluck it out.
It is better for you to enter the kingdom of God with one eye, rather than having two eyes, to be cast into hell fire… And the fire is not quenched." Mark 9: 39, 47-48

Everlasting fire for the devil
"Then He will also say to those on the left hand, 'Depart from Me, you cursed, into the everlasting fire prepared for the devil and his angels." Matthew 25: 41
Then I saw an angel coming down from heaven, having the key to the bottomless pit and a great chain in his hand. He laid hold of the dragon, that serpent of old, who is the Devil and Satan …and he cast him into the bottomless pit… Revelation 20: 1-3
The devil, who deceived them, was cast into the lake of fire and brimstone… Revelation 20:10

Those on the left cursed
But the cowardly, unbelieving, abominable, murderers, sexually immoral, sorcerers, idolaters, and all liars shall have their part in the lake

the Fire: as often as their skins are roasted through.
We shall change them for fresh skins, that they may taste the penalty…
17 The Israelites,97; 4 The Women,56

Fire for the hosts of Iblis
"...for those who resist Allah, is the penalty of the Fire…they will be thrown headlong into the (Fire) – they and those straying in Evil, And the whole hosts of Iblis together."
8 The Spoils of War, 14; 26 The Poets,94-95

Whoever, forsaking Allah, takes Satan for a friend, of a surety has suffered a loss that is manifest. Satan makes them promises, and creates in them false desires; but Satan's promises are nothing but deception. They (his dupes) will have their dwelling in Hell, and from it they will find no way of escape. 4 The Women, 119-121

The left-hand: the wrong-doers
The Companions of the Left Hand…in the midst of a fierce Blast of Fire…such is our requital for those who do wrong.
56 The Inevitable Event, 41, 7 The Heights, 41

which burns with fire and brimstone, which is the second death.
Revelation 21: 8

Then He (Jesus ed.) will also say to those on the left hand,
'Depart from Me, you cursed, into the everlasting fire prepared for the devil and his angels:
for I was hungry and you gave Me no food; I was thirsty and you gave Me no drink; was a stranger and you did not take Me in, naked and you did not clothe Me, sick and in prison and you did not visit Me.'
Matthew 25: 41-43

(Jesus said ed.)...whoever is angry with his brother without a cause...shall be in danger of hell fire." Matthew 5: 22

And the tongue is a fire, a world of iniquity. The tongue...is set on fire by hell. James 3:6
Their punishment will be eternal destruction, and they will be kept far from the presence of our Lord and his glorious strength.
2 Thessalonians, 1:9

To it (Hell ed.) are seven Gates: for each of those Gates is a (special) class (of sinners) assigned.
15 The Rocky Tract,44

...nor kill... yourselves... If any do that in rancor and injustice – soon shall We cast them into the Fire:
Those who unjustly eat up the property of orphans, eat up a Fire into their own bodies...
Do not eat up your property among yourselves in vanities...
4 The Women, 29-30; 10; 29

And there are those who bury gold and silver and spend it not in the Way of Allah...heat will be produced out of that (wealth) in the fire of Hell... 9 Repentance, 34-35

Hypocrites deserve hell

Then Jesus spoke...saying: "Woe to you, scribes and Pharisees, hypocrites! serpents, brood of vipers! How can you escape the condemnation of hell?"

Matthew 23:1-2, 29, 33

Faith no guarantee

There are...many among the priests...who in Falsehood devour the substance of men and hinder (them) from the Way of Allah. The Hypocrites...enjoin evil, and forbid what is just... Allah has promised the Hypocrites men and women...the fire of Hell.

9 Repentance, 34, 67-68

Unbelievers, Jews, Samaritans

But the...unbelieving... shall have their part in the lake which burns with fire... Revelation 21: 8

A certain man... fell among thieves, who stripped him of his clothing, wounded him, and departed, leaving him half dead.

...a certain priest came down that road. And when he saw him, he passed by on the other side.

...a certain Samaritan, as he journeyed, came where he was. And when he saw him, he had compassion. So he went to him and bandaged his wounds... and took care of him . Luke 10:30-31, 33-34

Unbelievers People of the Book

The Unbelievers spend their wealth to hinder (men) from the path of Allah...they will be gathered together to Hell. 8 The Spoils of War, 36

And indeed Hell surrounds the Unbelievers. 9 Repentance 49

They do blaspheme who say: "God is Christ the son of Mary." But Christ said: "O Children of Israel! worship God, my Lord and your Lord." Whoever joins other gods with Allah, - Allah will forbid him the Garden, and the Fire will be his abode. There will for the wrong-doers be no one to help.

5 The Table spread, 72

Those...who follow the Jewish (scriptures),... and the Christians – any who believe in Allah and the Last Day, and work righteousness – on them shall be no fear, nor shall they grieve. 5 The Table Spreads, 69

Forgiveness and its limits

O Israel, return to the Lord your God, for you have stumbled because of your iniquity; Say to Him, "Take away all iniquity; Receive us graciously…" Hosea 14:1-2

I…confess my transgressions to the Lord and you forgave the iniquity of my sin. Psalm 32:5

…all sins will be forgiven the sons of men, and whatever blasphemies they may utter; but he who blasphemes against the Holy Spirit never has forgiveness, but is subject to eternal condemnation. Mark 3:28-29

...the Father…has delivered us from the power of darkness and conveyed us into the kingdom of the Son of His love, in whom we have redemption through His blood, the forgiveness of sins. Colossians 1:12-14

Limits of forgiveness

Our Lord!...forgive us, then, our sins, and save us from the agony of the Fire."- 3 Al-'Imran,16

"We have wronged our own souls: if You do not forgive us and do not bestow upon us Your Mercy, we shall certainly be lost." 7 The Heights, 23

Do they not know that Allah accepts repentance…? For Allah blots out sins and forgives again and again. 9 Repentance,104; 4 The Women, 43

Allah does not forgive that partners should be set up with Him… to set up partners with Allah is to devise a sin most heinous indeed… But He forgives whom He pleases other sins than this… 4 The Women,48, 116

…For Allah is Oft-Forgiving, Most Merciful 3 Al-'Imran, 89

25. The Heavenly City/ Gardens of Paradise

Both the Qur'an and the Bible hold out the prospect of a reward for the faithful and the righteous which they will receive when they are raised from death. The images used to describe this afterlife differ.

The Hebrew Bible offers the image of the new Jerusalem, coupled to a new heaven and a new earth. In Revelation, this beautiful city has twelve pearly gates. In it a river flows bordered by the tree of life. The New Testament speaks of paradise only occasionally.

It is Paradise which in the Qur'an is the main focus. The everlasting gardens or *Jannah* to which the faithful and righteous may aspire are sometimes called the garden of Eden, implying a return to the paradise garden that humankind originally inhabited. Such gardens are mentioned in the Qur'an countless times, usually together with Jahannam, the fires of hell. The word paradise comes from the Persian, originally meaning 'walled garden'. On judgment day the walls open up like wide portals The paradise gardens are verdant and shady, provided with abundant water and filled with plenty, fowl and fruit. Wine is served by young men with beautiful pearly eyes. This wine which does not intoxicate. Nor does the milk turn sour, which together with the honey is reminiscent of the Bible's promised land.

Both the sparkling city and verdant gardens are intended for the faithful and the righteous; the men and women on the right. The New Testament uses the word sheep, as opposed to the sinister goats that proceed to hell. In this chapter the virtues which make someone eligible for heaven are lightly touched upon. In chapter 29 a more extensive description of virtues is given.

In both books 'martyrs', that is those who suffered (death) for their faith are given special treatment. As shown in the previous chapter, suicide bombers killing innocent life are explicitly excluded, committing as they do the double crime of killing innocent people and killing themselves.

A question hotly discussed is whether members of other religions are allowed into one's own heavenly or paradisiacal abode.

The Qur'an starts by mocking the idea that only Jews and Christians will go to heaven. It broadens the concept to allow Muslims to enter. They may relate there peacefully with Christians and Jews who remain faithful to their own scriptures.

Jesus also gives a broad and charitable view of paradise, explicitly admitting sinners and criminals to heaven.

In the Qur'an Paradise is promised to both men and women who are just and submit to God. It is characterized by peaceful human relations, also between the sexes. Just as on earth, there are couples in heaven, but they remain forever young. According to tradition, they become as tall as Adam, as beautiful as Joseph, as melodious as David, and of the same age (33) Jesus was when he was taken up on high by God, - and finally as wise as Muhammad.

In the Biblical image of heaven there are no sexual differences. People exist as shining angels, free from troubling erotic desires. Words such as bride and groom take on a spiritual meaning, as in the image of the bride Jerusalem.

Both Paradise and the Kingdom of Heaven, the New Jerusalem are filled with radiantly happy people, living forever in the close presence of God.

Heavenly City/Eternal Gardens, Eden

Bible

Heavenly Kingdom, Holy City
For behold, I create new heavens and a new earth…I create Jerusalem as a rejoicing, and her people a joy. Isaiah 65: 17-18

I saw a new heaven and a new earth…Then I, John, saw the holy city, New Jerusalem, coming down out of heaven from God, prepared as a bride adorned for her husband. The twelve gates were twelve pearls: And the street of the city was pure gold, like transparent glass. Revelation 21:1-2, 21

Repent, for the kingdom of heaven is at hand.

…and behold, a throne set in heaven, and One sat on the throne… and there was a rainbow around the throne, in appearance like an emerald.
Matthew 4: 17,Revelation 4: 2-3

And he (an angel) showed my (John) a pure river of water of life, clear as crystal, proceeding from the throne of God… on either side of the river, was the tree of life,

Qur'an

The Gardens of Eternity
But those who repent…and do what is right shall enter paradise…the gardens of Eden, which the Merciful has promised… 19 Mary, 61 (Dawood)

…for the righteous, is a beautiful Place of (Final) Return – Gardens of Eternity, whose doors will (ever) be open to them; 38 Saad, 49-50

...a Garden whose width is that (of the whole) of the heavens and of the earth... 3 Al-'Imran, 133

In a Garden on high…Therein will be a bubbling spring: Therein will be Thrones (of dignity), raised on high, goblets placed (ready), and cushions set in rows, and rich carpets (all) spread out.
88 The Overwhelming Event: 10-16

They will be) on Thrones encrusted (with gold and precious stones), reclining on them, facing each other. Round about them will (serve) youths of perpetual (freshness), with goblets, (shining) beakers, and cups (filled) out of clear-flowing fountains: no after-ache will they do not receive therefrom, nor will they suffer

which bore twelve fruits…the leaves of the tree were for the healing of the nations. Revelation 22:1-2
..to him who overcomes I will give to eat from the tree of life, which is in the midst of the Paradise of God." ' Revelation 2:7

…today you will be with Me in Paradise." Luke 23: 43

intoxication: And with fruits, any that they may select: and the flesh of fowls, any that they may desire.
56 The Inevitable Event, 15-21

In it are rivers of water incorruptible; rivers of milk of which the taste never changes; rivers of wine, a joy to those who drink; and rivers of honey pure and clear. In it there are for them all kinds of fruits; and Grace from their Lord. 47 The Prophet,15

The sheep on the right

When the Son of Man comes to His glory …He will sit on the throne…and He will set the sheep on his right hand… Matthew 25:31,33
…the saints of the Most High shall receive the kingdom, and possess the kingdom forever, even forever and ever. Daniel 7:18
Blessed are those who are persecuted for righteousness' sake, for theirs is the kingdom of heaven.
Matthew 5:3,10

Adorned in green garments

Those who are given their record in their right hand will read it (with pleasure), and they will not be dealt with unjustly in the least.
17 The Israelites, 71

Upon them will be green garments of fine silk and heavy brocade, and they will be adorned with Bracelets of silver; "Verily this is a Reward for you, and your Endeavour is accepted and recognised."
76 Time; or Man 21-22

I saw the souls of those who had been beheaded for their witness to Jesus and for the word of God… they lived and reigned with Christ… Revelation 20:4
Blessed are the poor in spirit, For

If you (but) establish regular Prayers (Salat ed.), practise regular Charity (Zakat ed.) believe in My Messengers…and loan to Allah a beautiful loan...
verily I will admit you to Gardens

theirs is the kingdom of heaven.
...whoever humbles himself as this little child is the greatest in the kingdom of heaven. Matthew 18:4

with rivers flowing beneath;
5 The Table Spread, 12

Those who have...suffered harm in My Cause, or fought or been slain – verily, I will admit them into Gardens with rivers flowing beneath; 3 Al-'Imran,195

A sinner in paradise

Jesus said to... the chief priests and the elders of the people...,
"Assuredly, I say to you that tax collectors and harlots enter the kingdom of God before you."
Matthew 21:21, 23,31

Then one of the criminals who were hanged blasphemed Him, saying,
"If You are the Christ, save Yourself and us."
But the other, answering, rebuked him, saying,
"... this Man has done nothing wrong."
Then he said to Jesus,
"Lord, remember me when You come into Your kingdom."
And Jesus said to him,
"Assuredly, I say to you, today you will be with Me in Paradise."
Luke 23: 39, 40-43

Jews /Christians in paradise?

And they say: "None shall enter Paradise unless he be a Jew or a Christian." Those are their (vain) desires. Nay–whoever submits his whole self to Allah and is a doer of good– he will get his reward with his Lord; on such shall be no fear, nor shall they grieve.
2 The Heifer, 111-112

If only the People of the Book had believed and been righteous, We should indeed have... admitted them to Gardens of Bliss. If only they had stood fast by the Law, the Gospel, and all the revelation that was sent to them from their Lord, they would have enjoyed happiness from every side. 5 The Table Spread, 65-66

As Angels

For in the resurrection they neither marry nor are given in marriage, but are like angels of God in heaven.
Matthew 22:30

Then I, John, saw the holy city, New Jerusalem, coming down out of heaven from God, prepared as a bride adorned for her husband.
Revelation 21: 2

Then the kingdom of heaven shall be likened to ten virgins who took their lamps and went out to meet the bridegroom. And at midnight a cry was heard: "Behold, the bridegroom is coming; go out to meet him!"
And… the bridegroom came, and those who were ready went in with him to the wedding; and the door was shut. Matthew 25: 1, 6, 10

God with the people

…God is with men, and He will dwell with them, and they shall be His people. God Himself will be with them and be their God.

Men and women together

If any do deeds of righteousness – be they male or female - and have faith, they will enter Heaven...
4 The Women,124

You enter the Garden, you and your wives, in (beauty and) rejoicing. 43 Gold Adornments, 70
And (there will be) Companions with beautiful, big, and lustrous eyes – like unto Pearls well-guarded. 56 The Inevitable Event, 22-23
...and they have therein companions pure (and holy); and they abide therein (for ever).
2 The Heifer, 25

We have created (their Companions) of special creation. And made them virgin-pure (and undefiled), beloved (by nature), equal in age, for the Companions of the Right Hand 56 The Inevitable Event, 35-38

The brightness of bliss

For them will be a Home of Peace in the presence of their Lord: He will be their Friend, because they practiced (righteousness).
6 The Cattle, 127

Their salutation on the Day they meet Him will be "Peace!"; and He has prepared for them a generous Reward. 33 The Confederates, 44

God will wipe away every tear from their eyes; there shall be no more death, nor sorrow, nor crying. There shall be no more pain, for the former things have passed away.
Revelation 21: 3-4

I (God ed.) will rejoice in Jerusalem, And joy in My people; The voice of weeping shall no longer be heard in her, Nor the voice of crying. Isaiah 65:19

Those who are wise shall shine like the brightness of the firmament, And those who turn many to righteousness like the stars forever and ever. Daniel 12:3

You will recognize in their faces the beaming brightness of Bliss.
83 The Dealers in Fraud, 24

Now no person knows what delights of the eye are kept hidden (in reserve) for them - as a reward for their (good) deeds.
32 The Adoration: 17

Some faces that Day will be beaming, (bright) Laughing, rejoicing.
80 He Frowned, 38-39

xii. Are Christians allowed into the Paradise Gardens?

Intermezzo by Marlies ter Borg

My father, Frits Neervoort, was born in what was then the world's second largest Muslim majority country, the Kingdom of the Netherlands, specifically in its colony, the Dutch East Indies. He grew up in Bandung as the child of parents who met in the Lutheran orphanage in the Hague. He was in his eighties when he and I discovered together that the figure, central to his faith, also played an important role in the Qur'an - Jesus. In the meantime, back in Holland, he had in his eighties, befriended an Afghan refugee who helped him with chores in house and garden. They reached an understanding: you pray for me on Friday, I'll pray for you on Sunday. In the last year of his life (just after 9/11) Frits showed a never-faltering interest in 'our' Qur'an and Bible project.

On his deathbed he was suddenly gripped by that old fear, that he would not be allowed to pass through Heaven's gate, and neither would his wife who believed only a little bit of everything.

I told him about the Gardens.

"You can both enter the gardens of paradise, as a couple."

"If that's true," the mortally ill 86-year-old cried, half in joke:

"I will convert to Islam," he said chuckling. "Call an imam!"

"There is no need, Dad, Christians and Jews may enter paradise as People of the Book; and there are so many gates that there is really no wall left."

That very moment, a cleaning lady came in, wearing a headscarf. I asked her to refrain from too rigorous a cleaning, as my father would soon be going to was soon going paradise.

"We will all go to paradise," the Muslima answered.

My father sank back into his pillow, a blissful glow in his tired eyes.

Part Five

Legal and ethical Issues

The search for God's law must attempt to pursue, express, promote, and re-create God's beauty.

Khaled Abou El Fadl [p.xix]

26. The position of Women

Equality and partnership of men and women

That men and women were created as equals is indicated by quotes from Bible and Qur'an. The stories of the creation of humankind show that men and women were created together, or separately from one another and for one another, to live as pairs in mutual care and protection. Paul writes that through their faith in Jesus men and women are equal. The Qur'an states that it is equitable that the rights of women be similar to those of men.

In the stories men play the dominant role. However Martha Frederiks shows us several impressive Biblical woman who also play a remarkable role in the Qur'an. The first of these is the Biblical Eve, the mother of life. Referred to in the Qur'an as Adam's wife, she receives the name Hawwa in Islamic tradition. Barbara Stowasser shows how the image of Hawwa became twisted into a negative Biblical mold. To Mary fell the high spiritual honor of giving virgin birth to Jesus. The Qur'an relates of her education at the hands of the priest Zacharias. Some Muslims see her as the equivalent of a prophet. The angel Gabriel gave to her God's creative word as he did to Moses and Muhammad.

Jesus makes no distinction between men and women. He takes women very seriously, protecting them from such harsh treatment as stoning, or forced divorce. He calls a woman 'the daughter of Abraham', an honor that the Hebrew Bible reserves for men. Mary Magdalene is his close disciple, loyal to Jesus until the end, the first to see him resurrected from the dead. The Acts of the Apostles recount the conversion of 'not a few...prominent women.' [7:12]

Although not mentioned in the Qur'an, Muhammad was first married to a highly independent and well-educated woman called Khadijah, who ran her own business. She helped him cope with his first revelations, gave him the financial space means to develop his new religion and became his first convert.

Inequality?

The oppression of woman is criticized both in Bible and Qur'an. In Genesis, the story of Paradise Lost implies that the actual dominance of men over women is a punishment, not an ideal situation. The Qur'an speaks with abhorrence about the gruesome habit of polytheists to bury their undesired baby girls alive. Women seem prone to mistreatment more than men. On the other hand, the story of Moses shows that the physical strength of men can make them prone to slaughter.

Depending on translation and interpretation, it seems as if the supposed inferiority of women sometimes seeps into the Holy Books themselves. Thus, Paul refers to the creation of Eve out of Adam, and her responsibility for the first sin, as legitimate grounds for the dominance of men. (Paul to)1 Timothy 2:13-14

The Qur'an grants men and women similar rights but adds that men have a degree of right or advantage over them.

Hitting wives?

The Qur'an contains a much-debated passage in which a man is supposedly granted permission, if not ordered, to beat a disobedient wife. 4 The Women, 34 This passage has been used to legitimize much suffering on the part of women. However, it can and has been interpreted and translated in a variety of ways.

Abdullah Yusuf Ali, whose translation is used in this book, speaks of the duty of a man to protect and support his wife and of a woman to take responsibility in his absence. If she falls short, the husband may not resort to brutally venting his anger.

Even the comment in the Saudi Arabian authorized version of Yusuf Ali's translation stresses that cruelty should be avoided.

Four steps mentioned are: Note 547 to 4 The Women, 34 p. 220

"1. Perhaps verbal advice or admonition may be sufficient
2. If not, sex relations may be suspended;
3. If this is not sufficient, some slight physical correction may be administered; but Imam Shafi'I considers this unadvisable, and all authorities are unanimous in depreciating any sort of cruelty, even of the nagging kind.
4. If all this fails, a family council is recommended".

This is a far cry both from the wife bashing that goes on both in Muslim and non-Muslim countries; and from what both extremist Muslims and Islam bashers would have us believe. On the contrary, the verse is an admonition to men to restrain themselves not correct their wives without good reason, without first trying to reason things out and observing a cooling-off period. Only if all this fails is the man authorized to administer at most a light blow, restraining himself from verbal violence. If she mends her ways, her husband may not harm her. In other words, a man must control himself.
Laleh Bakhtiar[6] holds that the relevant word *'wa'dribuhunna means* '*to go away'* rather that '*to beat'*, implying that the passage contains rules on initiating a divorce procedure. Ahmed Ali [7] translates the term as 'to make love,' as the camels do, by the male getting on top of the female.
Abou El Fadl argues that hitting one's wife is ugly, running counter to the search for God's beauty. He notes that the Prophet never hit his wives. p.108-9 Indeed, Muhammad forbade the hitting of any woman: "Never beat God's handmaidens" . Abu Dawud, Al-Nasai, Ibn Majah and Ahmad
The '*disobedience'* for which the wife is to be punished refers to God, not the husband. The women is to guard in her husband's absence not what her husband, but *'what Allah would have her guard.'* Disobedience to one's mate cannot itself be held a sin. In some cases obedience to God might even call for saying no to a husband. The example in the Qur'an is that of

[6] Laleh BakhtiarThe Sublime Qur'an, Kazi Publications Inc. first translation by a Woman
[7] Ahmed Ali, Al-Qur'an: A Contemporary Translation, Princeton University Press

the Pharaoh's wife, who opposed her husband's oppressive policies. So, the verse must refer to a grave transgression of divine rules rather than against the capricious will of the husband. As a tentative conclusion, (what more have human beings to offer?) Abou El Fadl, notes that in the case of such a grave transgression, it is up to the state, not the husband, to administer the punishment, after due process of course. [109-113]

So there is quite a variety of translations and interpretations. None of them, however, sanctions brutal and uncontrolled violence against women.

The religious, social and economic position of women

What do the Books have to say on the position of women outside the family circle? The apostle Paul bars women from positions requiring speaking in church or perhaps even in public, such as teaching. [1 Timothy, 2:12]
This has led Church authorities to reserve priesthood for males, although several Protestant denominations do permit women to hold positions of leadership. Although the Qur'an contains no comparable statement banning women from positions of responsibility, the position of Imam is reserved for males, at least when leading a male or mixed congregation. This is opposed by liberal Muslima's. Thus, the internal debate within Christianity and within Islam on the acceptability of women leading religious ritual shows similarities, even though the Scriptures differ.

As for economic liberties, the Hebrew Bible presents a mixed picture. On the one hand, women are limited in their economic freedom, because their decisions are subject to the veto of their father or husband. On the other hand the Bible book of Proverbs paints a picture of women as competent and independent in their economic dealings.

The Qur'an emphasizes the financial independence of women. They are paid for the work they do, just as men are. A married woman is free to dispose of her husband's dowry as she sees fit. In Europe, the dowry, now a forgotten concept, used to be brought into the marriage by the woman, to be managed by her husband. In the Qur'an, the man offers the dowry to the woman for her own disposal. He is obliged to support his wife, especially during her maternity leave, which can last, should she desire, up to two

years. She is not required to contribute to the family income. Divorced women and their children also have a right to support from the former husband. The obligation to support a wife and children can justify the inheritance by boys of twice as much as girls- a rule nowadays abrogated when women are financially independent.
In the Qur'an, some doubt is cast on a woman's ability in the commercial sphere, since her trustworthiness to act as a witness is valued at half that of a man. This verse refers to commercial transactions, where women might have insufficient knowledge. In areas in which women are experts, a woman's witness will be valued higher than that of a man. In any case, both sexes are eligible to serve as witnesses, asking for support from their own sex as the need arises.

The ambivalence of sex
Of course, sex plays a major role in male and female relationships. The evaluation of sex is ambivalent in both books: it can lead to joy and pain. The Song of Songs from the Hebrew Bible praises eroticism. In the New Testament Paul speaks of a more sober and moral love between men and women. He warns against lust, which can bring with it a whole series of evils, from jealousy to murder. In the Qur'an, spouses are a gift of God. Their relationship is one of love and compassion. The earthly love between men and women can find its example and completion in Paradise. But, it can also lead men and women astray. One should resist temptation as Joseph did.

Marriage
Therefore, sex should be limited to marriage. This point of view, strongly emphasized in both books, is understandable. At the time of writing, no effective contraceptives were available. In this way, marriage protects the unborn child from a miserable life as the bastard of an unmarried woman. Muhammad's concern for children without parents is not surprising, given that his mother was widowed before his birth and died when he was still a boy. His position is not anti-sex as such. On the contrary. In the Qur'an,

man fulfills his divine destiny in an erotically satisfying marriage. God does not demand celibacy, as practiced by Christian monks.

The book of Proverbs in the Hebrew Bible praises the good wife as a precious treasure on whom the husband depends. To Paul, marriage, desirable as a remedy for promiscuous lust, is a relationship of reciprocity. In the final analysis, however, celibacy is, for Paul, superior to marriage, which brings a whole set of new problems, deflecting one's attention from God.

Dress code

In the Qur'an, the dress code for men and women is linked to the ambivalent attitude toward sexual desire. So as to avoid seduction outside of marriage, both are required to dress and behave modestly in public, in order not to seduce the other sex. Clothing in the Qur'an has neither a primarily religious nor a hierarchical but a practical significance. The Qur'an is explicit about the need for women to cover their breasts, not about the need to cover their head. The relevant verses are open to diverse interpretations, as many as the variety of headgear worn or not worn) by Muslimas. They often look to the Hadith for further guidance. Special attention is paid to the women of the Prophet, who must have been more vulnerable to assault than other women.

The Bible is more explicit about covering the head, but the motives are hierarchical, and religious women with hats express their subservience to the man and to God. Women should dress modestly, and, especially when going to church, should cover their head to express their subservience to the man and to Jesus. Some Muslims refer to Paul when arguing for Muslimas to cover their heads.

Paul and Islam

In both Christianity and Islam, Paul is a controversial character. He is honored as the architect of Christianity; his passages on love are often read at wedding ceremonies. However some Christians criticize Paul for looking down on women and denouncing homosexuals. The attitude of Muslims to Paul is also ambivalent. On the one hand, he is rejected as a 'self acclaimed' prophet, who pushed himself in between Jesus and Muhammad. Paul is seen as the corrupter of the original message of Jesus and is accused of creating a wedge between Christians and Muslims. Paul is understood to have written negatively about Muhammad and the angel Gabriel who recited the Qur'an to him.

"I pray that God will punish anyone who preaches anything different from our message to you! It doesn't matter if that person is one of us or an angel from heaven. I have said it before, and I will say it again. I hope God will punish anyone who preaches anything different from what you have already believed." Galatians 1:8-9

On the other hand, Muslims sometimes refer to Paul as St, short for Saint, and cite his letters in arguing for harsh policies toward women and homosexuals not found in the Qur'an. For instance, on a website from Iran, we read the following:

"The headcovers are clearly mentioned not in the Qur'an but in the BIBLE as St. Paul's instructions: *'But every Woman who prays or prophesies with HER HEAD UNCOVERED dishonors her head, for that is one and the same as if her head were shaved. For if a woman is not covered, let her also be shorn. But if it is shameful for a woman to be shorn or shaved, LET HER BE COVERED.'* "(Paul to the) 1 Corinthians 11:5-6 Imam Reza Network /www.imamreza.net/eng/imamreza.php?id=6407

As for condemning homosexuals, St Paul's letter to the Romans 1:22-27 is cited to explain the spread of AIDS as a rightful punishment of God for 'unnatural' sex. www.imamreza.net/eng/imamreza.php?id=3280

As noted, the Qur'an contains no general condemnation of homosexuals and no specific condemnation of homosexual love. The Bible does.

Motherhood

Motherhood plays an important role in both Books. In Genesis, the pain women may bear in delivery is explained as a punishment for the sin of Eve. Proverbs says that children praise their mother with good reason. The Qur'an mentions a mother's pain as a good reason for her child to be kind to her.

The joys of motherhood are expressed in the stories about two remarkable women: Elizabeth, the mother of John (the Baptist), and Mary, the mother of Jesus. The Qur'an tells the same tale of the miracle of these unexpected pregnancies. The Qur'an says God is directly involved in the birth of every human and that He closely follows the beginning and end of each woman's pregnancy.

In the Qur'an, children and grandchildren are gifts from God. Depending on the translation - and in line with the rejection of the murder of baby girls - this phrase is understood to include daughters and granddaughters.

Adultery

Adultery is a threat to marriage and is strongly rejected in both Books. In the Hebrew Bible the punishment for adultery is stoning to death. Jesus rejects this, saying:

"Let him who is without sin throw the first stone."

In the Qur'an, the death penalty is reserved for murderers and those who cause wanton destruction. For adultery the punishment must therefore be milder. Both parties to adultery receive lashes of the whip, but only after due process, involving four witnesses instead of the usual two. They are allowed to remarry with other adulterers or unbelievers. If they repent, God is forgiving. Women are protected against false accusations.

Divorce

In the Hebrew Bible, a man is allowed to cast out his wife simply by giving her a 'divorce letter′ Jesus rejects this custom. He states that the union between man and wife is sanctioned by God and cannot be broken by humans. Paul echoes the words of Jesus, arguing that divorce as the breaking up of a divinely sanctioned union is forbidden. He considers remarrying after divorce as tantamount to adultery. Divorce is allowed (to new converts) only if one's partner is not a Christian.

The Qur'an also takes a stance against the ease with which men in those days could throw out their wives. Divorce is not encouraged, but is possible, after a just procedure. A woman has the right to complain about her husband, secure in the knowledge that God hears her words. If a man or a woman and their relatives have done everything they can to bring about reconciliation, they are entitled to ask for a divorce. This is granted only after a procedure that leaves room for reconciliation and protects the woman's interests. In any event, nothing should be rushed as long as the woman could still be carrying the man's child. Even after divorce, a man is obligated to support his wife and children. The interests of both parties are safeguarded as far as possible by the involvement of relatives from each side. The divorce should take place in a friendly atmosphere. Afterwards, both parties are allowed to remarry.

Polygamy

In the Hebrew Bible, having more than one official wife is described as a legitimate state for persons of wealth and high position. Kings such as David and Solomon were allowed many wives. Polygamy also has a social function. A married man may marry his brother's wife after his death. However, a man with more than one wife may not give preferential treatment to the children of his favorite wife. In the New Testament, polygamy is not rejected outright, although monogamy becomes the norm, certainly for church officials.

In the Qur'an, polygamy is allowed for a social goal, i.e., to ensure that war widows and their children are provided for. Of course, the stepfather must take good care of both the children and their possessions. Because of the financial burden a marriage places on the man, the number of wives is limited to a maximum of four. A polygamist must treat his different wives equally in all respects, even though it is acknowledged that, in practice, this is impossible. Indeed polygamy is hardly practiced, and nowadays is often considered by the family as a shameful state. A woman can divorce if her husband takes another wife, especially when she has inserted this as a condition in her marriage contract.

Women in paradise?

In Bible and Qur´an, whoever believes and acts well is promised everlasting rewards. The differences concern the sexual state of the inhabitants of paradise. As Jesus says, sexual differences will evaporate in heaven. In the afterlife, men and women will be without sex, like angels. Erotic images used in the Bible in connection with heaven refer to the New Jerusalem, not to a woman.

The Qur'an on the other hand, explicitly promises deserving women an afterlife in Paradise, on the basis of their own merit.

The Greek philosopher Plato, who represented the state of the art religious thought for centuries, reserves heaven for men, with noble women first to be reincarnated as male before reaching the stars. Plato Timaeus , 42B

The Qur'an however invites women to strive for paradise to which they will be welcomed as women. There they can enjoy ecstatic happiness as men can. In the Gardens of Paradise, people retain their sex, experience rejuvenation, and dwell as loving couples.

Qur'an not as mysogynous as often thought

Thanks to extremists on both sides, the Qur'an has the reputation for misogyny. This chapter demonstrates that the Qur'an contains less oppressive statements about women than is often assumed. The Bible, on the other hand, contains more statements about the inequality of women than many Christians or Jews are prone to believe. If noticed at all, many Christians and Jews see these misogynic verses as outdated, abrogated by the principles of equality and love in the Bible and by generally-accepted human rights.

On the other hand, many Muslims seem to take inequality farther that the Qur'an allows. Might they be taking their cue from certain Bible passages rather than from their own Holy Book? Muslims are allowed to go the the Bible when the Qur'an offers no conclusive statement, on the basis of the Qur'an verse

"So if you are in doubt about what We have revealed to you, ask those who have been reading the scriptures before you." 11 Hud,94, (Haleem 2004)

So Muslim interpreters have a legitimate reason for turning to the more conservative passages on Women in the Bible. Often these passages have already been incorporated into the Hadith, giving them the respected status of words Muhammad spoke outside of the divinely revealed Qur'an. Ironically, the more liberally-minded People of the Book reject the oppressive verses about women in the Hebrew Bible and the Letters of Paul that fundamentalist Muslims unwittingly rely upon. In repressing women, the more traditionally-minded Muslims are, - to paraphrase the French saying, 'plus royalist que le Roi' 'more royalist than the King'- more Biblically correct than the People of the Bible.

Bible Women Qur'an

Male and female equal
So God created humans to be like himself; he made men and women. Genesis 1:27

...the LORD made a woman out of the rib. The LORD God brought her to the man, and the man exclaimed, "Here is someone like me! She is part of my body, my own flesh and bones." Genesis 2:22-23
Faith in Christ Jesus is what makes each of you equal with each other, whether you are...a man or a woman. Galatians 3:28

Man and woman from one soul
It is He Who created you from a single person, and made his (her? ed.) mate of like nature, in order that he (she? Ed.) might dwell with her (him? ed. (in love).
7 The Heights,189

And women shall have rights similar to the rights against them, according to what is equitable; but men have a degree (of advantage) over them. 2 The Heifer, 228

Man and woman depend on each other
...men and women need each other. It is true that the first woman came from a man, but all other men have been given birth by women.
1 Corinthians 11:11-12

Men and women in pairs
And Allah...made you in pairs.
35 The Originator of Creation, 11

The Believers, men and women, are protectors one of another.
9 Repentance,71

Slaughtering baby boys
...the king, (Pharaoh ed.) gave a command to everyone in the nation, "As soon as a Hebrew boy is born, throw him into the River Nile! But you can let the girls live."
Exodus 1: 22

Herod...gave orders for his men to kill all the boys who lived in or near

A daughter a disgrace?
When news is brought to one of them, of (the birth of) a female (child), his face darkens, and he is filled with inward grief! With shame he hides himself from his people, because of the bad news he has had! Shall he retain it on (sufferance and) contempt, or bury

Bethlehem and were two years old and younger. Matthew 2:16

He will rule over you

Then the LORD said to the woman, "You will suffer terribly when you give birth. But you will still desire your husband, and he will rule over you." Genesis 3:16

(Adam said ed.) "She came from me, a man. So I will name her Woman!" Genesis 2:23

Women who claim to love God should do helpful things for others, and they should learn by being quiet and paying attention. They should be silent and not be allowed to teach or to tell men what to do. After all, Adam was created before Eve, and the man Adam wasn't the one who was fooled. It was the woman Eve who was completely fooled and sinned. (Paul to) 1 Timothy 2:10-14

If you are a wife, you must put your husband first. 1 Peter 3:1

A wife should put her husband first, as she does the Lord. A husband is the head of his wife... When God's people meet in church, the women must not be allowed to speak. They must keep quiet and listen, as the Law of Moses teaches. If there is

it in the dust? Ah! what an evil (choice) they decide on?

16 The Bee, 58-59

Men have an advantage

And women shall have rights similar to the rights against them, according to what is equitable; but men have a degree (of advantage) over them. 2 The Heifer, 228

Men are the protectors and maintainers of women, because Allah has given the one more (strength) than the other, and because they support them from their means. Therefore the righteous women are devoutly obedient, (to Allah ed.) and guard in (the husband's) absence what Allah would have them guard.

As to those women on whose part you fear disloyalty and ill-conduct, admonish them (first), (next), refuse to share their beds, (and last) beat (leave, or sleep with ed.) them (lightly); but if they return to obedience, do not seek against them means (of annoyance).

4 The Women,34

If a wife fears cruelty or desertion on her husband's part, there is no blame on them if they arrange an amicable settlement between themselves; and such settlement is

something they want to know, they can ask their husbands when they get home. It is disgraceful for women to speak in church.
(Paul to the) Ephesians 5:22-23;

1 Corinthians 14:33-35

best; even though men's souls are swayed by greed. But if you do good and practice self-restraint, Allah is well-acquainted with all that you do. 4 The Women, 128

Economic position of women

These are the laws that the LORD gave Moses about husbands and wives, and about young daughters who still live at home. Numbers 30: 16

Suppose a young woman who is still living with her parents makes a promise to the LORD…if he hears about it and objects, then she no longer has to keep her promise. The LORD will forgive her, because her father did not agree with the promise. Suppose a woman makes a promise to the LORD and then gets married…if her husband hears about the promise and objects, she no longer has to keep it, and the LORD will forgive her.

Numbers 30: 2-3, 5-6, 8,13

Women who claim to love God should do helpful things for others, and they should learn by being quiet and paying attention. They should be silent and not be allowed to teach or to tell men what to do. After all, Adam was created before Eve, and

Economic position of women

Whoever works righteousness, man or woman…to him will We give a new Life, a life that is good and pure, and We will bestow on such their reward according to the best of their actions. 16 The Bee, 97

To men is allotted what they earn, and to women what they earn.

4 The Women, 32

And give the women (on marriage) their dower as a free gift; but if they, of their own good pleasure, remit any part of it to you, take it and enjoy it with right good cheer.

4 The Women,4

The mothers shall give suck to their offspring for two whole years… the father… shall bear the cost of their food and clothing on equitable terms. If they both decide on weaning…there is no blame on them. 2 The Heifer, 233

For divorced women maintenance (should be provided) on a

the man Adam wasn't the one who was fooled. It was the woman Eve who was completely fooled and sinned. (Paul to) 1 Timothy 2:10-14

A truly good wife is... like a sailing ship that brings food from across the sea. She knows how to buy land and how to plant a vineyard, and she always works hard. She knows when to buy or sell, and she stays busy until late at night. She makes clothes to sell to the shop owners. She is strong and graceful...Her words are sensible, and her advice is thoughtful. Show her respect-praise her in public for what she has done. Proverbs 31: 10-11,14-18,24-26,31

Drunk with love; love is kind
Kiss me tenderly! Your love is better than wine, and you smell so sweet. All the young women adore you; the very mention of your name is like spreading perfume.
Songs of Solomon 1:2-3

And you, my love, are an apple tree among trees of the forest. Your shade brought me pleasure; your fruit was sweet. You...showered me with love. Refresh and strengthen me...
I am hungry for love!
Song of Solomon 2:3-5

reasonable (scale). This is a duty on the righteous. 2 The Heifer, 241

From what is left by parents and those nearest related there is a share for men and a share for women, whether the property be small or large, -a determinate share.
Allah (thus) directs you as regards your children's (Inheritance): to the male, a portion equal to that of two females. 4 The Women, 7,11
And get two witnesses, out of your men, and if there are not two men, then a man and two women, such as you choose, for witnesses. So that if one of them errs, the other can remind her. 2 The Heifer, 282

Love...hints of paradise
It is He Who created you from a single person, and made his (her? ed.) mate of like nature, in order that he (she? ed.) might dwell with her (him? ed.) (in love).
7 The Heights 189

And among His Signs is this that He created for you mates from among yourselves, that you may dwell in tranquility with them, and He has put love and mercy between your (hearts). 30 The Roman Empire, 21

My darling, you are perfume between my breasts. Songs of Solomon 1:13

You are a princess, and your feet are graceful in their sandals. Your thighs are works of art, each one a jewel; your navel is a wine glass filled to overflowing. Your breasts are like twins of a deer. …your hair is so lovely it holds a king prisoner. You are beautiful, so very desirable! You are tall and slender like a palm tree, and your breasts are full. I will climb that tree and cling to its branches. I will discover that your breasts are clusters of grapes…Kissing you is more delicious than drinking the finest wine. Songs of Solomon 7:1-3 5-9

In the same way, a husband should love his wife as much as he loves himself. A husband who loves his wife shows that he loves himself. Ephesians 5:28

Love is kind and patient, never jealous, boastful, proud, or rude. Love isn't selfish or quick-tempered. It doesn't keep a record of wrongs that others do. Love rejoices in the truth, but not in evil. Love is always supportive, loyal, hopeful, and trusting. 1 Corinthians 13:4-7

Allah has promised to Believers, men and women, Gardens under which rivers flow, to dwell therein, and beautiful mansions in Gardens of everlasting bliss. 9, Repentance, 72

And (there will be) Companions with beautiful, big, and lustrous eyes, - Like unto Pearls well-guarded.

And made them virgin - pure (and undefiled), - Beloved (by nature), equal in age, - For the Companions of the Right Hand.

Round about them will (serve) youths of perpetual (freshness)…

56 The Inevitable Event, 22-23; 36-38,17

Dark side of love

Lusting for sex at pagan shrines has made you unfaithful to me, your God. Hosea 4:12

Don't be controlled by your body. Kill every desire for the wrong kind of sex. Colossians 3:5

If you are guided by the Spirit, you won't obey your selfish desires. The Spirit and your desires are enemies of each other. People's desires make them give in to immoral ways, filthy thoughts, and shameful deeds.
(Paul to the) Galatians 5:16-17,19

Relativity of earthly love

Fair in the eyes of men is the love of things they covet: women…heaped-up hoards of gold and silver…Such are the possessions of this world's life; but in nearness to Allah is the best of the goals… 3 Al-'Imran,14

"The wife of the (great) Aziz is seeking to seduce her slave (Joseph ed.) from his (true) self: Truly he has inspired her with violent love: we see she is evidently going astray." 12 Yusuf, 30

Marriage - flesh of my flesh

...and the man exclaimed. "Here is someone like me! She is part of my body, my own flesh and bones. She came from me, a man... That's why a man will leave his own father and mother. He marries a woman, and the two of them become like one person. Genesis 2: 23-24

A truly good wife is the most precious treasure a man can find! Her husband depends on her, and she never lets him down. She is good to him every day of her life… Proverbs 31:10-12

Marriage - created in pairs

O mankind! reverence your Guardian-Lord, Who created you from a single person, created, of like nature, his mate, and from them twain scattered (like seeds) countless men and women.
4 The Women,1

He has made for you pairs from among yourselves…
42 The Consultation,11

And Allah has made for you mates (and companions) of your own nature, … 16 The Bee, 72

It is true that anyone who desires to be a church official wants to be something worthwhile. That's why officials must have a good reputation and be faithful in marriage. [1 Timothy 3:1]
Well, having your own husband or wife should keep you from doing something immoral. Husbands and wives should be fair with each other about having sex. A wife belongs to her husband instead of to herself, and a husband belongs to his wife instead of to himself. So don't refuse sex to each other, unless you agree not to have sex for a little while, in order to spend time in prayer. Here is my advice for people who have never been married and for widows. You should stay single, just as I am. But if you don't have enough self-control, then go ahead and get married. [1 Corinthians 7:2-5, 8-9]

And among His Signs is this, that He created for you mates from among yourselves, that you may dwell in tranquility with them, and He has put love and mercy between your (hearts). [30 The Roman Empire, 21]

Marry those among you who are single…if they are in poverty, Allah will give them means out of His grace. [24 the Light,32]

We sent…Jesus the son of Mary, and bestowed on him the Gospel; and We ordained in the hearts of those who followed him compassion and mercy. But the Monasticism which they invented for themselves, We did not prescribe for them… [57 The Iron, 27]

A woman's head to be covered

A woman should wear something on her head. It is a disgrace for a woman to shave her head or cut her hair. But if she refuses to wear something on her head, let her cut off her hair. Men were created to be like God and to bring honour to God. This means that a man should

Chastity and clothing

O you Children of Adam! We have bestowed raiment upon you to cover your shame, as well as to be an adornment to you. But the raiment of righteousness, - that is the best.
[7 The Heights, 26]

not wear anything on his head. Women were created to bring honour to men. It was the woman who was made from a man, and not the man who was made from a woman. He wasn't created for her. She was created for him. And so, because of this…a woman ought to wear something on her head…
1 Corinthians 11:6-9

Women must not pretend to be men/ wear men's clothing. The LORD your God is disgusted with people who do that. Deuteronomy 22:5

Your beauty should not come from outward adornment, such as braided hair and the wearing of gold jewelry and fine clothes. Instead, it should be that of your inner self, the unfading beauty of a gentle and quiet spirit, which is of great worth in God's sight. 1 Peter 3:3-4
Don't depend on things like fancy hairstyles or gold jeweler or expensive clothes to make you look beautiful. Be beautiful in your heart by being gentle and quiet. This kind of beauty will last, and God considers it very special.
1 Timothy 2: 9-10

Say to the believing men that they should lower their gaze and guard their modesty; that will make for greater purity for them… Allah is well acquainted with all that they do.

And say to the believing women that they should lower their gaze and guard their modesty; that they should not display their beauty and ornaments except what (must ordinarily) appear thereof; that they should draw their veils over their bosoms and not display their beauty except to their husbands, their fathers, their husbands' fathers…and that they should not strike their feet in order to draw attention to their hidden ornaments.
24 The Light, 30-31

O Prophet! Tell your wives and daughters, and the believing women, that they should cast their outer garments over their persons (when abroad): that is most convenient, that they should be known (as such) and not molested.
33 The Confederates, 59

Motherhood

The man Adam named his wife Eve, because she would become the mother of all the living. Genesis 3:20

Then the LORD said to the woman, "You will suffer terribly when you give birth. But you will still desire your husband, and he will rule over you." Genesis 3:16

…and the man Adam wasn't the one who was fooled. It was the woman Eve who was completely fooled and sinned. But women will be saved by having children.
1 Timothy 2:14-15

When Elizabeth heard Mary's greeting, her baby moved within her. The Holy Spirit came upon Elizabeth. Then in a loud voice she said to Mary: God has blessed you more than any other woman! He has also blessed the child you will have.
Luke 1:41-42

(A truly good mother ed.)…takes good care of her family and is never lazy. Her children praise her, and with great pride her husband says, "There are many good women, but you are the best!" Proverbs 31: 27-29

Motherhood

Read! (or Proclaim!) in the name of your Lord and Cherisher, Who created man, out of a (mere) clot of congealed blood. 96 Read, 1-2
It is He Who brought you forth from the wombs of your mothers when you knew nothing. 16 The Bee, 78
He makes you, in the wombs of your mothers, in stages, one after another, in three veils of darkness.
39 The Crowds, 6

And no female conceives, or lays down (her load), but with His knowledge. 35 The Originator of Creation, 11
Allah knows what every female (womb) bears, by how much the wombs fall short (of their time or number) or do exceed.
Every single thing is before His sight, in (due) proportion.
13 The Thunder 8

We have enjoined on man kindness to his parents: in pain did his mother bear him, and in pain did she give him birth.
46 The Winding Sand-tracts, 15

And Allah has made for you mates (and companions) of your own nature, and made for you, out of them, sons and daughters and grandchildren… 16 The Bee,72

Monogamy preferable

After David moved to Jerusalem, he married more women... 1 Chronicles 14:3

Suppose two brothers are living on the same property, when one of them dies without having a son to carry on his name...his widow...must marry her late husband's brother... Deuteronomy 25:5

And the king must not have a lot of wives - they might tempt him to be unfaithful to the LORD.
Deuteronomy 17:17

Well, having your own husband or wife should keep you from doing something immoral.
(Paul to the) 1 Corinthians 7:2

That's why officials must have a good reputation and be faithful (monogamous ed.) in marriage.
(Paul to) 1 Timothy 3:2

Polygamy, only if...

If you fear that you shall not be able to deal justly with the orphans, marry women of your choice, two or three, or four; but if you fear you shall not be able to deal justly (with them) then only one...to prevent you from doing injustice.
4 The Women, 3

You are never able to be fair and just as between women, even if it is your ardent desire. 4 The Women, 129

Sex outside marriage

Be faithful in marriage. Exodus 20:14

If any of you men have sex with another man's wife, both you and the woman will be put to death.
Leviticus 20:10

Suppose a man starts hating his wife soon after they are married. He might tell ugly lies about her, and say, "I married this woman, but

Sex outside marriage

Let those who find not the wherewithal for marriage keep themselves chaste... 24 The Light, 33

Nor come near to adultery: for it is a shameful (deed) and an evil, opening the road (to other evils).
17 The Israelites, 32

The woman and the man guilty of adultery or fornication, - flog each

when we slept together, I found out she wasn't a virgin." If this happens, the bride's father and mother must go to the town gate to show the town leaders the proof that the woman was a virgin… if the man was right and there is no proof that his bride was a virgin, the men of the town will take the woman to the door of her father's house and stone her to death.

Deuteronomy 22:13-15, 20-21

But I tell you that if you look at another woman and want her, you are already unfaithful in your thoughts. Matthew 5: 28

The Pharisees and the teachers of the Law of Moses brought in a woman who had been caught in bed with a man who wasn't her husband….they said (to Jesus ed.), "Teacher, this woman was caught sleeping with a man who isn't her husband. The Law of Moses teaches that a woman like this should be stoned to death! What do you say?" (Jesus ed.) stood up and said, "If any of you have never sinned, then go ahead and throw the first stone at her!" The people left one by one, beginning with the oldest. Finally, Jesus and the woman were there alone. Jesus…asked her, "Where is

of them with a hundred stripes:

Let no man guilty of adultery or fornication marry any but a woman similarly guilty, or an Unbeliever.

And those who launch a charge against chaste women, and produce not four witnesses (to support their allegations), - flog them with eighty stripes; and reject their evidence ever after: for such men are wicked transgressors.

Those who slander chaste women, indiscreet but believing, are cursed in this life and in the Hereafter: for them is a grievous Penalty.

24 The Light, 2-4, 23

everyone? Isn't there anyone left to accuse you?" "No sir," the woman answered. Then Jesus told her, "I am not going to accuse you either.
John 8: 3-11

Divorce

Suppose a woman was divorced by her first husband because he found something disgraceful about her. He wrote out divorce papers, gave them to her, and sent her away. Deuteronomy 24: 1-4

Some Pharisees wanted to test Jesus. They came up to him and asked, "Is it right for a man to divorce his wife for just any reason?"
Jesus answered, "Don't you know that in the beginning the Creator made a man and a woman? That's why a man leaves his father and mother and gets married. He becomes like one person with his wife. Then they are no longer two people, but one. And no one should separate a couple that God has joined together. I say that if your wife has not committed some terrible sexual sin, you must not divorce her to marry someone else. If you do, you are unfaithful."
Matthew 19:3-9

I instruct married couples to stay together, and this is exactly what the

A serious breach

Allah has indeed heard (and accepted) the statement of the woman who pleads with you concerning her husband and carries her complaint (in prayer) to Allah and Allah (always) hears the arguments between both sides among you. 58 The Woman who Pleads, 1
If you fear a breach between them…appoint(two) arbiters, one from his family, and the other from hers; if they wish for peace, Allah will cause their reconciliation…
4 The Women, 35

Divorced women shall wait concerning themselves for three monthly periods. Nor is it lawful for them to hide what Allah has created in their wombs… And their husbands have the better right to take them back in that period, if they wish for reconciliation.
2 The Heifer, 228

When you divorce women…do not turn them out of their houses…so give them a present. and set them

Lord himself taught. A wife who leaves her husband should either stay single or go back to her husband. And a husband should not leave his wife. 1 Corinthians 7:10-11

It is a terrible sin for a man to divorce his wife and marry another woman. It is also a terrible sin for a man to marry a divorced woman. Luke 16:18

A wife should stay married to her husband until he dies. 1 Corinthians 7:39

free in a handsome manner. 65 The Divorce, 1; 33 The Confederates, 49

For divorced women maintenance (should be provided) on a reasonable (scale). This is a duty on the righteous.

When you divorce women... do not prevent them from marrying... 2 The Heifer, 241, 232

Men and women as angels

When God raises people to life, they won't marry.

They will be like the angels in heaven. Matthew 22:30

Then I saw New Jerusalem, that holy city, coming down from God in heaven. It was like a bride dressed in her wedding gown and ready to meet her husband. Revelation 21: 2

Men and women in paradise

If any do deeds of righteousness, be they male or female - and have faith, they will enter Heaven... 4 The Women,124

Allah has promised to Believers, men and women, Gardens under which rivers flow, to dwell therein...Gardens of everlasting bliss. 9 Repentance, 72

You enter the Garden, you and your wives, in (beauty and) rejoicing. 43 The Gold Adornments, 70

xiii. Inspiring Women in Bible and Qur'an

Intermezzo by Martha Frederiks

As a child I loved to make show-boxes. Fabricated out of a plain carton shoe-box, the outside looks somewhat boring. But to those who take the trouble to peer inside, suddenly a colorful and surprising world opens up and the viewer suddenly meets e.g. hobbits in lush greens rubbing shoulders with fairies amidst beautiful flowers.
The image of a show-box comes to mind when reflecting on women in the Qur'an. For though there are many Qur'anic verses that deal with the rights and obligations of women, narratives that put women in the spotlight are rare. Mary, the mother of Jesus is the only woman mentioned by name in the Qur'an. All other women seem at best minor actors, and at worst just a reference in passing - in stories about men. Thus, the feminist critique that women tend to be written out of history, applies not only to the Bible but also – and possibly even more so - to the Qur'an. Qur'anic narratives indeed tell hís-story rather than hér-story.
But whosoever takes the trouble to look beyond the scarce references in the Qur'an, can unearth a wealth of colorful, entertaining and inspiring stories about women. A perceptive reader for example, with some knowledge of the Judeo-Christian traditions, needs no more than the mere hint [14 Ibrahim,37] to uncover the inferred tale of Hagar and Ishmael being abandoned in the desert. Likewise, that reader might recognize [2 The Heifer,158] another reference to the Hagar story, the tale of her desperate search for water and God's miraculous intervention on behalf of this discarded woman. According to the Islamic tradition Mother Hajar is one of the most exemplary persons of faith.

Her active search to change her situation, combined with her absolute trust in God (*takwa*), makes her a model for all believers. And her life predicaments are to this very day remembered during the pilgrimage in the rite of *sa'y*, when pilgrims run seven times between the hills of Safa and Marwah, imitating Hagar's search for water.

Not all stories about women in Bible and Qur'an however need such detection skills. Several women feature more or less prominently in stories, though they are solely referred to by their function. This holds for the illustrious queen of Saba or Sheba in the Qur´an, [27,The Ants,20-44, 1 Kings 10:1-13, 2 Chron. 9:1-12] known in Islamic tradition as Bilqis, and Zulaikha. It holds for the woman who tried to seduce the prophet Joseph. [Gen. 39:1-20 and 12,Yusuf, 21-34] These two women are key actors in the stories of Joseph and Solomon respectively. Both ladies prove to be strong women: beautiful, powerful and not easily disposed of!

Yet, the Islamic tales are not a mere repetition of Judeo-Christian stories. The crux and details of stories often differ; at times the Biblical stories are more elaborate, at times the Islamic traditions give more details. The Qur'anic story of the Egyptian woman, who according to Bible and Qur'an, saved baby Moses from the Nile [Ex. 2:5-7] and [28,The Narration,7] does not end with her rescue of Moses. Known in the later tradition as Asiya, Qur'an commentators identify her with the 'wife of Pharaoh', who is set as an example to all believers. The verse:

"O my Lord! build for me, in nearness to You, a mansion in the Garden, and save me from Pharaoh and his doings, and save me from those that do wrong". [66,The Holding,11]

refers to the story that Asiya later in her life was martyred for her faith. Tradition tells that when she spoke out against the wicked and idolatrous actions of her husband, the Pharaoh, he had her executed. But instead of being afraid, Asiya persevered in her faith (*sabr*) and in the hour of her death spoke only about her yearning to dwell in God's presence.

Thus Asiya, like several other women, becomes an example for all believers.
The stories of women that feature in both Bible and Qur'an are not many. But the person who takes the trouble to explore their tales, suddenly finds him- or herself meeting women that can inspire believers and non-believers to this very day.

27. Penal Law - Crime and Punishment

In every society, crimes are committed, usually only by a fraction of the population. In present-day secular states, religion is no longer of direct importance to penal law, although it can have an impact on the basic mentality underlying the law, on certain law-making issues, and, last but not least, on personal and group ethics.
The Bible and the Qur'an were written when the ties between religion and penal law were much more stringent. The laws in the two books define in various ways what is considered an offense, and how it should be punished. Much depends on interpretation. The variety of opinions between the faiths is matched by varieties within them, so that a liberal Muslim can seem closer to a liberal Christian than to a fundamentalist of his own creed. Here, the French expression 'les extremes se touchent' -"the extremes touch each other" seems valid. 'Fundamentalists' or 'Puritans' from each faith emphasize the letter of the law whilst 'Moderates 'or 'Liberals' focus on the historic context making harsh rules obsolete, and concentrate on the underlying mentality that guides moral behavior. Christians and Jews still recognize the Ten Commandments, the basic rules of the Law of Moses. For Christians, the Law is complementary to conversion, valid for prescribing behavior, if not sufficient for salvation. There is, however, quite a variety in how these commandments are interpreted, and how essential they are thought to bc in practice. Differences of opinion circle around questions such as capital punishment, abortion and the rights of homosexuals.

The harshness of the Law of Moses, with its high frequency of the death penalty for all kinds of offences, is mitigated by the 'Great Commandment in the Hebrew Bible':

Stop being angry and don't try to take revenge. I am the LORD, and I command you to love others as much as you love yourself. Leviticus 19:18

For Christians, the words of Jesus are relevant:

"But I am giving you a new command. You must love each other, just as I have loved you." John 13:34

The Qur'an explicitly builds on both the Hebrew Bible and the New Testament. The Law of Moses is still accepted as a source of Islamic law, valid unless specifically abrogated by specific verses in the Qur'an.

"It was We who revealed the Torah (to Moses): therein was guidance and light." 5 The Table Spread, 44

In stressing repentance and forgiveness, the Qur'an also builds upon the Bible. The relationship between the Bible and the Qur'an concerning penal law is therefore complex. It is touched upon here only lightly. In the same superficial way present day legal practices are mentioned, acknowledging that in so doing immense complexity and diversity is compressed into a mere handful of statements.

In all three books, murder is considered a major crime. Jews and Christians must obey the sixth commandment: You shall not murder. The Qur'an underscores the importance of this precept with a Jewish saying that declares the enormous impact of taking and of saving a life. Killing a human being is allowed in the Qur'an only as a punishment for murder or wanton destruction. Murder deserves the death penalty.

It is curious, given the importance of the sixth commandment, to see the death penalty so liberally dealt out in the Hebrew Bible. First and foremost insulting God must be punished by death.

"And warn the others that everyone else who curses me will die in the same way, whether they are Israelites by birth or foreigners living among you." Leviticus 24:16

Such a statement is considered obsolete in modern Jewish and Christian circles as too cruel to be associated with a Living and Loving God.
The phrase "*and slay them wherever you catch them*" 2 The Heifer,191 is often quoted as proof that Muslims are obliged to the kill unbelievers wherever and whenever they are stumbled across. Read as a whole the passage refers to a command valid only in war for civilians in a situation of peace. It is therefore dealt with in the next chapter.
In both books, murder is distinguished from accidental or unintentional killing. The Law of Moses promises those who kill by accident protection from revenge. The Qur'an calls for compensation to the victim's family.
Theft is punished in the Law of Moses by compensation (several times the worth of the stolen goods). In the Qur'an the thief's hand is to be cut off, unless he or she repents. In practice this severe punishment is rare, due to stringent conditions which are hardly ever met. For example, those guilty of theft due to hunger or provoked jealousy are exempt from this punishment.

Sexual transgressions are dealt with harshly in the Law of Moses. Those guilty of adultery, of losing their virginity before marriage and of homosexual behavior receive the death penalty. It is from this punishment that Jesus saves a woman caught in adultery. The Qur'an formulates a much lighter punishment for adulterers: whipping, not stoning. Culprits are allowed to live on and even remarry, although not with an upright believer. In other words social sanctions accompany physical ones. Punishment cannot be without proof, delivered by four witnesses. False witnesses are likewise punished. In practice, the whipping is often symbolic. The Qur'an is less clear about lost virginity before marriage. In certain extreme cases the Law of Moses is called upon by Muslims to legitimize capital punishment for lost virginity, either by the state or next of kin. This is inconsistent with the general approach to capital punishment in the Qur'an, which is reserved for those who themselves kill or create havoc in the land. Harsh words against homosexuals are found in the Hebrew Bible and the Letters of Paul. Death is their penalty. These statements are considered by many Jews and Christians to be abrogated by the Biblical command to love one's neighbor, without regard to his or her sexual behavior. Sexual relations between consenting adults have been removed from penal law. Emphasis now is on the legal protection of the young and weak from any kind of sexual harassment. In this light, the Biblical story of Lot or Lut is interpreted in terms of his attempt to protect his angelic visitors from mass rape; not as a condemnation of homosexual relations as such. Paul is seen, in the historical context, to have opposed homosexual exploitation of the young and weak by Greeks and Hellenized Jews, rather than condemning homosexual love relations between consenting adults. Today, the issue is no longer punishment of homosexual behavior, but giving homosexuals the right to marry.

Unlike the Bible, the Qur'an does not seem to deal with homosexuality in a general way, or mention the punishing homosexual behavior as such. The verse:

If two men among you are guilty of lewdness, punish them both.
4 The Women, 16

is usually translated as referring to two persons, to adultery between a man and woman, rather than just to men.

Most Muslims debating the subject refer to verses taken from the story of the prophet Lut. As described above, that story only relates how Lut tried to protect his angelic guests from the lustful masses. This does not imply a condemnation of homosexual love or sex between consenting adults. The lack of a clear statement in the Qur'an on homosexuality is sometimes compensated for by turning to the Bible, in accordance with advice given in the Qur'an:

"If you were in doubt as to what We have revealed to you, then ask those who have been reading the scriptures before you..." 10 Yunus, 94 Haleem, 2008

Thus, punishing homosexuals in Islamic law is ultimately based on the Law of Moses, and on the statements of Paul, not on the Qur'an. Here again, some Muslims are seen to be striving to be more biblically correct than the adherents of the Bible themselves. In some countries with a Muslim majority, homosexuality is still included in the penal law. In practice, however, the conditions for a conviction are so stringent, (i.e. four witnesses of the deed) that actual punishment of homosexuals takes place only in extreme cases. Liberal Muslims treat homosexuals as human beings who should be treated with respect, even if their sexual practices are considered unnatural.

Child abuse, considered a serious crime today, is not specifically mentioned in any of the books. In the Hebrew Bible sons are admonished not to abuse their parents, rather than the other way round.

"Don't have sex with your own mother. This would disgrace your father." Leviticus 18: 7

Sex of fathers with their daughters is not mentioned in the list of sexual crimes in the Hebrew Bible, although sex with a daughter-in-law and granddaughter is forbidden. The prophet Lut had sex with his two adult daughters, on their initiative it would seem; an incident not related in the Qur'an. A son who has sex with his mother (or another of his father's wives) was to be stoned, as indeed was his mother. Leviticus 20:11 Bad luck for the boy, but striking or even cursing a parent would have had the same outcome for him. Leviticus 20:9

The Qur'an does not mention child-abuse as such, but does prohibit a man to marry his mother or daughters. 4 The Women,23 As sex outside marriage falls under the general prohibition of fornication, this amounts to a veto on abuse by a father of his daughter. Abuse of sons falls under the general prohibition of homosexual acts. Both are to be punished with flogging. [24 The Light, 2]

However very little attention has been paid to child-abuse in Islamic law or literature and practice can and does depart from the intention of the Qur'an. Sometimes the abused children are ordered to acquiesce on the grounds of a misinterpretation of the quote: *Be kind to parents.* [17 The Israelites, 23] Or parents who abuse or mistreat their child escape punishment on the grounds of a farfetched interpretation of the words:

"*No mother shall be treated unfairly on account of her child. Nor father on account of his child…*" [2 The Heifer, 233]
Again the Muslim legal practice sometimes lags behind the Qur'an, whilst on the other hand the Western legal regime is miles ahead of the Laws in the Hebrew Bible. Both in Western and Muslim societies the actual banning of child-abuse is still an uphill struggle.

An Eye for an Eye or Forgiveness?

The Qur'an refers to the principle of limited, controlled punishment formulated in the Hebrew Bible, in terms of 'an eye for an eye a tooth for a tooth'. Excessive punishment is to be avoided, as it leads to uncontrollable spirals of revenge and destruction. However, this rule is overruled by the principle of remorse and forgiveness. In the Hebrew Bible, this principle is instituted in the Great Day of Forgiveness. Jesus speaks of turning the other cheek. The Qur'an states that whoever shows remorse after committing a crime is granted forgiveness by God. In Islamic law, they receive a lighter punishment. As stressed in the Hebrew Bible, the New Testament and in the Qur'an, forgiving is better than revenge.

xiv. The experience of child abuse

To honor the many victims of child abuse in Jewish, Christian and Muslim societies throughout the ages we present here the story in her own words by an anonymous young woman who sought the advice of Khaled Abou El Fadl.

He murdered her soul

After an uncomfortable pause, she tells me (Abou el Fadl ed.) that as a child she learned that love is a service.

"The warmth and love of a parent that you take for granted came to mean the price of my soul.

She senses the anxiety on my face and she says: "Yes, I was sexually molested by my father most of my life." … I learned early on that my body was not my own – it was simply a price to be paid in return for attention and affection. I learned to hate and sacrifice my body and to cower each time in shame. I was locked into a cycle of degradation and bitter self-hate … But who talks about me in your dignified world? Now, I refuse to be a victim … Every waking moment I try to empower myself, to reclaim myself, and to assert the right to say no. "

In Search of Beauty in Islam, p.28-29

Murder

Do not murder. Exodus 20:13

...Death is also the penalty for murder... Leviticus 24:17

Therefore, the human being (*Adam*) was created alone, to teach you that anyone who destroys one soul from the sons of Man (*benei Adam*) is reckoned by scripture as if he destroyed the whole world; and anyone who saves one soul from the sons of Man, is reckoned by scripture as if he had saved the whole world... Mishnah Sanhedrin, 4.5

Who kills one kills humankind

If a man kills a Believer intentionally, his recompense is Hell, to abide therein... and the wrath and the curses of Allah are upon him, and a dreadful penalty is prepared for him. 4 The Women, 93

On that account: We ordained for the Children of Israel that if any one slew a person

- unless it be for murder or for spreading mischief in the land –

it would be as if he slew the whole people:

and if any one saved a life, it would be as if he saved the life of the whole people.

The law of equality is prescribed to you in cases of murder: the free for the free, the slave for the slave, the woman for the woman. But if any remission is made by the brother of the slain, then grant any reasonable demand, and compensate him with handsome gratitude.

5 The Table Spread, 32, 2 The Heifer, 178

Accidental killing

... you must choose three of your towns to be Safe Towns... Then, if

Unintentional killing

Never should a Believer kill a Believer; but (it so happens) by

one of you accidentally kills someone, you can run to a Safe Town and find protection from being put to death. Deuteronomy 19: 2,4

mistake, (compensation is due): if one (so) kills a Believer…he should free a believing slave, and pay compensation to the deceased's family, unless they remit it freely. 4 The Women,92

Compensating theft

If you steal an ox… you must replace it with five oxen... Exodus 22:1

We don't put up with thieves, not even with one who steals for something to eat. And thieves who get caught must pay back seven times what was stolen and lose everything. Proverbs 6:30-31

Cutting off the thief's hands?

As to the thief, male or female, cut off his or her hands: a punishment by way of example, from Allah, for their crime…

But if the thief repents after his crime, and amends his conduct, Allah turns to him in forgiveness; for Allah is Oft-Forgiving, Most Merciful. 5 The Table Spread, 38-39

Adulterers stoned to death

If any of you men have sex with another man's wife, both you and the woman will be put to death, (by stoning ed.). Leviticus 20:10

They kept on asking Jesus about the woman (adulteress). Finally, he (Jesus ed.) stood up and said, "If any of you have never sinned, then go ahead and throw the first stone at her!" John 8. 7,11

Suppose a man starts hating his wife soon after they are married. He might tell ugly lies about her, and say, "I married this woman, but

Adulterers whipped

The woman and the man guilty of adultery or fornication- flog each of them with a hundred stripes: Let not compassion move you in their case, in a matter prescribed by God….

Let no man guilty of adultery or fornication marry any but a woman similarly guilty, or an Unbeliever.

And those who launch a charge against chaste women, and produce not four witnesses… flog them with eighty stripes; and reject their evidence ever after: for such men are

when we slept together, I found out she wasn't a virgin." If this happens, the bride's father and mother must go to the town gate to show the town leaders the proof that the woman was a virgin…if the man was right and there is no proof that his bride was a virgin, the men of the town will take the woman to the door of her father's house and stone her to death. This woman brought evil into your community by sleeping with someone before she got married, and you must get rid of that evil by killing her.

Deuteronomy 22:13-15, 20-21

The Virgin Mary
a narrow escape

Against the background of this legal practice it becomes clear what a narrow escape Mary had, when she became pregnant before marriage.

It explains her fear when the angel told her of her pregnancy, her defense that she had never slept with a man. Joseph, to whom she was engaged had the legal possibility of having her stoned because she was so obviously no longer a virgin. He decided not to accuse her, to let her off quietly.

wicked transgressors- unless they repent thereafter and mend their conduct, for Allah is Oft-Forgiving, Most Merciful. 24 The Light,2-5

"Then Joseph her husband, being a just man, and not wanting to make her a public example, was minded to put her away secretly." Matthew 1:19
It was only when the angel Gabriel reveled to Joseph that she had become pregnant without sex that Joseph could marry her.

Homosexuals
It's disgusting for men to have sex with one another, and those who do will be put to death, just as they deserve. Leviticus 20:13

(Paul about Greco-Romans, Hellenized Jews ed.) God let them follow their own evil desires. Women no longer wanted to have sex in a natural way, and they did things with each other that were not natural. Men behaved in the same way. They stopped wanting to have sex with women and had strong desires for sex with other men. They know God has said that anyone who acts this way deserves to die. But they keep on doing evil things, and they even encourage others to do them.

Romans 1: 26-27,32

Lut to the lustful mass
(We also sent) Lut (as a Messenger): "behold," he said to his people: "Do you do what is shameful though you see (its iniquity)? Would you really approach men in your lusts rather than women?

Of all the creatures in the world, will you approach males, and leave those whom Allah has created for you to be your mates? Nay, you are a people transgressing!..."

27 The Ants, 54-55, 26 The Poets,165-166

An eye for an eye

Personal injuries to others must be dealt with in keeping with the crime- [20]a broken bone for a broken bone, an eye for an eye, or a tooth for a tooth. ...death is the penalty for murder. [22]I am the LORD your God, and I demand equal justice both for you Israelites and for those foreigners who live among you.

Leviticus 24:19-22

A tooth for a tooth

It was We who revealed the Law (to Moses) therein was guidance and light.

We ordained therein for them: "Life for life, eye for eye, nose or nose, ear for ear, tooth for tooth, and wounds equal for equal."

5 The Table Spread, 44-45

Day of Forgiveness /other cheek

The tenth day of the seventh month is the Great Day of Forgiveness.

Leviticus 23:27

You know that you have been taught, "An eye for an eye and a tooth for a tooth."

But I (Jesus ed.) tell you not to try to get even with a person who has done something to you. When someone slaps your right cheek, turn and let that person slap your other cheek·

Matthew 5:38-39

Ask God to bless anyone who curses you, and pray for everyone who is cruel to you. Luke 6:28

Forgiving preferable

But if any one remits the retaliation by way of charity, it is an act of atonement for himself.

5 The Table Spread, 45

The recompense for an injury is an injury equal thereto (in degree): but if a person forgives and makes reconciliation, his reward is due from Allah. 42 The Consultation,40

For Allah blots out sins and forgives again and again. 4 The Women, 43

28. International law, war and peace

This chapter deals with the topic of aggression between different groups, faiths or nations in legal terms; with what is permissible and what is forbidden.

Jihad - the Good Fight

In this context, a misunderstanding must be cleared up about the word *Jihad*. It is often associated with aggressive war and criminal terrorism. Actually, it means quite the opposite. In most instances, *Jihad* has nothing to do with violence. It is based on the root j-h-d and means '*making a great effort to achieve an objective*'. Muhammad is recorded in the Hadith (tradition) to have told his followers after battle:

"You have arrived with an excellent arrival, you have come from the Lesser Jihad to the Greater Jihad - the striving of a servant (of Allah) against his desires."

Thus the peaceful struggle against evil, or the Satan in oneself, the striving for the good against odds, can be considered as the Greater Jihad, a duty for every Muslim. Hadith recorded by Imaam Khateeb al-Baghdaadi in *Taareekh Baghdad*, Hafiz al-Daylami (ra) in *al-Firdaws* and al-Bayhaqi in *al-Zuhd*. *Faydhul Qadeer* vol.4 pg.511 The well-known expression '*al-jihad fi sabil*' or 'Strive *on the way of Allah.*' is for most Muslims not a call for violence, but for effort directed towards the virtues encouraged by God. In the same sense, the Bible calls for fighting the good fight.

As for the use of violence, it is only allowed in carefully determined circumstances. A particular war can be considered just only if it is waged according to the legal principles stipulated in the Qur'an. This Lesser Jihad, *Jihad bis Saif* (striving with arms), is a defensive, limited war.

Historical wars as a context in Bible and Qur'an

Many of the passages on war in Bible and Qur'an should be read in their historical context. Jewish, Christian and Muslim traditions alike are haunted by the humiliating experience of a people driven from home, of followers of a faith maltreated. For the Jews, slavery in Egypt and the deportation to Babylon was the basic experience; for the early Christians it was persecution by the Roman authorities; for Muslims, this primal humiliating experience is the migration from Mecca. For all three religious traditions these remained deeply rooted memories evoking fear and bitterness.

In all three traditions, redress was sought by taking up arms against what was perceived as the incarnation of Evil. Hope was drawn from military success. If the Battle of Jericho for the Promised Land was for Jews a consoling memory, for early Christians it was the promised recapture or resurrection of a (New) Jerusalem; for Muslims it was the conquest of Mecca.

Historical wars in the Hebrew Bible

The Hebrew Bible relates the stories of wars involving the Children of Israel. The heroic tales of Moses and his successor Joshua, who vanquished Jericho, are spun in gruesome and sometimes genocidal detail. The idea that 'all is fair in war' was not a Jewish invention, but a widely practiced way of expelling law from the sphere of warfare. Most contemporary Jews and Christians are unable to relate to such unrestrained violence, especially if the weak - women, children, and animals – are victimized. The idea that God sanctions such mass murder runs counter to their image of God the Creator, the God of Love and Righteousness.

Christians and Jews now perceive the link of Godto mass destruction as highly antiquated.
The same sentiment holds true for the idea expressed in the Book of Deuteronomy that religious differences legitimize total destruction. The notion that God could order the massacre of the elderly, women and children for religious reasons is considered totally outdated.
Other militant passages in the Hebrew Bible lament the downfall of Jerusalem and rejoice at the subsequent downfall of the powers oppressing the Jews, such as Babylon. The emphasis is on confrontation, on 'us versus them', with the enemy defined as the ultimate evil. The identification of Babel, the historical enemy of Israel, with evil as such is echoed in the Qur'an.
During the course of the writing of the Hebrew Bible over many centuries, the image of God developed in a milder direction. War may no longer be as totally destructive as it was at Jericho. After a victory, the defeated population is no longer exterminated, but is forced to labor or deported. God favors the weaker party. He protects David from the superior strength of the giant Goliath. However when David, as anointed king, waged war too readily and too roughly, God punished him. He was forced to cede to his wise son Solomon the honor of building God's temple.

Humanitarian aid for the enemy… the Bible

This development in the direction of mildness is reflected in the humane passages on aiding the enemy.
"If your enemies are hungry, give them something to eat. And if they are thirsty, give them something to drink." Proverbs 25:21 Romans, 12:20

The Revelation of a heavenly war in the name of Christ

However in the last book of the New Testament total warfare reappears on a scale more vast than found in the Hebrew Bible. The war, encompassing the whole universe, was predicted in the Revelation to a Christian named John. It is the only extensive description of war in the New Testament. It is a war to be waged by the heavenly hosts commanded by the war angel

Michael against the icons of evil: the Beast, the False Prophet, the Devil and the Whore of Babylon.

This book was written when the early Christians had much to fear from persecution by the Romans. It is full of understandable bitterness and hatred, but it does contradict the teaching of Jesus. It has inspired Christians over the ages to go to war against whoever was at the time considered as 'the Antichrist', under the banner of the very man who preached love towards the enemy. The heavenly wars of the Last Day are now often understood in metaphorical terms.

The pacifism and tolerance of Christ

In the Gospels, the development towards a milder image of God which started in the Hebrew Bible is continued, but, at the same time, a major leap is made. Jesus seeks to break with confrontational thinking, with the notion of us-versus-them, by turning the other cheek, and loving even the enemy. Jesus himself did not resist being arrested and put to death. He warned that he who lived by the sword would die by it.

Muhammad versus the polytheists of Mecca

The Qur'an contains many verses about Muhammad's historic struggle against the so-called pagans, or unbelievers. The term 'unbeliever' refers to the Quraish, and their allies the Bakr, the most important tribes in Mecca, the town of Muhammad's birth. They were champions of polytheism. They made life extremely difficult for the prophet of monotheism. In the end, Muhammad and the followers of the new faith migrated to Medina. From there, they engaged in armed struggle against the polytheists of Mecca. The first decisive victory of the Muslims at the Battle of Badr in March 624, or Ramadan 2AH, is mentioned in the Qur'an. The sometimes violent conflict between Muhammad and the polytheists of Mecca offers a historical explanation of the term 'unbeliever'. It cannot simply be applied to the 21st century, but must be understood in its historic context. The last also holds for the violent conflict with Jews living in Medina, which was of a political rather than a religious nature.

In the war between Muhammad and the inhabitants of Mecca, peaceful principles also play an important role. In the historical context, this is understandable. After all, Muhammad was fighting his own countrymen, with whom he hoped to settle down peacefully after the war. As a result, refraining from all-out destruction was advisable.
Muhammad and his followers returned on two occasions to their hometown of Mecca, carrying only light arms, as was the custom for pilgrims. At first, they held what would today be called a peaceful sit-in. Muhammad simply demanded to be allowed to pay his reverences to the Ka'aba, an unalienable right for all pilgrims. A compromise was reached, allowing Muhammad to return to visit the sanctuary a year later. Treaties were signed, and only after they had been violated did renewed fighting break out. Muhammad was exhorted to intensify violence step by step. He was urged to grant the opponent a cooling-off period, to try persuasion first, then deterrence and to resort to armed conflict only if these principles had no effect. Once hostilities were resumed, Muhammad was obliged to limit the means of warfare: taking the enemy prisoner rather than totally destroying him, and keeping open options for a peaceful settlement. In the end, Mecca was captured with relatively little bloodshed; those who did not resist were spared. They were not forced to convert to Islam. As it is stated in the Qur'an:

"Let there be no compulsion in religion." 2 The Heifer, 256

Likewise the 'People of the Book', Christians and Jews living in areas conquered by Islam, were not subject to forced conversion or expulsion, but were protected by Muslim rulers in exchange for a special tax.
Thus, out of the historic situation, and what was known about the Bible, Divine inspiration led to a Qur'anic approach to war was developed, which remains relevant today. On the issue of war, one could say that the Qur'an represents a middle ground, between the extremely destructive passages in the Hebrew Bible and Revelation on the one hand, and the pacifism of Christ on the other. This becomes visible as aggressive verses in the Qur'an are typically enveloped in milder statements about repentance and forgiveness.

International law and war/ Jihad

Bible

Fight the good fight
Try your best to please God and to be like him. Be faithful, loving, dependable, and gentle. Fight a good fight for the faith and claim eternal life. 1 Timothy 6:11-12
I have fought well. I have finished the race, and I have been faithful.
2 Timothy 4:7

We live in this world, but we don't...fight our battles with the weapons of this world. Instead, we use God's power that can destroy fortresses. We destroy arguments and ...capture people's thoughts...
2 Corinthians 10:3-5

Qur'an

Greater Jihad – strive for good
To each is a goal to which Allah turns him; then strive together (as in a race) toward all that is good.
2 The Heifer,148

And strive in His cause as you ought to strive, (with sincerity and under discipline). 22 The Pilgrimage,78
Then fight in the cause of Allah...
2 The Heifer, 244

And those who strive in Our (Cause)- We will certainly guide them to Our Paths: For verily Allah is with those who do right.
29 The Spider, 69

Historic wars in the Bible

Moses and Joshua
Moses sent them off to war. The Israelites fought against the Midianites, just as the LORD had commanded Moses. They killed all the men...They also burned down the Midianite towns and villages. Moses became angry with the army commanders and said,

Historic wars in the Qur'an

War against Muhammad
The punishment of those who wage war against Allah and His Messenger, and strive with might and main for mischief through the land is:
execution, or crucifixion, or the cutting off of hands and feet from opposite sides, or exile from the

"I can't believe you let the women live! You must put to death every boy and all the women who have ever had sex. But do not kill the young women who have never had sex. You may keep them for yourselves." Numbers 31: 6-7, 14-15, 17-18
Meanwhile, the people of Jericho had been locking the gates in their town wall because they were afraid of the Israelites. No one could go out or come in.
With my help, you and your army will defeat the king of Jericho and his army, and you will capture the town. Here is how to do it: march slowly around Jericho once a day for six days. But on the seventh day, march slowly around the town seven times while the priests blow their trumpets. Then the priests will blast on their trumpets, and everyone else will shout. The wall will fall down, and your soldiers can go straight in from every side.
The walls of Jericho fell flat. Then the soldiers rushed up the hill, went straight into the town, and captured it. They killed everyone, men and women, young and old…They even killed every cow, sheep, and donkey.
Joshua 6: 1-5, 20-25

land: that is their disgrace in this world, and a heavy punishment is theirs in the Hereafter;
Except for those who repent before they fall into your Power: in that case, know that Allah is Oft-Forgiving, Most Merciful.
5 The Table Spread, 33-34

Allah had helped you at Badr, when you were a contemptible little force; 3 Al-'Imran,123
But if they (polytheists of Mecca ed.) violate their oaths after their covenant, (with Muhammad ed.) and taunt you for your Faith, - you fight the chiefs of unfaith: for their oaths are nothing to them: that thus they may be restrained. Will you not fight people who violated their oaths, plotted to expel the Messenger, (Muhammad ed.), and took the aggressive by being the first (to assault) you? 9 Repentance,12-13
And slay (fight ed.) them wherever you catch them, and turn them out from where they have turned you out. 2 The Heifer,191

King David

David defeated Goliath with a sling and a rock. He killed him without even using a sword. 1 Samuel 17:50 David…captured the city. David made the people…tear down the city walls [with iron picks and axes, and then he put them to work making bricks.[2 Samuel 12: 29, 31]

…David stood up and said: "I wanted to build…a temple, but the LORD has refused to let me build it, because he said I have killed too many people in battle. The LORD said to me, 'Your son Solomon will build my temple, and it will honour me. Solomon will be like a son to me, and I will be like a father to him.'"[1 Chronicles 28: 2, 3, 6]

David and Goliath

...the faithful ones… said: "This day we cannot cope with Goliath and his forces." But those who were convinced that they must meet Allah said: "How oft, by Allah's will, has a small force vanquished a big one? Allah is with those that steadfastly persevere." By Allah's will they routed them; and David slew Goliath.[2 The Heifer, 249,251]

We bestowed Grace…on David…And We made the iron soft for him, (Commanding) "You make coats of mail, balancing rings of chain armor, and you work righteousness; for be sure I see…all that you do."[34 The City of Saba,10-11]

It was We Who taught him the making of coats of mail for your benefit, to guard you from each other's violence: will you then be grateful?[21 The Prophets, 80]

Carried into captivity

Babylonia

King Nebuchadnezzar of Babylonia sent troops to attack Jerusalem soon after Jehoiachin became king. Jehoiachin immediately surrendered…He also led away as prisoners the Jerusalem officials, the military leaders, and the skilled

Driven from home

The evil Babylon

…the evil ones, teaching men magic, and such things as came down at Babylon…[2 The Heifer 102]

Martyrs

Those who have left their homes, or been driven out therefrom, or suffered harm in My Cause, or

workers - ten thousand in all. Only the very poorest people were left in Judah. 2 Kings 24:10,12, 14

Beside the rivers of Babylon we thought about Jerusalem, and we sat down and cried.

Babylon, you are doomed! May the Lord bless everyone who beats your children against the rocks! Psalm 137:1

Religious wars

Whenever you capture towns in the land the LORD your God is giving you, be sure to kill all the people and animals. He has commanded you to completely wipe out the Hittites, the Amorites, the Canaanites, the Perizzites, the Hivites, and the Jebusites. If you allow them to live, they will persuade you to worship their disgusting gods, and you will be unfaithful to the LORD.

Deuteronomy 20:17-18

Children, this is the last hour. You heard that the enemy of Christ would appear at this time, and many of Christ's enemies have already appeared. And a liar is anyone who says that Jesus isn't truly Christ. Anyone who says this is an enemy of Christ and rejects both the Father and the Son. 1 John 2:18,22

fought or been slain,- verily, I will blot out from them their iniquities, and admit them into Gardens with rivers flowing beneath- a reward from the Presence of Allah, and from His Presence is the best of rewards. 3 Al-'Imran 195

Legitimate goals of war against unbelievers

Fight in the cause of Allah those who fight you, but do not transgress limits; for Allah does not love transgressors. And slay them wherever you catch them, and turn them out from where they have turned you out…Such is the reward for those who suppress faith.

But if they cease, Allah is Oft-Forgiving, Most Merciful…but if they cease, let there be no hostility except to those who practise oppression. 2 The Heifer, 190 -193

And why should you not fight in the cause of Allah and of those who, being weak, are ill-treated (and oppressed)? - men, women, and children, whose cry is: "Our Lord! rescue us from this town, whose people are oppressors; and raise for us from You one who will protect;

Revelation of heavenly war

A war broke out in heaven. Michael and his angels were fighting against the dragon…But the dragon lost the battle. Yes, that old snake…is known as the devil and Satan.

Revelation, 12:7-

[9]One of the seven angels…said to me, "I will show you how God will punish that shameless prostitute... The woman was dressed in purple and scarlet robes, and she wore jewelry made of gold, precious stones, and pearls. In her hand she held a gold cup filled with the filthy and nasty things she had done.

and raise for us from You one who will help!" 4 The Women,75

Did not Allah check one set of people by means of another, there would surely have been pulled down monasteries, churches, synagogues, and mosques, in which the name of Allah is commemorated in abundant measure. Allah will certainly aid those who aid His (cause).

22 The Pilgrimage, 40

Means of war limited

Fighting is prescribed for you, and you dislike it.

…do not transgress limits.

2 The Heifer, 216, 190

(But the treaties are) not dissolved with those Pagans with whom you have entered into alliance and who have not subsequently failed you in anything, nor aided any one against you. So fulfill your engagements with them to the end of their term: for Allah loves the righteous. 9

Repentance, 4

If you fear treachery from any group, throw back (their Covenant) to them, (so as to be) on equal terms.

On her forehead a mysterious name was written: I AM THE GREAT CITY OF BABYLON, THE MOTHER OF EVERY IMMORAL AND FILTHY THING ON EARTH.
Revelation 17: 1, 4-5

I also saw the beast and all kings of the earth come together. They fought against the rider on the white horse and against his army. But the beast was captured and so was the false prophet. The beast and the false prophet were thrown alive into a lake of burning sulphur. But the rest of their army was killed by the sword that came from the mouth of the rider on the horse. Then birds stuffed themselves on the dead bodies.
Revelation 19:19-21

Against them make ready your strength to the utmost of your power, including steeds of war, to strike terror into (the hearts of) the enemies… [8The Spoils of War, 58, 60]

If one amongst the Pagans ask you for asylum, grant it to him…and then escort him to where he can be secure. [9 Repentance, 6]
Therefore, when you meet the Unbelievers (in fight), smite at their necks; at length, when you have thoroughly subdued them, bind a bond firmly (on them)…until the war lays down its burdens…thereafter (is the time for) either generosity or ransom.

47 The Prophet, 4

Jesus: love your enemies

You know that you have been taught, "An eye for an eye and a tooth for a tooth." But I (Jesus ed.) tell you not to try to get even with a person who has done something to you. When someone slaps your right cheek, turn and let that person slap your other cheek.
You have heard people say, "Love your neighbors and hate your enemies." But I (Jesus ed.) tell you

War termination

Fight those who do not believe in Allah nor the Last Day, nor hold that forbidden which has been forbidden by Allah and His Messenger, nor acknowledge the Religion of Truth, (even if they are) of the People of the Book, until they pay the Jizya tax ed.) with willing submission, and feel themselves subdued. [9 Repentance, 29]
But if the enemy incline towards peace, you (also) incline towards

to love your enemies and pray for anyone who ill-treats you. Then you will be acting like your Father in heaven." Matthew 5:38-39, 43-45

Jesus replied, "My friend, why are you here?" The men grabbed Jesus and arrested him. One of Jesus' followers pulled out a sword. He struck the servant of the high priest and cut off his ear. But Jesus told him, "Put your sword away. Anyone who lives by fighting will die by fighting. Matthew 26:50-52

If your enemies are hungry, give them something to eat. And if they are thirsty, give them something to drink. Proverbs, 25:21

The Scriptures also say, "If your enemies are hungry, give them something to eat. And if they are thirsty, give them something to drink. Romans 12:20

peace, and trust in Allah...

8 The Spoils of War, 61

It may be that Allah will grant love (and friendship) between you and those whom you (now) hold as enemies. For Allah has power (over all things); And Allah is Oft-Forgiving, Most Merciful.

60 The Woman to be Examined, 7

And fight them until there is no more tumult or oppression, and there prevail justice and faith in Allah; but if they cease, let there be no hostility except to those who practise oppression. 2 The Heifer, 193

God ends war and brings peace

God brings wars to an end all over the world. He breaks the arrows, shatters the spears, and burns the shields. Psalm 46:9

The Lord said, "I will go with you and give you peace." Exodus 33:14

A child has been born for us. His names will be Wonderful Advisor…Mighty God…Prince of Peace… peace will last forever. Isaiah 9:6-7

God blesses those people who make peace. They will be called his children! Matthew 5:9

Allah guides to peace

…and that He will change (their state), after the fear in which they (lived), to one of security and peace: 24 The Light, 55

Allah is He…the Source of Peace…the Preserver of Safety… 59 The Gathering, 23

…Allah calls to the Home of Peace. 10:Yunus,25

…Allah guides all who seek His good pleasure to ways of peace and safety… 5 The Table Spread, 16

For them will be a Home of Peace in the presence of their Lord. 6 The Cattle, 127

xv. War and international law in the Qur'an

Intermezzo by Marlies ter Borg

The roots of international law, now laid down in the United Nations charter, can be traced to Roman thinkers as Cicero. Elements leading to a theory of just and limited war are mainly associated with Christian philosophers such as: Augustine, Thomas Aquinas and Hugo Grotius. From this tradition stems such concepts as:

- *jus ad bellum,* which identifies legitimate reasons for going to war, such as self-defense or aiding others against aggression and oppression,

- *jus in bello*, which establishes what is forbidden during war, such as the killing of civilians and prisoners of war.

A lesser known but equally respectable tradition of thought on international law is present in Islam, beginning with the *Introduction to the Law of Nations* by Muhammad al-Shaybani at the end of the 8th century. These theories of limited and defensive war are based on the basic Qur'anic rules, which determine under which conditions people may take up arms, and what is permissible, what forbidden in war.
Thus, the concept that 'all is fair, all is permissible in war' is rejected in the Qur'an and by Muslim thinkers as it is by Christian and Jewish philosophers. Both traditions can be seen as forerunners of the laws set down in the Geneva Convention and the United Nations Charter.
Of course, in Islam, as among nations with a Christian or Jewish background, these principles are often violated. An unjust war is experienced as a terrible ordeal, or *fitna.* In the Muslim tradition, *fitna* means overwhelming wanton destruction, by foreign forces or in civil war. The word is derived from f*atana*, meaning to grind, to tear apart in

order to test. It refers to a situation of grave imbalance, generated internally, or by friction from the surroundings.

A similar image is found in the Bible. People can be tested and even purified by extreme circumstances, like precious metals in the crucible of life.

For He is like a refiner's fire ...a purifier of silver; He will purify the sons of Levi, and purge them as gold and silver. Malachi 3:2-3

Being the victim of war is everywhere considered a terrible ordeal, (fitna)

Rules of war in the Qur'an

In the Qur'an, war is a destructive process in which men participate reluctantly. It is never holy, sometimes just, but often unjust. Only in a just war fought with limited means are those who lose their life martyrs. A Muslim is not allowed to take up arms, even against unbelievers, without legitimate cause. He should not respond aggressively to every insult. He must exercise patience, trusting God to punish the unbeliever, if not during his life, then after his death.

The initial response to aggression is diplomacy -allowing the enemy time to think and then deterring him from violence by a show of arms.

One must have a very good reason to ultimately take up arms. Even against unbelievers, armed conflict is only permitted if they behave aggressively – if it is they who initiate the violence. Imperialist ambitions or terrorist actions are not sanctified by God. Self defense on the other hand is a legitimate goal of war. Other legitimate goals are helping the oppressed or those who have been driven from their homes; and protecting mosques, synagogues, churches and monasteries.

The Lesser Jihad, *Jihad bis Saif* (striving with arms), a defensive war with limited goals, must be fought with limited means.

According to the *Hadith,* destruction of the landscape and setting fires to towns and villages are strictly forbidden.

War is not directed at a people, but only at those who actually take up arms.

Muhammad is said to have elaborated rules to protect civilians in times of war.

"Do not kill any man far advanced in years, nor a child, a baby, or a woman." Abu Dawud 202 – 275

Suicide terrorism in which innocent civilians are killed is expressly Forbidden; it piles crime upon crime, murder upon suicide.

"...nor kill yourselves...If any do that in rancor and injustice – soon shall We cast them into the Fire:" 4 The Women, 29-30

According to the Qur'an, God grants immunity to members of the enemy-group, who refrain from fighting. Only on the battlefield is killing allowed. Massacre of the enemy is forbidden. As soon as one gains the upper hand on the battlefield, one must take and treat the adversary as a prisoner , to release him after the war.

The Qur'an stipulates rules not only for the start of war, but also for its termination. The enemy's request for peace must be complied with.

Who is the enemy?

It is often believed – on both sides - that an inevitable and unending enmity exists between Muslims on the one hand and Christians and Jews on the other.

In the Bible, no explicit statements can be found concerning Muslims, for the simple reason that Muslims did not exist at the time of writing. There are, however, several harsh passages in the Hebrew Bible on how to deal with people of another faith. In The New Testament, disdainful words are spoken about the followers of the anti-Christ, people who deny that Jesus is the Son of God. In the last book of the Bible, the false prophet is destroyed. Throughout history, this evil false prophet and the antichrist have been identified as Muhammad.

In contrast, Jesus himself is very mild and tolerant towards people of another faith, holding up the Good Samaritan as an example. He shows that it is not as much the professed faith as the good deed that counts. He teaches men to love their enemies.

Pagans and unbelievers

The Qur'an speaks of pagans, of those who praise many gods, of unbelievers as the prime enemy. At this point, it is useful to discuss the term 'unbeliever' in more detail. At first glance, it can be taken to mean simply anyone who is not a Muslim, anyone who does not believe that *'There is no God but God and Muhammad is his prophet';* a sentence not found in the Qur'an.

The term 'Muslim' also has a wider meaning, referring not to followers of a particular faith, but to men and women who follow the right way. It points to the natural moral intuition all men are in principle endowed with. In that sense, all people are or can be Muslim. On the other hand, some people who are Muslim in name stray from God's guidance. They become unbelievers. For the term 'unbeliever' has an ethical dimension. The pre-eminent unbeliever is Satan. He does not deny the existence of God – he even talks to Him – but he is disobedient. He acts contrary to God's just rules. Satan is, therefore, the enemy of man. He leads people, Muslims and non-Muslims alike, into temptation, into behavior that runs counter to their moral intuition.

The People of the Book

Historically speaking, the term 'unbeliever' refers to the polytheists from Mecca, not to the Israelites or Christians. They are called the 'People of the Book', *those to whom We had already given Scripture,* because they received the message of the one God even before Muhammad did. This implies that there is a basic affinity that makes it worthwhile for Muslims to enter into peaceful dialogue with Christians and Jews.

"(Believers), argue only in the best way with the People of the Book, except with those who act unjustly. Say. "We believe in what was revealed to us and what was revealed to you; our God and your God are One." Haleem 29 The Spider,46

According to the Qur'an, the Israelites are God's chosen people.

"O Children of Israel! Call to mind the favor which I bestowed upon you, and that I preferred you to all others for My Message." 2 The Heifer,47

According to the Qur'an Christians have a special relationship with God.

From those, too, who call themselves Christians, We did take a covenant... 5 The Table Spread,14

Christians are closest to Muslims, for they both love Jesus Christ.

... nearest among them in love to the Believers (the Muslims ed.) will you find those who say: "We are Christians" because amongst these are men devoted to learning and men who have renounced the world, and they are not arrogant. And when they listen to the Revelation received by the Messenger (Muhammad ed.), you will see their eyes overflowing with tears, for they recognize the truth... 5 The Table Spread,82

But, the People of the Book can also depart from their own monotheistic path and become unbelievers. The Qur'an joins the great Jewish prophets in their criticism of the Jewish people.

Curses were pronounced on those among the Children of Israel who rejected Faith, by the tongue of David and of Jesus the son of Mary, because they disobeyed and persisted in excesses. 5 The Table Spread,78

However, their rejection of pure monotheism as defined in the Qur'an is no legitimate reason to go to war against the People of the Book. It is only in extreme cases, when Jews or Christians actually start aggression against Muslims that armed resistance against them is allowed. Even then, the Laws limiting war laid down in the Qur'an must be followed.

Promise of Peace

If one dwells excessively on the warlike passages found in the earlier parts of the Hebrew Bible, the end of the New Testament and in the Qur'an, one gets the wrong impression. For in each book, the promise of peace appears repeatedly. This chapter is concluded with famous and much-loved passages on peace, celebrated in three languages:

Hebrew:	Shalom	שָׁלוֹם
Greek:	Irènè	ειρήνη
Arabic:	Salaam	عليكم السلام

Bible

Peace, Shalom

Blessed are the peacemakers: for they shall be called children of God. St.Matthew 5:9

...and they shall beat their swords into plowshares, and their spears into pruninghooks: nation shall not lift up sword against nation, neither shall they learn war anymore. Isaiah 2:4

For unto us a child is born, unto us a son is given, and his name will be called...Prince of Peace. Isaiah,9: 6

Glory to God in the highest and earth peace, goodwill toward men. Luke 2:14

But I (Jesus ed.) say to you, love your enemies, bless those that curse you, do good to those that hate you... Matthew 5:44

Qur'an

Peace, Salaam

But Allah calls to the Home of Peace: 10 Yunus, 25

...Allah guides all who seek His good pleasure to ways of peace and safety. 5 The Table Spread,16

And make not Allah's (name) an excuse...against doing good or acting rightly or making peace between persons. 2 The Heifer, 224

But if the enemy incline toward peace, you (also) incline towards peace... 8 The Spoils of War, 61

It may be that Allah will grant love between you and those whom you hold as enemies.
60 The Woman to be examined, 7

29. Common Values and Virtues

"So strive as in a race in all virtues" 5 The Table Spread, 48

The limits of the law are not sufficient to produce a society that is happy and thriving in a friendly environment. Law must be complemented by ethics. The Hebrew Bible, New Testament and Qur'an are full of ethical advice. This chapter is an attempt to compress some of the central values held in common into a single table. They concern what people throughout the world long for, though often fail to attain. These values, the Books argue, cannot be realized without the utmost effort, and must be taught to the young. They contain the notion that men and women must actively strive towards them, even if total realization is not possible in earthly life. Both acting in contradiction to them, and even by sheer negligence life can become a hell. The books demonstrate a sense of urgency.

The values presented here do not generally contradict human rights; rather they complement them. Whereas human rights provide the legal framework of the good life, ethics provide their contents. In some cases, the values run parallel to or even support the enactment of human rights. For instance, the Qur'an contains the notion that there can be compulsion in religion.

In this chapter, I have, out of necessity, been even more selective than in the previous ones. I omit guidelines that are outdated and concentrate on what is relevant today.

In presenting these common values, I begin where I left off in the last chapter, with Peace-Shalom in Hebrew, Salaam in Arabic. Lasting peace is unattainable without reconciliation and forgiveness. It must be based on tolerance, especially in religious affairs. The Qur'an is explicit about religious tolerance. The dialogue must be performed with beautiful words. In the Hebrew Bible, much wisdom is found on how to conduct a dialogue. Both books urge that those with whom discussion is useless must be passed by in peace.

Peace must also be accompanied by justice. Justice, in its turn, must be tempered by mercy and charity. Strangers and wayfarers are explicitly included in this realm of charity.

Bible and Qur'an stress the importance of using one's wealth and talents to achieve these values. Burying one's talents or wealth is rejected. Of course the relevance of values changes with the socio-cultural context. Some values such as hygiene are so obvious today, shared by believers and non believers alike, that its religious origin is forgotten.

Thus Allah 'loves *those who keep themselves pure and clean.*' [3 Al-'Imran,76]
Washing has to do with honoring. Thus Jesus *"began washing his disciples' feet and drying them with the towel he was wearing."* [*CEV* John 13:5]
Other contemporary values, of great importance in the crowded, technologically advanced societies of today, were hardly relevant in the cultures in which the Books were written. Environmental concern is an obvious example. Although the vulnerability of nature was not an issue at the time, today's environmentalists can find unexpected inspiration in certain Bible and Qur'an passages. The stories of the creation and the great flood, told in both Books, can be seen as reminders of the wonder of nature and of its vulnerability. Other passages relevant to environmental concerns are quoted below.

Certain values pertain to the character of individuals. In the Qur'an and the Bible being successful or wealthy is of less importance than being truthful, just, steadfast and kind. As Proverbs argues, kindness should be shown to people and to animals. Tradition has it that Muhammad criticized his wife Aisha for being cruel to her camel.

And, last but certainly not least, the Books value a family life in which parents are honored and children are a source of wealth and joy.

Peace, Shalom

Blessed are the peacemakers: for they shall be called children of God. St.Matthew 5:9

...and they shall beat their swords into plowshares, and their spears into pruninghooks: nation shall not lift up sword against nation, neither shall they learn war anymore. Isaiah 2:4

Peace, Salaam

But Allah calls to the Home of Peace: 10 Yunus, 25

...Allah guides all who seek His good pleasure to ways of peace and safety. 5 The Table Spread,16

But if the enemy incline toward peace, you (also) incline towards peace... 8 The Spoils of War, 61

Love and forgiveness

Thou shalt not hate thy brother in thine heart. Thou shalt not avenge, nor bear any grudge... but thou shalt love thy neighbour as thyself:.. Leviticus 19:17-18

And forgive us our debts, as we forgive our debtors. St. Matthew 6:12

But I say unto you, That ye resist not evil: but whosoever shall smite thee on thy right cheek, turn to him the other also. St.Matthew 5:39

Love your enemies, do good to them which hate you. St.Luke 6: 27

Forgiveness and reconciliation

And He is the Oft-Forgiving, Most Merciful. Beginning of very sura except 9

The recompense for an injury is an injury equal thereto (in degree): but if a person forgives and makes reconciliation, his reward is due from Allah. 42 The Consultation, 40

Nor can Goodness and Evil be equal. Repel (Evil) with what is better: then will he between whom and you was hatred become as it were your friend and intimate!
41 Fussilat, 34

Don't blame the other

Judge not, and ye shall not be judged: condemn not, and ye shall not be condemned: forgive, and ye shall be forgiven:

Tolerance and self-criticism

... let every soul look to what he has sent forth for the morrow
59 The Gathering, 18

...those who repent and make

And why beholdest thou the mote that is in thy brother's eye, but perceivest not the beam that is in thine own eye? Either how canst thou say to thy brother,
"Brother, let me pull out the mote that is in thine eye,"
when thou thyself beholdest not the beam that is in thine own eye? Thou hypocrite, cast out first the beam out of thine own eye, and then shalt thou see clearly to pull out the mote that is in thy brother's eye.
St. Luke 6: 37,41-42

amends and openly declare (the Truth): to them I turn; for I am Oft-Returning, Most Merciful.
2 The Heifer, 160

And when they hear vain talk, they turn away therefrom and say: "To us our deeds, and to you yours; Peace be on you." 28 The Narration, 55
And the servants of (Allah) Most Gracious are those who walk on the earth in humility, and when the ignorant address them, they say: 'Peace!' 25 The Criterion, 63

Pluriformity and dialogue
For all people will walk every one in the name of his god, and we will walk in the name of the LORD our God for ever and ever. Micah 4:5

...the Ethiopians are no less important to me (God ed.) than you are. I brought you out of Egypt, but I also brought the Philistines from Crete and the Arameans from Kir.
CEV, Amos 9:7

But they shall sit every man under his vine and under his fig tree; and none shall make [them] afraid:
Micah 4:4

No compulsion in religion
Let there be no compulsion in religion. 2 The Heifer, 256

Will you then compel mankind, against their will, to believe! No soul can believe, except by the Will of Allah... 10 Yunus, 99-100

Argue only in the best way with the People of the book (Haleem)...
Say, 'We believe in what was revealed to us and in what was revealed to you; our God and your God are one; we are Devoted to Him. 29 The Spider, 46

He that is void of wisdom despiseth his neighbor, but a man of understanding holdeth his peace.
Proverbs 11:12

And whosoever shall not receive you, nor hear your words, when ye depart out of that house or city, shake off the dust of your feet.
Matthew 10:14

Just
Ye shall do no unrighteousness in judgment:..but in righteousness shalt thou judge thy neighbor. Leviticus 19:15

When the righteous are in authority, the people rejoice:
Proverbs 29:2

Merciful and caring
He that hath pity upon the poor lendeth unto the Lord; and that which he hath given will he pay him again. Proverbs 19: 17

Be ye therefore merciful, as your Father also is merciful. St.Luke 6:36

For, brethren, ye have been called unto liberty; only use not liberty for an occasion to the flesh, but by love serve one another. Thou shalt love thy neighbour as thyself.
Galatians 5:13-14

Say: O you that reject Faith! I do not worship that which you worship, nor will you worship that which I worship. To you be your Way, and to me mine.
109 Those Who Reject Faith, 1-3, 6

Righteous
...Allah loves the righteous.
...Allah loves those who judge in equity. 9 Repentance, 45 ; 5 The Table Spread, 42
Stand out firmly for justice, as witnesses to Allah, even as against yourselves, or your parents, or your kin, and whether it be (against) rich or poor: 4 The Women,135

Charitable
Be...regular in charity. 2 The Heifer, 110
And they feed, for the love of Allah, the indigent, the orphan, and the captive – (Saying), "We feed you for the sake of Allah alone: no reward do we desire from you, nor thanks." 76 Time, 8-9

Alms are for the poor and thc needy... for those in bondage and in debt...and for the wayfarer.
9 Repentance, 60

For I was hungred, and ye gave me meat: I was thirsty and ye gave me drink: Naked, and ye clothed me: I was sick and ye visited me: I was in prison and ye came unto me.
St..Matthew, 25:35-36

And strive in His cause as you ought to strive…give regular Charity and hold fast to Allah!
22 The Pilgrimage, 78

Love of strangers

Also thou shalt not oppress a stranger: for ye know the heart of a stranger, seeing ye were strangers in the land of Egypt. Exodus 23: 9

And if a stranger sojourn with thee in your land, ye shall not vex him. But the stranger that dwelleth with you shall be unto you as one born among you, and thou shalt love him as thyself; Leviticus 19:33-34

I was a stranger, and ye took me in.
St.Matthew, 25:35

Respect others, help wayfarers

O mankind! We…made you into nations and tribes, that you may know each other…
49 The Inner Apartments, 13

And render to the kindred their due rights, as (also) to those in want, and to the wayfarer. 17 The Israelites, 26

…To spend of your substance…for the wayfarer… 2 The Heifer, 177

So give what is due to…the wayfarer. 30 The Roman Empire, 38

Use your talents

And so he who had received five talents came and brought five other talents, saying, "Lord, you deliveredst unto me five talents; behold, I have gained beside them five talents more".

His lord said to him, "Well done, thou good and faithful servant:"

He also that had received two talents came and said, "Lord, thou deliveredst unto me two talents:

Trade and spend in God's way

…strive (your utmost) in the Cause of Allah, with your property…
61 Battle Array,11

…gold and silver…spend it in the way of Allah… 9 Repentance, 34

…do not eat up your property among yourselves in vanities, but let there be…trade by mutual good-will… 4 The Women, 29

behold, I have gained two other talents beside them. His lord said unto him,
"Well done, good and faithful servant;" Matthew 25:20-23

It is easier for a camel to go through the eye of a needle, than for a rich man to enter into the kingdom of God. Mark 10:25

Restore the property of the orphans to them (when they reach their age)... 4 The Women, 2

To those who reject Our Signs and treat them with arrogance, no opening will there be of the gates of heaven...
until the camel can pass through the eye of the needle. 7 The Heights, 40

Be truthful, steadfast, righteous
Thou shalt not raise a false report: put not thine hand with the wicked to be an unrighteous witness. Thou shalt not follow a multitude to do evil; Exodus 23:1-2
My heart is fixed, O God, my heart is fixed (steadfast ed.): Psalm 57:7
Therefore, my beloved brethren, be ye steadfast, unmoveable, always abounding in the work of the Lord... 1 Corinthians 15:58
And be ye kind to one another, tenderhearted, forgiving one another...... Ephesians 4:32
A righteous man regardeth the life of his beast: Proverbs 12:10

Be truthful firm and kind
And cover not Truth with falsehood, nor conceal the Truth when you know (what it is).
2 The Heifer, 42

But they never lost heart if they met with disaster in Allah's way, nor did they weaken (in will) nor give in. And Allah loves those who are firm and steadfast. 3 Al-'Imran, 146

...for Allah loves those who are kind. 5 The Table Spread, 13

It behooves you to treat the animals gently. Sahih Muslim 4;2536

Environment

God is Master of the earth

O Lord, how manifold are thy works! in wisdom hast thou made them all: The earth is full of thy riches. Psalm 104:24

...the land is mine, for ye are strangers and sojourners with me. And in all the land of your possession ye shall grant redemption of the land. Leviticus 25:23-24

And I brought you into a plentiful country, to eat its fruit thereof and the goodness thereof; but when ye entered, ye defiled my land and made mine inheritance an abomination. Jeremiah 2:7

The earth mourneth and fadeth away, the world languisheth...The earth also is defiled under the inhabitants therefof; because they have transgressed the laws, changed the ordinance, broken the everlasting covenant. Therefore hath the curse devoured the earth, and they that dwell therein are desolate: therefore the inhabitants of the earth are burned, and few men left.

Isaiah 24: 4-6

But ask the beasts, and they shall teach thee: and they shall teach thee;

Mischief on the earth

Man merely vice-regent

Behold, your Lord said to the angels: "I will create a viceregent on earth." 2 The Heifer,30

And remember how He made you inheritors...and gave you habitations in the land:..so bring to remembrance the benefits from Allah, and refrain from evil and mischief on the earth. 7 The Heights 74

O Children of Adam! wear your beautiful apparel...eat and drink, but do not waste by excess, for Allah does not love the wasters.

7 The Heights, 31

...in order that you may not transgress (due) balance.

5 The Most Gracious, 8

Do not do mischief on the earth, after it has been set in order...

7 The Heights, 56

Mischief has appeared on land and sea because of the meed (reward ed.) that the hands of men have earned, that Allah may give them a taste ot...their deeds.

30 The Roman Empire, 41

and the fowls of the air, and they shall tell thee: Or speak to the earth, and it shall teach thee: and the fishes of the sea shall declare unto thee.
Job 12:7-8

Parents and children

Honour thy father and thy mother... Exodus 20:12, St. Matthew 19: 19

...Jesus...said unto them: "Let the little children come unto me, and forbid them not: for of such is the kingdom of God". St. Mark 10:14

A woman, when she is in travail hath sorrow, because her hour is come; but as soon as she is delivered of the child, she remembereth no more the anguish, for joy that a man (human baby ed.) is born into the world. St.John 16:21

Correct thy son, and... he shall give delight unto thy soul. Proverbs 29:17

A wise son heareth his father's instruction: Proverbs, 13:1

Children's children are the crown of old men... Proverbs 17:6

Family life

It is He Who created you from a single person, and made his mate of like nature, in order that he might dwell with her (in love). When they are united, she bears a light burden and carries it about (unnoticed). When she grows heavy, they both pray to Allah their Lord, (saying): "If You give us a goodly child, we vow we shall (ever) be grateful."
7 The Heights, 189

Kill not your children on a plea of want- We provide sustenance for you and for them. 6 The Cattle, 151

Allah instructed you...concerning the children who are weak and oppressed: that you stand firm for justice to orphans. 4 The Women, 127

...Be good to your parents;
6 The Cattle, 151

...Be kind to parents. 17,The Israelites, 23

xvi. God is the End

Intermezzo by Khaled Abou El Fadl p.141

God is the ultimate, the consummate, the final, and the end. But the magnets of self-indulgence and arrogance hide in our moral fog and lead the compass of our soul astray. Without our inner compass, we are lost in the fog, but our merciful Lord places indicators along the way. The indicators point toward God, leading us back from where we came. The indicators become like signs on the foggy trail, consoling and warning the anxious traveler that the throne of God is where all the roads will eventually converge.

xvii. Who's talking? Intermezzo by Andrew Rippin

It's always an interesting experience getting first year undergraduate students to read some of the Qur'an: they are as close as one can ever get to a 'blank slate' when it comes to dealing with the text without any preconceptions. Frequently they immediately assume that it is Muhammad who is talking in the text and have some difficulty working through how God can be the "We" and the "I" and the "He" all at the same time. The challenges of the text are never so apparent as when one listens to such voices.

Omega

I am the Alpha and the Omega, the Beginning and the End, the First and the Last. Revelation 22:13

He is the First (Alpha) and the Last (Omega)... 57 The Iron, 3

Omega: attributes of God

It was difficult to assign a number to this final chapter. It deals with a theme that runs through all the previous chapters, starting even before the first day of creation and ending with the everlasting peace found in heaven, the ecstatic joy found in paradise. God is Alpha and Omega, the Beginning and the End. The idea of God as the first and the last is common to both Books. That is why the first and last chapters are not signified by numbers but by a letter, the first and the last in the Greek alphabet. Alpha is a tiny chapter, a start, not of God, but of human awareness of his attributes. The reader's sense of the divine is allowed to grow as he peruses the intermittent chapters. Omega as a final chapter summarizes the notions of God/Allah to be found in Bible and Qur'an.

I say explicitly notions. No absolute knowledge of God is available, to me at least. I can only record which aspects and characteristics have been attríbuted to God in Bible and Qur'an. I can also note that there are, between the notions of God and Allah in both books, substantial commonalities.

Unity or Trinity

As to the number, there is a difference of opinion between the Hebrew Bible and the Qur'an on the one hand and the New Testament on the other. In the Hebrew Bible, God is One, although sometimes the plural *Elohim* is used. Using the so-called majestic plural is still formal practice among earthly kings and queens. In the Hebrew Bible, we read: *The Lord our God, the Lord is one*! Deuteronomy 6:4

As the Hebrew Yigdal Hymn sings:

כְּיִחוּדוֹ יָחִיד וְאֵין אֶחָד.
לְאַחְדּוּתוֹ סוֹף אֵין וְגַם נֶעְלָם:

"He is One - and there is no unity like His Oneness - Inscrutable and infinite is His Oneness;"

As expressed in the New Testament

" *...there is no other God but one.* "1 Corinthians 8:4

However, the New Testament also sees the One God as Three.

"...in the name of the Father and of the Son and of the Holy Spirit." Matthew 28:19

Some of the attributes of God devolve upon Jesus. He is the Truth and the Light; He is the Judge, but also the Loving and Forgiving One, the Shepherd and the Savior.

In the Qur'an, the dogma of the Trinity is emphatically opposed and the unity of God is emphasized. The fact that the majestic plural, *We,* is often used when God speaks does not in any way affect His Oneness.

"And your God (Allah) is One God (Allah): there is no god but He..." 2 The Heifer, 163

"They do blaspheme who say: God is one of three in a Trinity: for there is no god except one God (Allah)." 5 The Table Spread, 73

In the Qur'an, Jesus is honored as a special prophet, born of the virgin Mary, who receives the Gospel as Moses had received the Torah. Jesus is not the son of God, for God has no sons. The Qur'an also mentions the spirit proceeding from God and inspiring Jesus. But the spirit is not in itself a divine principle.

"Christ Jesus...was (no more than) a Messenger of Allah, and his Word, which He bestowed on Mary, and a Spirit proceeding from Him. so believe in Allah and His Messengers. Do not say 'Trinity'...For Allah is One God: glory be to Him: (far Exalted is He) above having a son." 4 The Women, 171

In the Qur'an, some of the Divine attributes devolve onto the Holy Books. Thus the Qur'an, but also the Torah and the Gospel, are carriers of light.

The Unity/Trinity issue is the single most important difference between the Qur'an and the Bible. It has thrown its shadow over all the similarities. Over the ages, it has been used to legitimize bloodshed, and today is still a source of animosity.

Children of God

The phrase 'children of Allah' is sometimes used in the West in a figurative sense to refer to Muslims or even to humankind. It is not found in the Qur'an. The concept runs counter to very essence of Allah. The Qur'an speaks emphatically of the Children of Israel when referring to the Jews, or the Children of Adam when referring to humankind. Nowhere is a concession made to the principle that the self-sufficient God has no children.

"Say He is Allah, the One and Only... He begets not, nor is He begotten; And there is none like unto Him." 112 The Purity of Faith, 1, 3-4

In the Bible the expression 'children of God' is used in a figurative sense. Not only Jesus is the son of God. In the Hebrew Bible, this name is given for instance to the King Solomon:

"...I have chosen him to be My son, and I will be his Father. " 1 Chronicles 28: 6

Alternately, the people of Israel are called children of God:

"You are the children of the Lord your God." Deuteronomy 14:1

In the New Testament, this title is given to those who follow Jesus.

"...as many as received Him, to them He gave the right to become children of God, to those who believe in His name: who were born, not of blood, nor of the will of the flesh, nor of the will of man, but of God." John 1:12-13

The status of Jesus is an issue dividing Muslims and Christians fuelling centuries of animosity. This runs counter to the message of Jesus/'Isa. In both books he is a man of peace. Those who foster enmity or go to war to defend the Trinity against Allah, or vice versa – who set the Jesus against 'Isa - are forfeiting the honor of being called – in a metaphoric sense God's children.

"Blessed are the peacemakers, for they shall be called sons (children CEV) of God." Matthew 5:9

God and gender

Another point of debate is the gender of God. In principle, the Absolute cannot be limited by being of one sex rather than another. In practice, the Hebrew Bible, the New Testament and the Qur'an were written in patriarchal societies and in patriarchal languages, and have been translated in ways more or less patriarchal. For instance, the Hebrew word *Yahweh,* literally meaning *I am,* is translated into English as *the Lord*, thus more or less automatically applying the male gender. In the Hebrew Bible, as in the New Testament, God is called the Father.

"...thou, O LORD, art our Father." Isaiah 63:16

"Our Father which art in heaven" Matthew 6:9

In the Qur'an, God is never called the Father, since Allah has no children. However, Allah is specified by the gender neutral pronouns *I* and *We* but also by the pronoun *He*, just as in the Bible. On the other hand, it can been argued that the phrase denoting God at the beginning of nearly every Surah - *Most Gracious, Most Merciful* - is connected to the word womb, since the Arabic reads *Ar-Rahman Ar-Rahim,* and the Arabic word for womb is *Rahim*.

The names or attributes of God

As to God's name, here we see a great variety. The Jewish personal name for God, YHWH, 'I am who I am', translated in the Bible as Lord, is itself of a sacred nature, not to be spoken. In the Hebrew Bible God has many other names, describing various attributes.

The Qur'an speaks of Allah the One God, with many names.

To Him belong the Most Beautiful Names. [59 The Gathering, 24]

There are several lists of the names of Allah in circulation. Muslims speak of the symbolic number of 99. This implies that name 100 is forever unknown to man. God knows all; man certainly does not. He will never know the definitive or complete truth concerning the Divine. This calls for modesty.

God is All-knowing

All knowledge was thought to belong to God, and while God is all-knowing, human beings had to diligently seek this knowledge. Human beings, however, will never be able to attain but a fraction of God's truth, This did not necessarily mean that truth is relative, but it did mean that truth is partial.

Khaled Abou El Fadl, In Search of Beauty in Islam [p. xvii]

It is therefore with sincere modesty that I present below 13 attributes associated with or 'names' given to God in both Books. This selection is neither based on a thorough linguistic study of names used for God in Hebrew, Greek and Arabic, nor on a profound theological- philosophical

approach. My focus is pragmatic, geared to the recognition of similarities in the images of God in the Qur'an and the Bible which could appeal to modern human beings. The focus is not so much on abstract metaphysical attributes concerning the ultimate essence of God, but on His relations to humankind. As in the Jewish Yigdal Hymn I describe13 'names' or attributes of God, but my choice differs. Where there is an overlap with the Yigdal attributes I make thankful use of that beautiful hymn.
The 13 attributes presented here are clusters of a set of related characteristics. Thus, Rock, Fortress and Protector are grouped together, as are Judge and Witness, or Teacher and Guide. Admittedly, the selection of 13 attributes out of 99 names of God is somewhat arbitrary. It does happily span the 'Jewish' number of 13 and the Islam number of 99. And it is reminiscent of a touching passage in the Bible about Abraham and Ishmael.

"And Abraham took Ishmael his son... and circumcised the flesh of their foreskin in the selfsame day, as God had said unto him. Abraham was ninety years old and nine...And Ishmael his son was thirteen years old..."
Genesis 17:23-25

This presentation of attributes of God is not exhaustive, but does shows how very close the images of God are in Bible and Qur'an. Of course, the differences must also be given due consideration and respect. However the work on this chapter has given me the overwhelming impression that the similarities between 'God' and 'Allah' are much greater than animosities between the faiths would lead us to expect.

Everlasting, self-sufficient, incomparable The first attribute refers to a highly abstract cluster of characteristics. God is eternal, everlasting. As the Yigdal hymn sings: "*unbounded by time is His existence.*" He can bestow eternal life on people who accept His guidance. The Qur'an calls God self-sufficient. God is his own source. He is neither created nor begotten. The Bible states that God has no needs.
That idea that God is incomparable is found in both Books. Taken literally, this would mean the end of this chapter. For we humans can only describe

God by comparing him to something limited, something that we know from experience: a rock, a teacher, a light. The names of God/Allah are to be taken in a metaphorical or symbolic sense. However we choose to describe God - however He chooses to describe himself to us - that is only a small part of the story. This is can be taken as a warning against arrogant dogmatism that boasts of knowing the whole Divine truth, and of having the right to judge the beliefs of others.
That having been said, we can now happily proceed to describe the Divine attributes both Books have in common in terms we humans can understand.

Creator To begin at the beginning, God is the Creator of heaven and earth and all that therein is, and of men and women in particular. As such, we have already met Him. He not only created the world; He also sustains it; and explicitly in the Qur'an God continually creates and recreates.

Fortress and safeguard As the Qur'an states, God protects and preserves what He has created. In the Bible, He is compared to a rock on which to build a fortress providing safety. This attribute devolves upon Jesus, who is called the Rock.

Source of peace Peace is an important value in both Books. God is seen as its source. He calls men and women to a home of peace. In the Qur'an, Jesus asks that peace be upon him. The Hebrew Bible speaks of the Prince of Peace. Christians see this as referring to Jesus. God calls those who strive for peace His children.

All-knowing Knowledge and Truth are also important values. God is wise; he sees and hears and knows all. This should make us humans modest.
"He scrutinizes and knows our hidden most secrets - He perceives a matter's outcome at its inception;" Yigdal hymn: verse 10
In the New Testament, Truth devolves upon Jesus.

Teacher and guide God is ready to teach humankind. He guides men and women on the straight path. Speaking to a pastoral people, the Bible calls

God and Jesus the Shepherd. The Qur'an speaks of all three Books as the guide and relates how God teaches Moses, Jesus and Muhammad.

Savior In the Hebrew Bible, God saves from danger in specific historic situations, such as slavery in Egypt. He also saves more generally from sin. In the New Testament, the attribute Savior becomes a name for Jesus.
In the Qur'an, God saves men and women from punishment of hellfire, and lifts them up into the Gardens of Paradise.

Almighty This attribute is associated with absolute kingship as it existed in the Middle East and as it was introduced, for example, into Europe after the Middle Ages. The image of the all-powerful king unites legislative, judicial and military leadership. Today, many kings or queens are constitutional monarchs reigning under the rule of law, with no judicial power and symbolic legislative or military responsibilities at most. In that sense, the image of God as King is somewhat outdated. However, the image of God the Almighty remains.
This image can be consoling for those who suffer, for they can rely on God to save them in the end. However, it also raises questions. Why should a benign and almighty God allow men, women and even innocent children to suffer? How people struggle with this question was shown in chapter 16 on the underserved suffering of Job.

Two faces of God If God is Almighty, how can he allow even the righteous to suffer? In the Bible and the Qur'an, a God of love allows, or even brings, tragedy and destruction upon people. God has two faces. He causes both laughter and tears.
One meaning given to suffering is that of punishing the wrongdoers. This theme runs through this anthology, appearing in the story of Noah and the great flood; the destruction of Sodom in the story of Lot; the plagues sent to Egypt in the story of Moses; and the description of Hell, the fiery abode for those who do wrong.

If on other hand even good people face suffering, that must be a test, leading to a further a refining of character. This suggests that one can come out of a period of suffering as a better, wiser, milder person.
God values highly those who suffer undeservedly. In the Hebrew Bible, Job is the typical example. In the New Testament, it is Jesus, the Son of God, Himself the carrier of divine attributes, who suffers humiliation and death among criminals. His suffering is redemptive not only for himself but for all people (of good will).
The Qur'an rejects the crucifixion; the concept of a suffering God is foreign to the Qur'an. It shows the value of redemptive suffering in other ways. Prophets have always suffered, as has Muhammad.

Judge God is the judge who metes out reward and punishment to the deserving and undeserving both in this world and in the life to come.

"He recompenses man with kindness according to his deed
He places evil on the wicked according to his wickedness;" Yigdal Hymn

Again, in the New Testament, Jesus takes on this divine attribute. He becomes the judge. In the Qur'an, he is witness; God is judge. Here, God the Judge acts as a righteous, even generous merchant, who repays men liberally for the good they have done.

Forgiving This aspect of God, as the righteous and sometimes harsh judge, is softened by the aspect of forgiveness, stressed in all three books. God is forgiving and merciful.

Loving The Hebrew Bible, New Testament and Qur'an all speak of the love of God towards humankind. Sometimes, Divine Love is seen as conditional, with God loving only those who love Him and follow His ways. The Qur'an offers a list of those whom God does and does not love because of their attitude and way of life. However, God is ready to forgive when they mend their ways. Other quotes, notably from the Hebrew Bible and the New Testament, give a picture of God's a priori and even unconditional love.

Light The step from love to light might not seem logical, but it is often made, especially by Mystics. God is Light as He is Love. He created light and can lead men and women out of darkness into light. In the New Testament, Jesus is the Light of the world. In the Qur'an, the light given by God to humankind is a book: the Torah, the Gospel and the Qur'an.

Truth, Light and Love

The truth of God ignites my life. The passion overwhelms me with visions of beauty – of light and enlightenment. The passion chases the shadows away from the niches of my mind. Illuminated by the light of the heavens and the earth, I am like a brilliant star. In this luminous state I discover true love – a light upon light.

Khaled Abou El Fadl *In Search of Beauty in Islam* p.114

Attributes of God/Allah

Bible

Eternal, Incomparable

And God said unto Moses,
"I AM THAT I AM.
...this is my name forever..."
Exodus 3:14-15

Thy throne is established of old; thou art from everlasting. Psalms 93:2

Now unto the King eternal, immortal...be honour and glory for ever and ever. 1 Timothy 1:17

There is none holy as the LORD: for there is none beside thee, neither is there any rock like our God. 1 Samuel 2:2

God...dwelleth not in temples made with hands; Neither is worshipped with men's hands, as though he needed anything...
The Acts 17:24-5

...the gift of God is eternal life through Jesus Christ our Lord.
Romans 6:23

Qur'an

Incomparable, Self-sufficient

He is Allah, the One and Only;
Allah, the Eternal, Absolute;
112 The Purity of Faith,1-2

There is no god but He, - the Living, the Self-subsisting, Eternal.
2 The Heifer,255

Your Lord is Self-Sufficient...
6 The Cattle,133

He is Self-Sufficient! His are all things in the heavens and on earth!
10 Yunus,68

And there is none like unto Him.
112 The Purity of Faith,4

Allah will say: ..."theirs are Gardens, with rivers flowing beneath - their eternal home:" 5 The Table Spread,119

Creator

…the everlasting God, the LORD, the Creator of the ends of the earth, fainteth not, neither is weary… Isaiah 40:28

…thou hast made heaven, he heaven of heavens, with all their host, the earth…the seas and all that is therein, and thou preservest them all; Nehemiah 9:6

All things were made by him; and without him was not anything made that was made. St.John, 1:3

Creator

We created the heavens and the earth and all between them in Six Days, nor did any sense of weariness touch Us. 50 Qaf, 38

He is Allah, the Creator, the Evolver, the Bestower of Forms…
59 The Gathering,24

It is Allah Who originates creation and repeats it. 10 Yunus,34

Praise be to Allah, the Cherisher and Sustainer of the Worlds;
1 The Opening,2

Rock and Fortress

For thou art my rock and my fortress; Psalms 31:3

He is the Rock... Deuteronomy 32:4

The name of the LORD is a strong tower: the righteous runneth unto it, and is safe. Proverbs 18:10

…and that Rock was Christ.
1 Corinthians 10:4

Protector and Guardian

O you people! Adore your Guardian-Lord… 2 The Heifer,21

For my Lord has care and watch over all things. 11 Hud,57

…Allah is the Protector of the Righteous. 45 Bowing the Knee,19

Prince of Peace

Praise the Lord, O Jerusalem; He maketh peace in thy borders…
Psalm 147:12,14

Source of Peace

Allah is…the Source of Peace…
59 The Gathering, 23

Peace!" - a Word… from a Lord, Most Merciful! 36 Ya-Sin, 58

Peace, peace to him that is far off and to him that is near," saith the LORD; Isaiah , 57:19

For unto us a child is born…and his name shall be called…
The Prince of Peace. Isaiah 9:6

Glory to God in the highest, and on earth peace, good will toward men!
St.Luke, 2:14

Now the Lord of peace himself give you peace always by all means.
2 Thessalonians 3:16

Grace be to you, and peace, from God our Father and from the Lord Jesus Christ. Ephesians 1:2

But Allah calls to the Home of Peace: 10 Yunus, 25

For them will be a Home of Peace in the presence of their Lord:
6 The Cattle,127

…Allah guides all who seek His good pleasure to ways of peace and safety… 5 The Table Spread,16

(Jesus said ed.) "So Peace is on me the day I was born, the day that I die, and the day that I shall be raised up to life (again)!" 19 Maryam, 33

Knowing and Wise

The LORD by wisdom hath founded the earth; by understanding hath he established the heavens.
Proverbs 3:19

For the Lord knoweth the way of the righteous: for he knoweth the secrets of the heart. Psalm 1:6; 44:21

for your Father knoweth what things ye have need of, before ye ask him. St.Matthew, 6:8

Talk no more so exceeding proudly; let not arrogancy come out of your

All-knowing, All-Seeing, Wise

For Allah has full knowledge and is acquainted with all things.
4 The Women, 35

…He is Allah…the Wise.
34 The City of Saba, 27

…Allah is the…Truth, that makes all things manifest. 24 The Light, 25

For Allah is well-acquainted with (all) that you do. 59 The Gathering,18

For Allah is He Who hears and sees all things…
Allah knows all. 4 The Women, 58,70

mouth: for the LORD is a God of knowledge, and by him actions are weighed. [1 Samuel 2:3]

Wisdom and knowledge are granted unto thee. [2 Chronicles 1:12]

…the truth is in Jesus.: [Ephesians 4:21] Jesus saith unto him, "I am…the truth… [St. John 14:6]

But Allah knows, and you know not. 2 The Heifer, 216

High above all is Allah…the Truth!...say "O my Lord! advance me in knowledge." [20 Ta-Ha, 114]

Guide, Teacher, Shepherd

I will instruct thee and teach thee in the way which thou shalt go: I will guide thee with mine eye. [Psalm 32:8]

And the LORD shall guide thee continually, and satisfy thy soul in drought…and thou shalt be like a watered garden… [Isaiah 58:11]

Thou shalt guide me with thy counsel, and afterward receive me to glory. [Psalm 73:24]

The Lord is my shepherd; I shall not want. He maketh me to lie down in green pastures: he leadeth me beside the still waters. [Psalm 23:1-2]

…our Lord Jesus, that great shepherd of the sheep… [Hebrews 13:20]

And he (Jesus ed.) began again to teach by the sea side: [St. Mark 4:1]

Guide, teacher

It is Allah Who gives guidance toward Truth.
Allah…guides whom He pleases to a Way that is straight. [10 Yunus, 35,25]

Those who believe, and work righteousness, - their Lord will guide them because of their Faith: beneath them will flow rivers in Gardens of Bliss. [10 Yunus, 9]

His name will be Christ Jesus…And Allah will teach him the Book and Wisdom, the Law and the Gospel, [3] Al-'Imran, 45,48

Ramadhan is the (month) in which was sent down the Qur'an, as a guide to, also clear (Signs) for guidance and judgment (between right and wrong). [2 The Heifer,185]

It is He Who sent down to you… in

For the Holy Ghost shall teach you… what ye ought to say. St. Luke 12:12

truth, the Book, confirming what went before it; and He sent down the Law (of Moses) and the Gospel (of Jesus) before this, as a guide to mankind… 3 Al-'Imran, 3

Savior, Redeemer

As for our redeemer, the LORD of hosts is his name, the Holy One of Israel. Isaiah 47:4

And Moses said unto the people, "Fear ye not, stand still, and see the salvation of the LORD, which he will shew to you to day…for the Egyptians whom ye have seen to day, ye shall see them again no more for ever. Exodus 14:13

Deliver me from all my transgressions;.. Deliver me from my bloodguiltiness, O God, thou God of my salvation… Psalms 39:8; 51:14

For unto you is born to you this day in the city of David a Saviour, which is Christ the Lord. St. Luke 2:11

Him hath God exalted with his right hand to be Prince and Saviour, for to give repentance …and forgiveness of sins. The Acts 5:31

Giver of Salvation

Our Lord! we have indeed believed: forgive us, then, our sins, and save us from the agony of the Fire; 3 Al-'Imran,16

For those who believe and do righteous deeds, will be Gardens, beneath which rivers flow: that is the great Salvation… 85 The Zodiacal Signs,11

Our Lord! Forgive us our sins, blot out… our iniquities…and save us from shame on the Day of Judgment: 3 Al-'Imran,193,194

We send down…in the Qur'an that which is a healing and a mercy to those who believe. 17 The Israelites,82

But Allah will deliver the righteous to their place of salvation: no evil shall touch them, nor shall they grieve. 39 The Crowds,61

Almighty King

...I am the Almighty God; Genesis 17:1

He that dwelleth in the secret place of the most High shall abide under the shadow of the Almighty. Psalm 91:1

The LORD hath prepared his throne in the heavens; and his kingdom ruleth over all. Psalm 103:19

For the kingdom is the LORD's: and he is the governor among the nations. Psalm 22:28

Thy kingdom is an everlasting kingdom, and thy dominion endureth throughout all generations. Psalm 145:13

Thy kingdom come. Thy will be done, as in heaven, so in earth. St. Luke 11:2

Then shall the King say unto them on his right hand 'Come, ye blessed of my Father, inherit the kingdom prepared for you from the foundation of the world. St.Matthew, 25:34

...Great and marvelous are thy works, Lord God Almighty; just and true are thy ways, thou King of saints! Revelation 15:3

All-Powerful

...for Allah is...All-Powerful. 16 The Bee, 70

Nor is Allah to be frustrated by anything whatever in the heavens or on earth: for He is... All-Powerful. 35 The Originator of Creation, 44

Wheresoever you are, Allah will bring you together. For Allah has power over all things. 2 The Heifer,148

Allah creates what He wills; for verily Allah has power over all things. 24 The Light,45

In the name of Allah, The King... of Mankind. 114 Mankind, 2

His Throne extends over the heavens and the earth, and He feels no fatigue in guarding and preserving them for He is the Most High, the Supreme (in glory). 2 The Heifer, 255

Don't you know that to Allah (alone) belongs the dominion of the heavens and the earth? He punishes whom He pleases and He forgives whom He pleases; and Allah has power over all things 5 The Table Spread, 40

Two Faces of God

Light and darkness

For everything there is a season…A time to weep, and a time to laugh, a time to mourn, and a time to dance… Ecclesiastes 3:1, 4

I form the light, and create darkness: I make peace, and create evil; I, the LORD do all these things. Isaiah 45:7

For he maketh sore, and bindeth up: he woundeth, and his hands make whole. Job 5:18

God punishes

…and I will cause it to rain upon the earth…and every living substance that I have made will I destroy from off the face of the earth. Genesis 7:4

Then the LORD rained upon Sodom and upon Gomorrah brimstone and fire from the LORD out of heaven; Genesis 19:24

But if ye will not hearken unto me, and will not do all these commandments…

I will even appoint over you terror,

Two Faces of Allah

Laughter and tears

That it is He Who grants laughter and tears; That it is He Who grants death and life. 53 The Star, 43-44

If Allah touches you with hurt, there is none can remove it but He: if He designs some benefit for you, there is none can keep back His favor. 10 Yunus,107

To Allah belongs the dominion of the heavens and the earth. He gives life and He takes it. 9 Repentance, 116

Allah destroys

But the Deluge overwhelmed them while they (persisted in) sin. 29 The Spider,14

How many towns have We destroyed (for their sins)? Our punishment took them on a sudden by night or while they slept for their afternoon rest. When (thus) Our punishment took them, no cry did they utter but this: "Indeed we did wrong." 7 The Heights, 4-5

Then those who reject faith in the Signs of Allah will suffer the severest penalty, and Allah is

consumption… and cause sorrow of heart: and ye shall sow your seed in vain, for your enemies shall eat it... Leviticus 26:14,16

The Son of man shall send forth his angels, and they shall gather out of his kingdom all things that offend, and them which do iniquity; And shall cast them into a furnace of fire: there shall be wailing and gnashing of teeth. St. Matthew 13:41-42

Exalted in Might, Lord of Retribution. 3 Al-'Imran, 4

…the man who draws on himself the wrath of Allah, and whose abode is in Hell? A woeful refuge! 3 Al-'Imran,162

Suffering, purification by fire

Thou, which hast shewed me great and sore troubles, shalt quicken me again, and shalt bring me up again from the depths of the earth.
Psalm 71:20

But who may abide the day of his coming? and who shall stand when he appeareth? for he is like a refiner's fire… and he shall purify the sons of Levi, and purge them as gold and silver… Malachi 3:2-3

For I reckon that the sufferings of this present time are not worthy to be compared with the glory which shall be revealed in us. Romans 8:18

But and if ye suffer for righteousness' sake, happy are ye… 1 Peter 3:14

Redemptive suffering

…a Day when they will be tried (and tested) over the Fire!
51 The Winds that Scatter,13

…and to be firm and patient, in pain (or suffering) and adversity and throughout all periods of panic. Such are the people of truth, those who fear Allah. 2 The Heifer 177

… We afflicted the nations with suffering and adversity, that they might learn humility.
6 The Cattle 42

To those who leave their homes in the cause of Allah, after suffering oppression - We will assuredly give a goodly home in this world; but truly the reward of the Hereafter will be greater. 16 The Bee,41

The Suffering of Christ

But they cried, saying, "Crucify him, crucify him!" St.Luke 23:21

Though he were a Son, yet learned he obedience by the things which he suffered; And being made perfect, he became the author of eternal salvation unto all them that obey him; Hebrews 5:8-9

...but if, when ye do well, and suffer for it, ye take it patiently, this is acceptable with God. For even hereunto were ye called: because Christ also suffered for us, leaving us an example, that ye should follow his steps: Who his own self bare our sins in his own body on the tree, (cross ed.) that we, being dead to sins, should live unto righteousness: by whose stripes ye were healed. 1 Peter 2:20-21,24

Thou therefore endure hardness as a good soldier of Jesus Christ.

2 Timothy 2:3

Jesus not crucified

That they said (in boast), "We killed Christ Jesus the son of Mary, the Messenger of Allah" - but they did not kill him, nor crucify him...for a certain they did not kill him.

4 The Women,157

Muhammad suffered

Or do you think that you shall enter the Garden (of Bliss) without such (trials) as came to those who passed away before you? They encountered suffering and adversity, and were so shaken in spirit that even the Messenger and those of faith who were with him cried: "When (will come) the help of Allah?" Ah! Verily, the help of Allah is (always) near!

2 The Heifer , 214

Righteous judge

Shall not the Judge of all the earth do right? Genesis 18:25

And he shall judge the world in righteousness, he shall minister judgment to the people in uprightness. Psalm 9:8

Then shall the trees of the wood

Judge in truth

O my Lord! You judge in truth!

21 The Prophets, 112

Allah is never unjust in the least degree: if there is any good (done), He doubles it... 4 The Women, 40

Shall I seek for judge other than

sing out at the presence of the LORD, because he cometh to judge the earth.[1 Chronicles 16:33]

For we must all appear before the judgment seat of Christ... 2 Corinthians 5:10

...the Lord Jesus Christ, who shall judge the quick and the dead at his appearing and his kingdom; 2 Timothy 4:1

Allah? - when He it is Who has sent to you the Book... [6 The Cattle, 114]

Our Lord...will in the end decide the matter between us... in truth and justice. [34 The City of Saba, 26]

But Allah will judge betwixt you on the Day of Judgment. [4 The Women,141]

Forgiving

...for it is a day of atonement, to make an atonement for you before the LORD your God. [Leviticus 23:28]

...O Lord, pardon mine iniquity, for it is great. [Psalms 25:11]

...saith the LORD: for I will forgive their iniquity, and I will remember their sin no more. [Jeremiah 31:4]

To the Lord our God belong mercies and forgivenesses though we have rebelled against him. Daniel 9:9

And forgive us our debts, as we forgive our debtors. [St. Matthew 6:12]

...the Son of man hath power upon earth to forgive sins... [St. Luke 5:24]

Forgiving

You should know that Allah is strict in punishment and that Allah is Oft-Forgiving, Most Merciful. 5 The Table Spread, 98

...I am...He that forgives again and again, to those who repent, believe and do right...[20 Ta-Ha, 82]

For Allah is One that blots out (sins) and forgives... [22 The Pilgrimage, 60]

Be quick in the race for forgiveness from your Lord...those...who restrain anger, and pardon all men;

- for Allah loves those who do good,-who ...pardon (all) men;
- ...and ask Allah for their forgiveness.

3 Al-'Imran,133-34; 24 the Light, 62

God is Love

I love them that love me... Proverbs 8:17

...for God loveth a cheerful giver. 2 Corinthians 9:7

...the Lord...loveth him that followeth after righteousness. Proverbs 15:9

He that loveth not knoweth not God; for God is love. 1 John 4:8

And walk in love, as Christ also hath loved us... Ephesians 5:2

God is love; and he that dwelleth in love dwelleth in God, and God in him.
We love him because he first loved us. 1 John 4:16,19

...and the God of love and peace shall be with you. 2 Corinthians 13:11

Light

...God said, "Let there be light"; and there was light...and God divided the light from the darkness. Genesis 1:3-4

Lo, all these things worketh God

Allah loves

If you do love Allah, Allah will love you... 3 Al-'Imran, 31

...Allah loves those who make themselves pure. 9 Repentance ,108

...Allah loves those who do good.
...Allah loves those who are firm and steadfast.
...Allah does not love those who do wrong. 3 Al-'Imran,76, 134, 146, 57, 31

On those who believe and work deeds of righteousness, (Allah) Most Gracious will bestow Love. 19 Maryam, 96

For my Lord is indeed full of mercy and loving kindness. 11 Hud, 90

...He has put love and mercy between your (hearts): verily in that are Signs for those who reflect. 30 The Roman Empire, 21

Light

Allah is the Light of the heavens and the earth.
The parable of His Light is as if there were a Niche and within it a Lamp...enclosed in Glass: the glass

oftentimes with man, To bring back his soul from the pit, to be enlightened with the light of the living. Job 33:29-30

Thy sun shall no more go down;.. for the Lord shall be thy everlasting light, and the days of thy mourning shall be ended. Isaiah 60:20

For thou art my lamp, O LORD; and the LORD will lighten my darkness. 2 Samuel 22:29

Then spake Jesus again unto them, saying, "I am the light of the world: he that followeth me shall not walk in darkness, but shall have the light of life." St.John, 8:12

That was the true Light, which lighteth every man that cometh into the world. John 1:9

The people which sat in darkness saw a great light; and to them which sat in the region and shadow of death light is sprung up…
St. Matthew 4:16

as it were a brilliant star... well-nigh Luminous, though fire scarce touched it:
Light upon Light! Allah guides whom He will to His Light. 24 The Light, 35

Praise be to Allah, Who…made the Darkness and the Light. 6 The Cattle,1

Allah is the Protector of those who have faith: from the depths of darkness He will lead them forth into light. 2 The Heifer, 257

It was We Who revealed the Law (to Moses): therein was guidance and light. …We sent Jesus the son of Mary, confirming the Law that had come before him: We sent him the Gospel: therein was guidance and light… 5 The Table Spread, 44,46

There has come to you from Our Messenger…a (new) light and a perspicuous Book. 5 The Table Spread,15

But those whose faces will be (lit with) white, - they will be in (the light of) Allah's mercy: therein to dwell (for ever). 3 Al-'Imran,107

Biographical Notes on the Contributors

Dr Marlies ter Borg is a free lance philosopher, public intellectual and and bridgebuilder. She was born in Indonesia on Christmas Eve, 1948, during the Indonesian War of Independence. Brought up in England and Holland, in a pleasant mix of protestant denominations, she does now not profess to a particular faith. She studied philosopy and sociology at Leiden and Amsterdam University, and received a PhD from the Free University of Amsterdam with a thesis on the 'Belief in Progress and Economic Growth'. She worked as parliamentary assistant for the Dutch Green Party; at the Scientific Council for Government Policy (WRR); and at the Free University of Amsterdam as polemologist. During the Cold War she organised bridge building seminars between experts from East and West, resulting in a timely publication with contributions from NATO and Warsaw Treaty experts. After the Cold War she initiated and led the Foundation Building for Peace, which ran a housing project for Russian military families returning home from Eastern Europe.
Marlies ter Borg initiated and compiled the anthology of Qur'an and Bible stories, published online in Dutch, English and Arabic on www.bibleandkoran.net by IKON and Radio Netherlands worldwide in 2007. The site received international attention, attracting over a million visitors in the first month.
For this revised and extended English print publication she collaborated with several experts in the field from Muslim, Christian, Jewish and neutral background: Andrew Rippin, Khaled Abou el Fadl, Babara Stowasser, Mehmet Pacaci, Moch Nur Ichwann, Martha Frederiks, Awraham Soetendorp, Karin Bisschop and Herman Beck.
Het husband works as professor of non-institutionalesed religion at Leiden University. She has two children and two grandchildren.

Karin Bisschop is a Dutch 'new' Muslima, who emigrated to Canada. She co-edited the Dutch Book *Koran en Bijbel in Verhalen*,on which this anthology is based. She initiated and acts as webmaster for www.moslima.nl and www.muslima.ca

Dr. Herman Beck is professor of Religious Studies, specifically Islam, and at present dean of the Faculty of Humanities at the University of Tilburg, the Netherlands. His research focuses on the identity of Muslims in the Netherlands. He held a special professorship at the Islamic State University (Institute Agama Islam Negeri) Sunan Kalijaga (SuKa) at Yogyakarta, Central Java. He was born in 1953 in former Dutch New Guinea, as the son of a Dutch religious Minister and a nurse. He is a professed Christian.

John Esposito John Esposito is University Professor, Professor of Religion and International Affairs and Professor of Islamic Studies at Georgetown University, Washington D.C. He is founding Director of the (Prince Alwaleed) Center for Muslim-Christian Understanding. Esposito was raised a Roman Catholic in an Italian neighborhood in Brooklyn, New York City, and spent a decade in a Catholic monastery.

Khaled Abou El Fadl (born in Kuwait) is a professor of law at the University of California Los Angeles School of Law where he teaches Islamic law, immigration, human rights, international and national security law. He holds degrees from Yale University (B.A.), University of Pennsylvania Law School (J.D.) and Princeton University (M.A./Ph.D.). He also received formal training in Islamic jurisprudence in Egypt and Kuwait. Abou El Fadl is a Muslim.

Reverend Dr. Martha Frederiks is special professor in Missiology at the University of Utrecht the Netherlands, and director of the Interuniversity Institute for Missiology and Oecumenica, IIMO . She was protestant missionary in Gambia, and advisor for the Project for Christian Muslim Relations in Africa (ProCMuRA).

Dr. Moch Nur Ichwan was KNAW (Dutch Royal Academy of Science) Post-Doctoral Fellow 2007-2009 and is now lecturer at the Sunan Kalijaga State Islamic University, Yogyakarta, Indonesia. He is researcher at the Center for the Study of Islam and Social Transformation (CISForm) of the same University and director of SAMHA Institute for the Study of Religion, Society and Human Rights, Yogyakarta. His current research is on "Ulama and Re-islamisation of the Public Sphere in Indonesia" and "Politics of Shari`atization in Aceh". He is a professed Muslim.

Ruud Lubbers, a Christian Democrat from a Roman Catholic background, was Prime Minister of the Netherlands for more than a decade and United Nations High Commissioner for Refugees. He is co-founder with Michael Gorbachev of the Earth Charter. He was professor at the Dutch Universities of Tilburg and Rotterdam, and is honorary doctor of Georgetown University, Washington D.C.

Dr. Mehmet Pacaci Dr. Mehmet Pacaci is professor at Ankara University Turkey. His specialty is Tafsir or interpretation of the Qur'an. His Ph.D is on comparative eschatology - exploring the synergies and distinctions amidst Muslim, Jewish and Christian Holy Scriptures on eschatology. He is specifically interested in hermeneutical problems of interpreting and understanding the Qur'an. Historical setting of the Qur'an, pre-Islamic Arabian and Semitic culture as a background of the Qur'anic message, modern approaches in the commentary of the Qur'an in comparison to classical understanding of Islam are among his interests. He is currently attached to the Embassy of Turkey in Washington D.C., visiting scholar at George Mason University Ali Vural Ak Center for Islamic Studies and Scholar in Residence, the Wesley Theological Seminary, Washington D.C.

Andrew Rippin is professor of History, and specialist in Islamic Studies with an interest in the Qur'an and the history of its interpretation, at the University of Victoria, British Columbia, Canada. He is fellow of the Royal Society of Canada.

Awraham Soetendorp was rabbi of the Reformed (Liberal) Jewish Community of The Hague, and rabbi of the Union of Dutch Reformed Jewish Communities. Born in 1943 in Amsterdam, the Netherlands, Rabbi Soetendorp survived as a "hidden child". After the war he found his parents and the family lived in Israel from 1948 until 1953. Rabbi Soetendorp has been active in a wide variety of progressive, humanitarian, and interfaith organizations and meetings including the Anne Frank Foundation, the World Economic Forum Annual Meeting, the World Council of Religious Leaders, the Earth Charter, 'Water for Life' and the Global Forum of Spiritual and Parliamentary Leaders. He is President of the Jacob Soetendorp Institute of Human Values.

Dr Barbara Freyer Stowasser is Sultanate of Oman Professor in Arabic and Islamic Literature at Georgetown University, Washington D.C. United States of America. She studied at UCLA and Ankara and gained a PhD from the University of Münster, Germany. She was the 34th president of the Middle East Studies Association.
At present, Dr. Stowasser is working on a book on Gender Discourses in the Tafsir and Fatwa Literatures, a textbook on the Islamic Tafsir, and a book on Islam and Time.

Acknowledgements

This book is like a little medieval cathedral. Many people worked to build it, each providing their specific contribution. Some of them are named and thanked below. Many receive no mention. Some are unknown even to me. These include all those who have, diligently and without any ulterior motive, added to the expanding sea of knowledge on internet, those pieces of text and information without which this project would have been impossible.

CreateSpace
First I would like to thank the team at CreateSpace,who printed this book and designed the outside cover, for their enthusiasm, help and personal attention. They made the process formally designated as 'self-publishing' into what seemed like interactive publishing. CreateSpace's combination of state of the art print on demand technology, with excellent management, responsiveness to the authors needs, and personal attention, are a wonder in the world of publishing. CreateSpace applies the saying 'for the people and by the people' to books; placing the author at the center of the publishing proces, demanding only the limited, non-exclusive right to print, while leaving the author in full possession of his or her rights. By saving money with technology and good organisation, CreateSpace enables the author to gain a generous return on his or her relatively small initial investment. Most important however is that the author stays in control, with CreateSpace only offering a variety of services from which the author can take his or her pick.
I would also like to thank Burke Gerstenschlager at Palgrave Macmillan, who sollicited two excellent peer reviews mentioned elsewhere in this book and led me through the mazes of academic publishing, to an enthusiastic board decision. Unfortunately the cooperation stranded on the cliffs of legal problems, due to the particular nature of this anthology as compared with standard contracts. My gratitude also goes to the two

anonymous reviewers, who wrote such kind and complimentary words, whilst supplying useful and detailed criticism. One wrote:

"One should appreciate a balanced and unbiased language and content of introduction parts for each topic. The passages from the either of the Holy Scriptures are selected carefully both to provide a proper content of them and to preserve neutrality over them."

The other commented: "*The academic world will be indebted to the author for this project. It is long overdue.*"

The Dutch book and website

This English anthology is an extended version of a Dutch book *Koran en Bijbel in Verhalen,* published in 2007. Here the contribution of Karin Bisschop was the most substantial. Her role as sparring partner ensured the high degree of non-partiality of the book, which was continued into the English version.

I would have liked to thank again the publishing and PR team at Unieboek | Het Spectrum Publishers, The Netherlands. Many thanks go to the IKON, (the Ecumenical Broadcasting Company of the Netherlands) who dared to put this anthology online in 2007 together with the full Bible and full Qur'an text; especially Marloes Keller, Peter Dekker, Mohamed el Aissati, Bas Buesink, Mirjam Nieboer, Annemiek Schrijver en Martin Fröberg.

I am likewise indebted to the management and editorial staff of Radio Netherlands Worldwide for bringing this initiative into the world by translating and publishing the anthology online in English and Arabic. An important and generous initiative.

Expert advice and moral support

One can debate what is of greater importance when compiling a novel anthology like this one: expert advice or moral support. I received plenty of both from several quarters. For the Dutch beginnings it was offered by Imam Muhammad Tahier and the theologian Eduard Verhoef. Their encouragement at an early stage was a great help. During the many

presentations I gave on a variety of themes in the anthology I learned a great deal from the discussions. Several experts took the trouble to review and advise on parts of the book. Cenay Senak gave me valuable feedback right at the start of the project. Memorable was her view on the afterlife, hell being rather thinly populated in her view. Gurkan Celik and Iris Creemers invited me to present the story of Mary just before Christmas at the interfaith Dialoog Academie which they lead, and Gurkan later gave valuable comments on Common Values and Virtues. [ch. 29] Reverend theologian Dr Antje van der Hoek, looked especially at the chapter on women, pointing to relevant passages from the book of Proverbs in the Bible. She organized an interfaith evening with Christians and Muslims which we all thoroughly enjoyed. Reverend Katrijne Bezemer, historian and theologian, allowed me to present my case to members of her congregation, and gave me both encouragement and critical comments on Job [ch. 16] and Jona [ch. 7] and the position of women. [ch.26]
Inspiring was the feedback I received on many other occasions. Memorable was the evening at a home for elderly nuns and priests at which I was honored to meet bishop Muskens. Equally inspiring was the weekend at the Lioba convent with Dutch Nuns and interfaith friends from Suffolk. It was there that the idea for the title of the book surfaced. I must give special mention to Cynthia Capey from the Suffolk Inter-Faith Resource and Manwar Ali, chief executive of Jimas for their willingness to put the story of Mary online in 2005, before anyone in Holland had practically heard of the project. Rev. Malcolm Weisman, Jewish Minister for Small Communities and Jewish Chaplain to HM Forces, taught me the Hebrew Yigdal Hymn about the thirteen attributes of God. Elahe Mojdehi explained how Persian tradition embroiders forth on the Qur'an, including Zarathushtra as a major Muslim prophet; and why the snake has no legs. With the enthusiastic support of Anja Seaton, the SIFRE group organized a hartwarming book launch in the Mary-le-tour church in Ipswich. Thanks go to Imam Rashed from the London Mosque for his view on the coma from which Jesus Awoke, and the escape op Mary and Jesus to the Far East.

The Qur'an
The Tahrike Tarsile Qur'an publishing Incorporation in New York deserve thanks for their cordial and quick permission to use The Qur'an Translation by Abdullah Yusuf Ali, 24th US Edition 2008 for the whole of the right column the Qur'an verses.

The Bible Translations
The situation with the Bible quotes, used in the left hand colomn, is more complex.
The quotes used in the chapters on *Common values virtues*, and *Alpha, Omega on Attributes of God* are extracts from the Authorized version of the Bible (The King James Bible), the rights in which are vested in the Crown, are reproduced by permission of the Crown's patentee, Cambridge University Press. Thanks are due for the genereous, speedy and eloquent way in which permission was given. It was joy to return to my childhood experience with the beautiful, age-old Biblical language from 1611, the days of Shakespeare. They are so perfect for the chapters which do indeed taste of eternity.

The Bible Contemporary English Version, Harper Collins 2000 was used for the 'modern' chapters on:
- The position of women
- Penal law - crime and punishment
- International law - war and peace
Although we stayed below the limit of 500 verses for which permission must be asked, I would nevertheless like to thank American Bible Society for making available the excellent contemporary translation over the years 1991-1995.The same holds for Thomas Nelson inc., of whose New King James version of 1982 an amount of verses below the 1000 limit for which persmissionis necessary.

Copy editing, checking and layout
The Bible and Qur'an verses were checked in several rounds. First in Dutch byTrix Santen and Dien Theunissen, both elderly ladies from a

Roman Catholic background. Thankyou very much for those happy hours of reminiscence and laughter. Ati Chr. Blom, Iris Hubrecht, Hetty Karman. Riet Kortmann, Joke ten Kate and Hilda Offerhuis all spent time checking the Dutch quotes. Thankyou to these soroptimist friends, in whose midst the idea for the Side by Side originated.
The Englsih version was diligently checked an rechecked by Robert Fickes and Janneke Tilma. Robert also helped out with the American English. Janneke stayed with me right up to the end, proofreding in an excellent and speedy fashion.
If a mistake has been overlooked, this cannot be due to any of these wonderful people.
The help of the Vorm op Maat team with layout and image problems was indispensable.

Academic Contributors
And last but not least I would like to thank Mehmet, Nur, Martha, and Herman for responding so speedily and eloquently to my rather strange wish: to write comments on some aspect or story from the anthology in way both professional and personal. Andrew deserves special thanks for his advice, moral support and general backing of the project. John Esposito's enthusaism was especially welcome, offering a book [resenation many months before the book was there. Thankyou Khaled for sharing so many thoughts with me in such a short space of time. And as the saying goes, behind every great man there stands a great woman. Special thanks go to Khaled's wife and executive director of his office, without whom my little ongoing 'conference' with Abou Eld Fadl would have been impossible: Grace Song.

Bibliograpy

It is my belief that of all God's wondrous creations, the intellect is the most wondrous of all, and it is also my belief that a book is the gift of God that preserves the intellect for generations to come.

Khaled Abou El Fadl [xvi]

In compiling this anthology, I was able to build on numerous studies investigating the historical context and interpretation of the Hebrew Bible, the New Testament and the Qur'an. I was encouraged by finding comparative studies on particular figures in both books, such as Jesus, Joseph or Job. All this work by others made it easier for me to compile my anthology. Only a handful of the relevant literature is mentioned in the bibliography.

-The authorized King James Version on the Holy Bible, the Church of England 1611, the Crown United Kingdom
-The Bible Contemporary English Version, Harper Collins 2000
- New King James Version, Thomas Nelson 1982

- *The Qur'an* Translation by Abdullah Yusuf Ali, Tahrike Tarsile Qur'an Inc New York, 24th US Edition, 2008
- *The Qur'an,* a new Translation by M.A.S. Abdel Halleem, Oxford University Press, 2004
- *The Koran,* Translated with notes by N.J. Dawood, Penguin Books, 1956/2006
- *The Qur'an, translated by* Ünal, Ali, with annotated interpretation in Modern English, Light, New Jersey 2006
-*The Holy Qur'an*, translated by Maulawi Sher 'Ali, Islam International Publications ltd. Holland 1955, Surrey 2004

- Al Imam Ibn Kathir, *The Stories of the Prophets,* (701 -774 AH) or (1301 -1372 AD).
- Beck, H. & G. Wiegers, *Moslims in een Westerse Samenleving, Islam en Ethiek,* Meinema ,2008
- Beck, H. *Les Musulmans d'Indonésie,* Turnhout: Editions Brepols 2003

- Borg, M.L.A. and K. Bisschop, *Koran en Bijbel in Verhalen*, Spectrum Unieboek 2007
- Brown, B.A. *Noah's other Son, bridging the gap between the Bible and the Qur'an,* Continuum, New York, 2007
- Declais, J.L. *David raconté par les musulmans*, Paris, Cerf, 1999
- Esposito, J. *The Future of Islam,* Oxford University Press 2010
- Esposito, J. *Islam: The Straight Path,* 4th ed., Oxford University Press 2010
- Esposito, J. *The Oxford Encyclopedia of the Islamic World*, Oxford University Press 2009
- Esposito, J & D. Mogahed, *Who Speaks for Islam,* Gallup Inc 2007
- Esposito, Editor-in-Chief, *The Islamic World: Past and Present,* 3 vols., Oxford University Press, 2004
- Esposito, Unholy War: *Terror in the Name of Islam*, Oxford University Press, 2002
- Abou el Fadl K. *The Search for Beauty in Islam: A Conference of the Books*, Rowan and Littlefield, 2006
- Abou el Fadl K., *The Great Theft, wrestling Islam from the extremists,* Harper, San Francisco, 2005
- Abou el Fadl, K., Speaking in God's Name: Islamic Law, Authority and Women: *Oneworld Publications,* 2001
-Frederiks, M.T.*Queens, seducers and friends of God. Islamic stories about women in Bible and Qur´an* Meinema 2010
- Frederiks, M.T. 'Hagar in the Islamic Tradition', in F.L. Bakker en J.S. Aritonang (eds), *On the Edge of Many Worlds*, Meinema 2006, 237-248.
- Jomier, J. T*he Bible and the Qur'an, Bible et Coran,* Les Éditions du Cerf, 1959, San Francisco: Ignatius Press. 2002
-Khalidi, T. *Un musulman nommé Jésus*, Albin Michel, Paris, 2003
- Reynolds G.S. *The Qur'an and its Biblical subtext,* Routledge 2010
- Lubbers, R. W. van Genugten,T. Lambooy *"Inspiration for Global Governance- the Universal declaration of Human Rigthts and the Earth Charter"* Kluwer, 10 December 2008 Human Rights Day
- Moch Nur Ichwan, "State, Scripture and Politics: the Official Translation of the Qur'an in Indonesia," in Henri Chambert-Loir (ed.), *History of Translation in Indonesia and Malaysia,* Paris, Cornell: EHESS and Cornel University Press
- Peters, F.E. *The Children of Abraham, Judaism, Christianity, Islam,* Princeton University Press 2004

- Plato, *Timaeus* Translated by R,G Bury, Loeb Classical Library. Harvard University Press,1975
- Reynolds, G.S. The Qur'an and Its Biblical Subtext. Routledge, 2001
- Rippin, A. *Defining Islam*: *A reader,* Equinox, London, 2007
- Rippin, A, ed. *The Blackwell Companion to the Qur'an,* Wiley-Blackwell, 2009
- Rippin, A. *Muslims - Their Religious Beliefs and Practices*, Routledge 2005
- Rippin, A. (ed.), *The Qur'an and its interpretative tradition*. Aldershot: Variorum, 2001
- Sahih Muslim, collection of Hadith by Muslim ibn al-Hajjai known as Imam Muslim, (202 AH- 261 AH) transl. Abul Hamid Siddiqi, 2007
- Simon, M. *Midrash Rabbah Genesis,* The Soncino pres,s 1961 http://www.archive.org/details/midrashrabbahgen027557mbp
- Stowasser, B.F. *Women in the Qur'an,Traditions and Interpretation.,* Oxford University Press, 1994
- Stowasser, B.F. & Haddad, Y.Y., *Islamic Law and the Challenge of Modernity*, Altamira Press, 2004
- Stowasser, B.F , *The Islamic Impulse,* Croom Helm,1987, reprinted 1989
- Stowasser, B.F. *Women In The Qur'an, Traditions, and Interpretation*, Oxford University Press, 1994
- Thyen, Johann-Dietrich *Bibel und Koran im Vergleich, und kleine Koran-Konkordanz.* Altenberge: Verlag für Christlich-Islamisches Schrifttum, 1984
- Thyen, J-D, *Bibel und Koran: Eine Synopse gemeinsamer Überlieferungen*. Cologne: Böhlau. 1989
- Wimmer, S. J. & / S. Leimgruber: *Von Adam bis Muhammad. Bibel und Koran im Vergleich.* Deutscher Katecheten-Verein München. Stuttgart: Katholisches Bibelwerk 2005.

CPSIA information can be obtained at www.ICGtesting.com
Printed in the USA
LVOW03s0100010814

396980LV00003B/8/P

9 781466 459816